CAMBODIA
A COUNTRY IN TRANSITION

Dedicated to my grandson, **Aaron.**

CAMBODIA
A COUNTRY IN TRANSITION

PRADIP PUTATUNDA

STERLING PUBLISHERS (P) LTD.
Regd. Office: A1/256 Safdarjung Enclave, New Delhi-110029.
Cin: U22110DL1964PTC211907
Mobile: +91 82877 98380/+91 120-6251823
e-mail: mail@sterlingpublishers.in
www.sterlingpublishers.in

Exclusive distributors in Cambodia

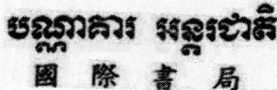

INTERNATIONAL BOOK CENTER
Importers, Wholesalers, Retailers of Office Stationery & Books
Address: No 250 Preah Monivong Blvd. Phnom Penh (IBC1-Preah Monivong)
Tel: (855-23) 221 788/221 799 Fax: (855-23) 221 768 E-mail: info@ibc.com.kh

Cambodia – A Country in Transition
©2021, Dr. Pradip Putatunda
ISBN 978 81 947772 8 1

All rights are reserved.
No part of this publication may be reproduced, stored in a retrieval system or transmitted, in any form or by any means, mechanical, photocopying, recording or otherwise, without the prior written permission of the original publisher.

Printed in India

Printed and Published by Sterling Publishers Pvt. Ltd.,
Plot No. 13, Ecotech-III, Greater Noida-201306, U P, India

PREFACE

Cambodia entered a new era of political stability and international recognition in 1993. After three decades of civil conflict and instability, a new phase of state-building began for Cambodia in 1991 with the Paris Peace Agreement and the 1993 elections for a Constituent Assembly. Over the past twenty-seven years, Cambodia underwent a significant transition, reaching lower middle-income status in 2015 and aspiring to attain upper middle-income status by 2030. Growth was achieved by transitioning to a market economy with openness to trade and capital flows, supported by development assistance, preferential market access to the European Union and the United States and, more recently, large foreign direct investments.

The structural transformation of Cambodia's economy, in recent years, is clearly underway with the declining share of agriculture in the country's GDP growth and employment. In turn, garments & footwear manufacturing and construction & real estate have been key sources of economic growth and job creation. In addition, Cambodia's travel and tourism industry has also become a vital engine of the country's economic growth. There is a magic about this charming yet confounding Kingdom where ancient and modern worlds collide to create an authentic adventure. Cambodia's recent macro-economic management is based on a prudent fiscal policy, high levels of de-facto dollarization and openness to trade and capital flows. Improved domestic revenue mobilizations enabled the government to expand public services while maintaining a conservative approach to borrowing.

Towards achieving its development goals, Cambodia advanced the 'open sky policy' that is reintegrating the country politically and economically into the region and the world. Cambodia's commitment to enhanced regional and international cooperation is seen through its active engagement in a number of regional and international forums such as, among others, the Association of Southeast Asian Nations (ASEAN), the Greater Mekong Subregion (GMS), ASEAN Regional Forum (ARF), United Nations, and WTO. Within Cambodia, it is expected that successful regional and international integration will improve the economy, and will generate opportunities to attract investments and reduce poverty.

However, the global shock triggered by the COVID-19 pandemic has significantly impacted Cambodia's growth momentum in 2020 at a time when Cambodia also faces the partial suspension of preferential access to the EU market under the 'Everything but Arms' initiative. The COVID-19 outbreak and slow recovery in global economic activity alongside prolonged financial market turmoil pose risks to Cambodia's growth outlook.

This text presents the narrative under five major concomitants of the Cambodian transition: historical setting, economic landscape (in agriculture and industrial sector), country strategy framework for overall growth and achievements so far, regional aspirations and foreign relations. The book also focuses on the imminent challenges for sustainable growth in Cambodia during the years ahead.

CONTENTS

	Preface	*v*
Chapter-One	: Introduction	1
Chapter-Two	: History of Cambodia and a Chronology of Evolution	26
Chapter-Three	: Rural Development through Rapid Transformation in Agriculture	51
Chapter-Four	: The Fact-Sheets of Industrial Performance and Development--A Review	70
Chapter-Five	: Achievements and Future Directions in Sustainable Inclusive Development	110
Chapter-Six	: New ASEAN Regionalism : Causes, Achievements, and Challenges	135
Chapter-Seven	: The Potentials and Challenges of Cambodia as a Member of ASEAN	163
Chapter-Eight	: Achievements on Poverty Reduction, Public Health & Health Services and Public Education during 1999-2019	184
Chapter-Nine	: Economic Perspectives of Industrialisation: 1989-2019	206
Chapter-Ten	: Cambodia's Foreign Relations — Politico and Socio-Economic Contexts	226
Chapter-Eleven	: COVID-19 : Health, Socio-Economic, and Geo-Political Consequences in the World	275
Chapter-Twelve	: Concluding Observations	298
	Appendix	*313*
	Abbreviation & Acronyms	*323*
	Bibliography	*331*

My sincere thanks to
Dr. Chea Vandeth,
Dr. Khlot Thyda,
and
Dr. Lek Bopha
for their inputs and inspirations.

CHAPTER-ONE
INTRODUCTION

Cambodia is an incredibly beautiful small country in Southeast Asia bordering gulf of Thailand. Cambodia is also having land boundaries with Laos, Thailand and Vietnam. The total length of land boundaries is 2,530km; out of which the individual lengths for each of the bordering countries are 555km with Laos, 817km with Thailand and 1,158km with Vietnam. Cambodia covers an area of 181,035 sq.km (69,898 sq.miles). Most of the country consists of a low-lying alluvial plain that occupies the central part of the country. To the south-east of the plain lies the delta of the Mekong river. To the east of the plain, ranges of undulating hills separate Cambodia from Vietnam. To the south-west, a mountain range, the Chuor Phnum Kravanh, fringes the plain and forms a physical barrier along the country's coast. Cambodia's highest peak, Phnom Aural (1,813 metre/5,948 ft.) rises in the eastern part of this range. To the north, the Chuor Phnum Dangrek mountains separate Cambodia from Thailand.

Geographically speaking, Cambodia is divided into six major regions: the western and north-western mountains rich in tropical forest, wildlife and fruit trees; the north-eastern plateau abounding with tropical forest, wildlife, waterfalls, diamonds; the central plain known as a large area of flat land for cultivating mainly rice, corns, and beans; for favoring fish and mangrove, there is the western and south-western coastal plain popular with tourists who sunbathe on the sandy beaches, and who consume seafood; the western and north-eastern valleys suitable for the development of hydro-electric power;

and the peninsula suitable for tin mining, rubber cultivation and fishing. Total population of Cambodia is 16,684,465 as of May 9, 2020, based on Worldometer elaboration of the latest United Nations data. Cambodia 2020 population is estimated at around 16.72 million people at mid-year according to UN data. Cambodia population is equivalent to around 0.21 percent of the total world population. Cambodia's population grew 1.41 percent from 2019 to 2020, adding over 232,000 people to the population. Cambodia ranks number 71 in the list of countries (and dependencies) by population. The population density in Cambodia is around 95 people per square kilometer (245 people per square miles). Khmer is the official language in Cambodia, coming in with 97 percent of the population using it on a regular basis, with other languages at only 3 percent.

Urban population (percent of total) in Cambodia was reported at 23.39 percent in December-end, 2018 according to the World Bank collection of development indicators, compiled from officially recognized sources. These numbers confirm that Cambodia is still over-whelmingly rural, but urbanization is rising. Urban population refers to people living in urban areas as defined by national statistical offices. It is calculated using World Bank population estimates and urban ratios from the United Nations World Urbanization Prospects. In Cambodia, population in the largest city i.e. in Phnom Penh (percentage of urban population) is 51.37 percent. Population in urban agglomerations of more than 1 million is 12.01 percent and the balance urban population in urban agglomerations of less than 1 million.

Buddhism is the official religion of Cambodia. According to the World Fact Book, in 2019, approximately 98 percent of Cambodia's population follows Theravada Buddhism, with Hinduism, Islam, Christianity, and the tribal animism making up the bulk of the small remainder. Buddhism in Cambodia has existed since at least the 5th century. Cambodia is the home to one of the only two Hindu temples dedicated to Brahma in the World. Angkor Wat of Cambodia is the largest Hindu temple of the World.

Introduction 3

ECONOMIC DEVELOPMENTS INDICATORS
AN OVERVIEW

Cambodia has undergone a significant transition over the past two decades, reaching lower middle-income status in 2015 and aspiring to attain upper middle-income status by 2030. Cambodia's economy, driven by garment exports and tourism, has sustained an average growth rate of 8 percent between 1998 and 2019, making it one of the fastest growing economies in the world. Growth remained strong, while easing slightly, at 7.1 percent in 2019, after the better than expected growth rate of 7.5 percent in 2018.

The global shock triggered by the COVID-19 pandemic has significantly impacted Cambodia's economy in 2020 at a time when Cambodia also faces the partial suspension of preferential access to the EU market under the 'Everything but Arms' initiative. The outbreak caused sharp deceleration in most of Cambodia's main engines of growth in the first quarter of 2020, including weakened tourism and construction activity. Growth is projected to slow sharply to -2.5 percent in 2020 under the baseline scenario. The COVID-19 outbreak and slow recovery in global economic activity alongside prolonged financial market turmoil pose risks to Cambodia's growth outlook.

Poverty continues to fall in Cambodia. As per the latest statistical data on poverty and socio-economic development in Cambodia, 12.9 percent of the population lives below the national poverty line in 2018 compared to 13.5 percent in 2014 and 47.8 percent in 2007. Unemployment rate in Cambodia is 0.7 percent in 2019. About 90 percent of the poor live in the countryside. Cambodia achieved in 2009 the Millennium Development Goal (MDG) of halving poverty. However, the vast majority of families who escaped poverty did so by a small margin. Around 4.5 million people remain near poor, vulnerable to falling back into poverty when exposed to economic and other external shocks.

Cambodia's robust economic growth continues. According to official data from the World Bank and projections from

Trading Economics, the Gross Domestic Product (GDP) in Cambodia was worth USD23.80 billion in 2019 compared to USD17.71 billion in 2015. The GDP value of Cambodia represents 0.02 percent of the world economy. The return of business and consumer confidence has driven domestic demand. As a result, consumption, accommodated by fast domestic credit growth, has risen significantly, buoying up economic expansion. Internal demand keeps strengthening because of low oil prices and increasing confidence in the construction and real estate boom. As data published by the authorities, in 2019, the consumption grew at a healthy rate of 4.8 percent, fueled by domestic demand. Driven largely by durable equipment and construction, in 2018, gross fixed capital formation growth was robust at 6.1 percent year on year (at constant prices). More clearly, Gross Fixed capital formation in Cambodia increased to 14019.50 KHR million in 2018 from 13213.80 KHR Million in 2017. In the context of a limited capital markets, Cambodia should be relatively shielded from financial volatility while it would still be suffering from the associated US dollar appreciation. It is evident that post-2008 global financial crisis, growth has been less volatile but remains below its pre-global financial crisis level. However, there are some downside risks which include further appreciation of the US dollar, a delay in economic recovery in Europe, and a slower trend of the Chinese economy. Slower Chinese economy could somewhat dampen growth prospects, mainly due to potentially lower Chinese tourist arrivals and investment inflows, while export dependency is low. Moreover, US dollar rate hike which is currently not visible, may trigger abrupt market reactions, causing capital inflows to fall sharply, bond spreads to rise steeply, and liquidity to tighten.

THE REAL SECTOR

(a) Construction and Real Estate

Construction remains the most dynamic engine of growth in Cambodia during the last decade i.e. during 2009 to 2019. From

Introduction

the international experience, we can observe that construction plays a unique role in economic growth and is often a key barometer of economic conditions. Construction increases a country's physical infrastructure, critical factor for long term growth. The performance of the construction sector both affects and is influenced by general economic conditions. According to an official report published on end-December 2019, Cambodia's construction sector attracted a total investment of USD9.35 billions in 2019, up 79 percent from USD5.22 billions in 2018. Released by the Ministry of Land Management, Urban Planning and Construction (MLMUPC), the report said that the ministry had granted licenses to 4,446 construction projects in 2019, up 55 percent from 2,867 projects in 2018. More than 1,000 companies are registered and operating in the construction sector, of which 485 are foreign companies from China, South Korea, Japan, Thailand, Vietnam, Singapore, Malaysia, France, the US, the UK, Australia, Canada, Germany and Spain, among other countries.

There is a broad-based surge of construction activities across different sub-sectors, including infrastructure, residential developments, commercial centers and retail outlets. Not surprisingly, the construction boom is mostly concentrated in and around Phnom Penh, the Cambodian capital and commercial hub. Looking ahead, Cambodia's construction activities are likely to continue apace, as the Cambodian government pushes infrastructure development and demand for property remains high owing to an expanding expatriate and middle-class population. Cambodia's central position in the Greater Mekong Sub-region (GMS) potentially makes it a key part of regional economic development, as it sits along the GMS Southern Economic Corridor, a key trade route linking Vietnam, Cambodia, Thailand and Myanmar. In order to take full advantage of regional integration and also to improve cross-border connectivity and road links between rural and urban areas within the country, the Cambodian government has placed infrastructure at the heart of it's development agenda. Already completed and on-going infrastructure developments cover the construction of major national roads and bridges, railway rehabilitation, airport expansion and power generation projects. Of these, the Cambodian government has set the improvement of main national roads as a priority, along with building link and ring roads to enhance land connectivity with rural and sub-urban areas via better access to the national arteries. Examples of these large-scale projects include the construction of the Phnom Penh – Sihanouk Ville Expressway, the upgradation of National Road No. 5 which is the main road connecting Phnom Penh to the town of Poipet on the Thai border, as well as upgrading National Road No. 1 which links Phnom Penh with the border town Bavet next to Vietnam.

To tackle one of Phnom Penh's most daunting challenges, traffic congestion, the Cambodia government is working on a new ring road project which is expected to finish completely by 2020. Regarding waste water management, Phnom Penh's drainage system was first built during the French colonial period. Subsequent upgradation and expansions have been made, but they are far from adequate in catering for the fast-growing population. In view of this, the Cambodian government is currently working with the Japan International Cooperation Agency (JICA) for a citywide master plan for Phnom Penh's sewage and drainage system, which is likely to run through to 2035. In the foreseeable future, therefore, the city is expected to carry out major upgradation of its sewerage and drainage facilities.

In the Real Estate area, since the passing of Foreign Ownership Property Law in 2010, which allows foreigners to buy condominiums in towers above the first floor of buildings, there has been a steady increase in number of foreign investors in Cambodia's real estate market. Real estate market, one of the Kingdom's economic backbones in terms of economic growth, has seen significant growth in the last few years. It grew anywhere from 10-15 percent in 2019 and is expected to be healthy in the coming years too. Real estate is one of the few sectors that business insiders consider to be a good trend for investors. By end-2019, real estate market appeared to be maturing and developing in a positive direction. Affordable residential development, hospitality and higher quality commercial developments will likely be the focus for the coming years. The demand for affordable residences is on the rise as the number of middle-income people is growing. The Cambodian government is making substantial efforts to focus more on attracting foreign investors in the country especially in the real estate sector.

(b) Garments

One of the key drivers of growth in Cambodia is garment and footwear exports. Cambodia's garment and footwear exports have grown at a solid pace in recent years, with a compound annual growth rate of 10.8 percent per annum over the 2014 – 2016 period. It grew rapidly to become a powerhouse for the Cambodian economy producing USD7.97 billion of exports in 2019. Cambodia is one of the top ten exporters of clothing in the world today. Cambodia's garment manufacturing industry is largely export-oriented and highly integrated into global supply chains.

With the help of trade privileges given by the United States and European Union, the industry has blossomed. It accounted for 74 percent of Cambodia's total merchandise exports in 2018. In 2018, it contributed 11.3 percent of the country's seven and half percent GDP growth. In 2019, a report from General Department of Customs and Excise of the Ministry of Economy and Finance said, Cambodia exported more than USD7.97 billion worth of garments, textile and footwear (GTF) products in the first nine months of the year, up 13.18 percent year-on-year from USD7.044 billion. The United States accounted for USD2.5 billion of the exports and the EU USD2.4 billion -- with USD670 million going to the United Kingdom, USD711 million to Japan, USD121 million to ASEAN member states, and USD1.5 billion to other countries.

Cambodia's garments exporting factories mainly operate to the cut-make-pack (CMP) model. They produce relatively low value added garments, with the design and production decisions made in other countries. In most cases, raw materials are imported from mainland China, Hong Kong, Taiwan, Japan, Vietnam and South Korea. The garments and footwear sector continues to be a major employer for Cambodia's labor force. In the first half of 2017, the sector provided on average 635,000 jobs per month in registered exporting factories, adding approximately four percent increase over the same period in the previous year. December 2019 figures are estimates, but industry sources have quoted numbers as high as 754,000 workers.

Most of Cambodia's garment factories have offshore owners. Garment Manufacturers' Association of Cambodia members come from mainland China (33 percent), Taiwan (20 percent), Hong Kong (12 percent), South Korea (11 percent), Japan (5 percent) and other states including Cambodia (19 percent). According to the Ministry of Labor and Vocational Training (MoLVT)report, in 2018, the number of operational garment factories in Cambodia rose to 625 from 556 in 2016. That's expected to increase to 745 by the end of 2021. However, Cambodia's National Social Security Fund registers all garment and footwear factories with eight employees or more, including subcontractors, regardless of whether they export or not. For 2018, it had 825 factories registered. The difference is most likely made up of non-exporting and sub-contracting companies.

Wages for garment workers were flat in the early 2000s, and for the first decade actually fell in real terms. Since 2010, however, wages have increased in both nominal and real terms. The minimum wage for the garment and textile industry, which is set each year, was USD80 per month in 2013; the figure for 2019 had been set at USD182. The sector's total wage bill reached an average of USD126 million per month over the first half of 2017, as compared to the monthly average of USD116 million over the same period in 2016.

Since 2001, the International Labor Organization's Better Factories Cambodia (BFC) program has carried out monitoring training and reporting around working conditions in Cambodian factories. The program helps manufacturers to understand and comply with national and international labor standards and help workers to be aware of their rights. In Cambodia, a garment factory must agree to BFC monitoring before the government grants it an export license. In 2017, analysis of statistics shows a growing number of subcontracting companies. These provide jobs and contribute to growth, but they can potentially be used as a way to undercut regulations and the minimum wage because subcontractors are not monitored by BFC and get less scrutiny from government bodies. Major global clothing brands typically have their own codes of conduct that they require factories to adhere to. These may include limits on hours worked, maximum temperatures and a ban on short-term contracts.

Cambodia's garment and footwear industry is also facing a number of challenges:

1. Increasing competition from other Asian countries, in particular from Myanmar and Bangladesh;

2. The free trade agreement between the EU and Vietnam that begins in 2018 and gradually drops Vietnam's 12 percent import tariff to zero;

3. Brexit. The United Kingdom bought nearly one-third of Cambodia's garment and footwear exports to the entire EU market in 2018;

4. A further significant challenge will come when the country inevitably grows out of the United Nations Least Developed Country status. When this happens, Cambodia may lose the duty-free access it currently has to some overseas markets, such as the EU.

Besides above challenges, there are positive chances too:

Cambodia has had duty-free access to the United States travel goods market since mid-2016 and production for that market is ramping up. Cambodia is having considerable success growing new markets. Japan took just 2.7 percent of Cambodia's total garment and footwear exports in 2010, but 9 percent in 2016. Canada took just 0.5 percent in 2010, but nearly 8 percent in 2016.

In the last 20 years, while Cambodia's garment and footwear industry has grown enormously, the textile industry – just producing fabric – has remained tiny. Textile production on a commercial scale requires a substantial investment in heavy machinery that requires a lot of energy to operate – energy that is relatively expensive in Cambodia. Two mills in Cambodia, one in Bavet and one in Kampong Chnnang, produce knitted fabrics.

(c) Tourism

Tourism sector acts as a growth engine of Cambodia's economic and overall development. Over 3.3 million tourists visited Cambodia in the first six months of 2019. According to the Ministry of Tourism's Data, it is an 11.2 percent hike on year-to-year bases. Out of the total number, Chinese tourists contributed 1.2 million visitors showing an impressive 38 percent increase. Growth of international tourist arrivals was sustained at 10.7 percent year-on-year in 2018, slightly lower than 11.8 percent in 2017, thanks mainly to the rising number of Chinese visitors. In 2018, arrivals from China were number one; it's 2.03 million visitors accounted for 32.6 percent of total visitor arrivals. This means the authorities achieved their target two years earlier. Under Cambodia's 'China Ready' strategy, which was launched in 2016, the authorities targeted receiving 2 million Chinese visitors by 2020. Far behind are tourists from other important source markets, i.e. Vietnam, Laos, and Thailand in the first half of 2019. In 2018, arrivals from Vietnam, Lao PDR, and Thailand were next to China, capturing 12.9 percent, 6.9 percent, and 6.2 percent of total arrivals respectively. Number of visitors from South Korea decreased significantly, by 20.2 percent, in 2019. Number of tourists from the United States declined insignificantly by 1.1 percent. Rather surprisingly, the country's main tourist draw, Siem Reap province, home to the famed Angkor Archaeological Park, welcomed 8 percent less foreign tourists in 2019 than in the previous year, 1.2 million in total. While tourists from several countries did visit Cambodia less than before in 2019, the overall growth was due to the increased number of visitors to Phnom Penh and coastal areas with 2 million overseas tourists visited the capital and nearly 600,000 visited the coastal provinces.

In 2018, almost a quarter of arrivals from China reported coming to Cambodia for business purposes. Thanks to the rapid increase in air travel. The three main international gateways – Phnom Penh, Siem Reap, and Sihanouk Ville airports – served more than 10 million passengers or a 25 percent increase in 2018 compared to 2017. In 2018, the three airports received more than 4 million foreign travelers, or 65.8 percent of total international arrivals. However, substantial untapped potential remains, given that only about 5 percent of tourists visiting Vietnam and 13.5 percent visiting Thailand, extended their visits to Cambodia. In 2018, while Cambodia received 6.2 million foreign tourists (10.7 percent year-on-year increase), Thailand 38.3 million (8.2 percent year-on-year increase) and Vietnam received 15.5 million (20 percent year-on-year increase).

Development and provision of tourism infrastructure is seen as a pre-requisite to become a popular tourist destination. An attractive tourist destination not only relies on its natural resources, but also on its available infrastructure, facilities, and service. For example, Vietnam is spending as much as USD24 billion during 2016-2020, of which the state budget accounted for 8 to 10 percent, focusing on building and upgrading tourism and transport infrastructure in provinces with key tourist landmarks. Tourist arrivals to Vietnam surged during the past three years, rising 56 percent to 15.5 million in 2018, up from 9.9 million in 2016. Until 2015, Vietnam attracted about 6 million tourists a year.

In Cambodia, to ensure the positive trend persists, in 2019 it was resolved that the government is going to join hands with the private sector to create new tourism products to encourage visitors to stay longer in the kingdom.

(d) Agriculture

Over the past decade, the agriculture sector in Cambodia has undergone a significant structural transformation. During the period, the agriculture sector has become more productive, i.e, agricultural land and labor productivity has increased while it has become less important in overall GDP. In 2019, Cambodia's overall GDP grew at 7.1 percent. However, agriculture in Cambodia grew by just 1.4 percent in 2019, noting that the Agriculture sector's contribution to Cambodia's GDP in 2019 decreased to 17 percent, compared to 22.01 percent in 2018. The share of agriculture in Cambodia's gross domestic product were 23.36%, 24.74%, 26.58%, 28.87%, 31.6%, 33.52%, 34.56% and 33.88% in the year 2017, 2016, 2015, 2014, 2013, 2012, 2011 and 2010 respectively. In 2018, rice production, which accounted for about half of agricultural GDP, grew by 3.5 percent (lower than the 5.7 percent growth rate in 2017), reaching 10.8 million metric tons, of which 2.0 percentage points were contributed by dry season rice and 1.5 percentage point by wet season rice productions. In 2018, the increase in yields accounted for 57 percent of rice production increase, while the rest was due to expansion of harvested land. In 2017, 93.2 percent of the rice production increase was contributed by land expansion, with better weather conditions. Thus, in 2018, the improvements in yields reflect better or more efficient use of agricultural inputs. Yields of wet and dry season rice production increased by 1.7 percent and 1.0 percent respectively.

Total rice cultivated area rose to 3,256 thousand hectares or 3.0 percent in 2019 largely due to the increase in cultivated area of rainy season rice. Rainy season rice's cultivated areas rose to 2,740 thousand hectares in 2018 (or a 3.4 percent increase), up from 2,650 thousand hectares in 2017. Dry season rice's cultivated areas, however, remained at 590 thousand hectares, likely reflecting challenges in the expanding irrigation system for rice production during dry seasons. Official statistics indicate that Cambodia's paddy rice surplus reached 5.8 million metric tons in 2019, or 3.7 million metric tons milled rice equivalent.

Introduction 13

Cambodia, however, exports its rice surplus mostly in the form of paddy rice, while milled rice exports accounted for 16.7 percent of total surplus. Cambodia's fragrant rice exports accounted for about 79 percent of total milled rice exports in 2018. While long grain rice accounted for 17 percent and long grain parboiled rice 4 percent. Cambodia's fragrant rice once again won the World's Best Rice Award in 2018 in the World's Best Rice Contest organized annually by The Rice Trader. Since 2009, Cambodian Jasmine rice has been competing globally, especially against Thai Jasmine rice, for the annual title of World's Best Rice. So far, Cambodia has won four awards, in 2012, 2013, 2014, and 2018, while Thai rice received five awards. United States rice, Myanmar rice, and Vietnam rice received one award each.

From January 2019, the European Commission (EC) imposed safeguard measures on Cambodia's rice. According to the EC, an investigation confirmed a significant increase in imports of Indica rice from Cambodia and Myanmar into the EU that was causing economic damage to European producers. In response, the EC decided to re-introduce import duties, which will be steadily reduced over a period of three years. Effective January 18,2019, the EU reinstated the normal customs duties of Euro175 per ton in year one, progressively reducing it to Euro150 per ton in year two and Euro 125 per ton in year three. As a result, in February 2019, Cambodia's milled rice exports to the EU reached only 10,080 tons or a 57.8 percent month-on-month decline. Cambodia exported 270,000 tons (or 43 percent of total milled rice exports) to the EU market in 2018. In contrast, China has increased its import quota for Cambodia's rice to 400,000 tons in 2019, up from 300,000 tons in 2018. However, Cambodia's actual milled rice exports in 2018 to China (which includes the mainland, Hong Kong SAR, China; and Macau SAR, China) reached 170,154 tons, or 27 percent of total milled rice exports. This was reportedly due to the slow process of granting permission by Chinese customs to export to China. The Chinese market, like the EU market, bought largely fragrant rice from Cambodia. In 2019, overall, the decline of

Cambodia's rice exports to the EU was more than offset by the increase in the country's rice exports to the Chinese market.

Cambodia is located within the neighborhood of commodity giants, namely, Malaysia, Thailand, and Vietnam. As a result, to remain in the competition, Cambodia has been strategically working during the last decade or so, toward quality differentiation and branding (rice, pepper), sustainability premiums ('green'), and improved food safety ('clean'), while advancing agro-processing (cashews, starch). In this regard, authorities have introduced the 'Malys Angkor' rice brand as well as Geographical Indication (GI) products such as Kampot pepper and Mondulkiri Coffee. Cassava processing plants are also being built. However, diversification toward production of animal products and fisheries remains less successful despite rising demand and prices. Rising income and urbanization with a rapid expansion of the tourism sector is changing household food consumption, particularly regarding its consumption of animal products. This is also true for it's export market. In this regard, Cambodia's national strategy to promote agricultural diversification could play a crucial role.

(e) Consumption, Income and Employment

Cambodia's latest socio-economic survey (CSES) found robust consumption and income growth over the last decade. The CSES findings reveal that the average monthly income of Cambodian households is estimated to have reached USD1,376.49 in December 2017, compared with the previous value of USD1,228.51 in 2016 and compared to the previous value of USD309.00 in 2012. Among the three geographically classified groups, namely 'Phnom Penh', 'Other urban', and 'Other rural' household groups, the incomes of the 'other urban' grew fastest during 2009-2019 period.

It is obvious that high income growth has also boosted consumption during the last decade. The statistic shows that in 2019, the private consumption growth amounted to 4.8 percent, compared to 4.4 percent growth in 2018. The consumption of

Introduction

'Phnom Penh' households grew fastest during the period. The construction and real estate sector boom is occurring largely in Phnom Penh and it would be reasonable to conclude that this might have fueled rapid consumption growth there.

Cambodia is also experiencing a rapidly growing labor force, accommodating expansion of domestic production. Survey found, consistent with National accounts data, that Cambodia's relatively young population gave rise to an increase in the working age population (15 – 64 years age group) in the period 2009-2019. Consequently, the dependency ratio declined. The rising labor force appeared to be well absorbed by high employment growth with increased demand for labor, particularly in the 'other urban' and 'other rural' geographical areas.

Cambodia's Socio Economic Survey also indicates an improvement in Cambodia's employment structure with rising 'paid-employee' and 'self-employed' category shares and shrinking 'unpaid family worker' category share. The 'other urban' geographical area has experienced the largest increase in self-employed category share during 2009-2019 at the expense of the unpaid family worker share. The 'other rural' geographical classification experienced a significant increase in its paid employment category share which surged at the expense of its unpaid family worker share. This implies expanding availability of paid employment in rural areas.

In terms of establishments' characteristics, the total establishments of 4,571 accounting for about 962,972 employments in 2017. Out of the total establishments, about 5.6 percent started their business before 1993, 6.6 percent started during 1993-1997, while other 87.7 percent started theirs after 1998, as per Survey conducted by Cambodia's National Employment Agency in May 2018. As compiled from officially recognized sources, the total employed population in 2019 in Cambodia was 9,230,114, compared to 7,951,000 in 2013 out of a total working age (15 – 64) population of 10,437,230 in 2019 compared to total working age (15 – 64 years) population of

9,604,000 in 2013. Cambodia's labor force participation rate was increased to 81.25 percent in December 2019, compared to 81.13 percent in 2018. In the latest report, unemployment rate of Cambodia dropped to 0.1 percent in December 2019.

THE EXTERNAL SECTOR

Healthy foreign direct investment (FDI) inflows remain supportive of Cambodia's external position and help boost consumption. FDI inflows grew exponentially in the last few years, due to healthy macro-economic policies, political stability, regional economic growth and freedom in terms of investment projects. Cambodia's Foreign Direct Investment (FDI) increased by USD933.9 million in December 2019, compared with an increase of USD921.8 million in the previous quarter. Cambodia's Foreign Direct Investment net flows data in USDis updated quarterly, available from March 2010 to December 2019. The data reached an all-time high of USD937.4 million in quarter ended June 2019 and a record low of USD291.0 million in quarter ended March 2010. The National Bank of Cambodia provides Foreign Direct Investment in local currency. CEIC converts quarterly Foreign Direct Investment into USD. However, certain sectors which require national participation or prior approval, are regulated, such as the production of cigarettes or films. Certain investment fields are completely banned, such as psychotropic drugs and narcotics.

The slump in oil prices has positive impacts on Cambodia's current account balance as the country is an oil importer. The slump helped to contain import growth, partly offsetting the slowdown in merchandise exports as garments export eased. Cambodia's total Imports grew 20.3 percent year-on-year in December 2019, compared with an increase of 18.1 percent year-on-year in the previous quarter. Cambodia's total imports growth from March 2011 to December 2019 with an averaged rate of 14.2 percent. The data reached an all-time high in June 2018 and a record low of 4.7 percent in June 2016. In the latest reports, Cambodia's total imports recorded USD5.7 billion in December 2019. Total exports reached USD3.8 billion in December 2019, which registered an increase of 22.2 percent year-on-year. Cambodia's Trade Balance recorded a deficit of USD279.5 million in January 2020. Current Account recorded a deficit of USD1.2 billion or KHR 4,814 billion in December 2019, compared with a deficit of USD820.8 million in the previous quarter. Current account is the sum of the balance of trade (exports minus imports of goods and services), net factor income (such as interest and dividends) and net transfer payments (such as foreign aid). Cambodia recorded a Current Account deficit of 15.60 percent of the country's Gross Domestic Product in 2019. There have been improvements in net services and net current transfers due to improved confidence, continued vibrant economic activity, and rising remittances during 2015-2019. On the other hand, trade deficit and negative net income persist. Cambodia attracted USD3,588 billion in foreign direct investment (FDI) in 2019, an increase of nearly 12 percent over 2018 as per National Bank of Cambodia report released in end-December 2019. As a result of continued healthy FDI inflows, gross international reserves further improved, reaching USD16.9 billion in December 2019, compared with USD15.8 billion in the previous month or 7 months of prospective imports. The International Monetary Fund provides Cambodia's monthly Foreign Exchange reserves in USD.

In terms of export, despite some initial successes in export product diversification, garment sector still captured almost 70 percent of total exports in 2019. Cambodia's exports to international markets reached more than USD10 billion in the first ten months of 2019, mainly from the garment, textile, footwear and travel products sectors. Garments exports were worth USD6.4 billion, textiles USD40 million and footwear USD905 million. In 2019, continued high export growth for footwear products and the resumption of robust milled rice and rubber export growth are encouraging.

In December 2019, in terms of imports, Cambodia's strong domestic demand continues to drive import growth. While the current construction boom has contributed to construction material imports growth, the recent decline in oil prices is supporting rising demand for petroleum and vehicle imports. Domestic demand is also stimulating consumption goods imports such as food and beverages. Cambodia's main import partners are China, Thailand, Hong Kong, Vietnam, Taiwan, and South Korea.

Inflation rate in Cambodia increased by 3.07 percent in December 2019 over the same month in the previous year as per data published monthly by Cambodia's central Bank. In Cambodia, the most important components of the Consumer Price Index (CPI) are: food and non-alcoholic beverages (44.8 percent), housing, water, electricity, gas and other fuels (17.1 percent), transport (12.2 percent), restaurants (5.9 percent), and health (5.1 percent). Other items include: clothing and footwear (3 percent), recreation and culture (2.9 percent), furnishing and household maintenance (2.7 percent). The index also takes into account miscellaneous goods and services (2.3 percent), alcoholic beverages, tobacco and narcotics (1.6 percent), education (1.2 percent) and communication (1.1 percent). Cambodia's regional countries' inflation have also been eased. Lower inflation in China, consistent with its slower growth trend, has also helped to subdue regional inflation. Given that Cambodia is an oil importer, the recent sharp decline in petroleum product prices has allowed households to spend less on transportation.

THE MONETARY SECTOR

a. Interest Rates, Exchange Rates and Monetary Aggregates

Interest rate caps are by definition a government intervention in the market place and a response to perceived market failures. Interest rate caps either target exploitative rates charged to the most vulnerable borrowers, or the overall cost of credit in some market segments or the entire economy. If interest rate caps are used as a policy tool to achieve certain socio-economic goals, such as lower overall cost of credit, ceilings are set at 'binding levels' intended to influence the market outcome. While evaluating interest rate caps, a simple question can arise of why lending rates are high in the first place. The interest rate charged on loans, in simplified terms, is the sum of five components, namely, costs of funds, overhead costs (e.g. administrative costs of the bank as well as costs of processing the loan), risk premium, profits and taxes. In Cambodia, both lending and deposit interest rates edged up slightly in 2014 and in 2015 due to rapid domestic credit growth. This trend has to be seen against a background in which heightened competition among banks has resulted in a significant drop in the short-term US dollar lending rate since 2012. Cambodia also implemented caps on the maximum rates charged by micro-finance institutions in 2017. Consequently, the interest rate spread – the difference between the nominal lending and deposit rates – has narrowed substantially as we observed in 2019 also.

Cambodian riel versus the US dollar exchange rate remains broadly stable, supporting overall price stability. Historically, the Cambodian Riel reached all time high of 4,269 in July of 2010. Riel depreciated slightly by mid-2015, reaching CR4,098 per dollar, which has helped to mitigate some of the losses in external competitiveness in agricultural commodities mainly whose prices are denominated in local currency. Nonetheless, the riel appreciated slightly against the Thai baht and the Vietnamese dong during the first half of 2015. Monthly average Cambodian Riel's exchange rate against USDwas reported at KHR4,069.182 per 1USDin April 2020. This recorded an increase from the previous number of KHR 4,055.773 per 1USDin March 2020. Accommodating economic expansion, broad money growth continues, albeit at a slower pace, with the rapid expansion of the banking and financial sector.

Cambodia's Money Supply M2 was reported at USD25.668 billion in December 2019. This recorded an increase from the previous number of USD25.218 billion for November 2019. Cambodia's Money Supply M2 data is updated monthly, averaging USD2.200 billion from January 1995 to December

2019, with 300 observations. The data reached an all-time high of USD25.668 billion in December 2019 and a record low of USD135.765 million in January 1995. CEIC converts monthly Money Supply M2 into USD. The National Bank of Cambodia provides Money Supply M2 in local currency. The National Bank of Cambodia's average market exchange rate is used for currency conversions.

Cambodia's Money Supply M1 was reported at USD3.432 billion in December 2019. This recorded an increase from the previous number of USD3.345 billion for November 2019. Cambodia's Money Supply M1 data is updated monthly, averaging USD431.358 million from January 1995 to December 2019, with 300 observations. The data reached an all-time high of USD3.432 billion in December 2019 and a record low of USD73.536 million in January 1995. The National Bank of Cambodia provides Money Supply M1 in local currency. CEIC converts monthly Money Supply M1 into USD. The National Bank of Cambodia's average market exchange rate is used for currency conversions.

b. The Banking Sector

Cambodia's banking industry had enjoyed strong growth in both loans and deposits in 2019. Outstanding loans rose by 26 percent year-on-year to 117 trillion riels (USD28.8 billion) in 2019, while customers' deposits increased by 25 percent to 124 trillion riels (USD30.5 billion), according to the latest report of the National Bank of Cambodia (NBC). The growth was driven by the rising loan demands in trade, real estate and construction, and also manufacturing, among others. Speaking at the opening of the NBC's annual meeting in January 2020, NBC governor said Cambodia's economy grew by 7.1 percent in 2019, with strong macroeconomic and financial stability despite some risks. The banking sector is healthy and has been actively contributing to financial inclusion, the improvement of livelihoods and the reduction of poverty for the Cambodian people.

Introduction

According to the NBC's report, on 31st December 2019, Cambodia had 43 commercial banks, 14 specialized banks and dozens of microfinance institutions. By December-end 2019, there were roughly 7.5 million deposit accounts and 3 million credit accounts at the country's banks and microfinance institutions.

THE FISCAL SECTOR

The Executive Board of the International Monetary Fund (IMF) concluded the Article IV consultation with Cambodia on December 6, 2019. Growth accelerated in 2019. Economic activity remains robust in 2019 owing to continued export growth and strong construction activity, while inflation remains stable at around 2.5 percent. The current account deficit widened to about 12 percent of GDP in 2018 and continued to widen in 2019. Robust Foreign direct Investment inflows, as well as an increase in short term inflows, nevertheless contributed to an accumulation of gross international reserves to about 7 months of prospective imports in August 2019.

Financial conditions had been accommodative both in 2018 and in 2019. Private sector credit, increasingly concentrated in the real-estate and construction sectors, accelerated in 2018 and also grew around 28 percent in 2019. Fiscal consolidation has been sustained as high revenue growth and largely contained expenditure continued to play a positive role.

a. Revenue Composition

Cambodia's revenue mobilization has improved markedly in recent years. Continued improvements in revenue administration have enabled high domestic revenue growth to be sustained. While in 2007, government revenue amounted to less than 10 percent of GDP, in 2018, government revenue in Cambodia amounted to approximately 17.8 percent of the country's gross domestic product, compared to 18.9 percent in 2017 and 17.6 percent in 2016. This is among the highest levels in ASEAN. The budgeted revenue (including grants) for the 2019 budget was conservative. Although domestic revenue was budgeted to increase to 19.3 percent of GDP in 2019, up from 18.6 percent of GDP in 2018 budget, it remained below the estimated revenue collection of 21.5 percent of GDP achieved for 2018. Public outlay was budgeted to be contained at 23.9 percent of GDP in 2019, only slightly lower than 24.0 percent of GDP in 2018 budget. The introduction and implementation of the revenue mobilization strategy (2014 – 2018) appropriately set out key priority areas, namely revenue administration and good governance, given the existing capacity of the revenue colleting agencies. However, Cambodia's revenue sources are skewed towards VAT and import taxes. Out of total tax revenue, 61 percent of total tax revenue is generated by the VAT. This is a relatively high share compared to regional peers. VAT is usually considered among the most regressive sources of taxation, since consumption makes out a larger share of income for poorer households (Peralta-Alva et al., 2018). On the other hand, revenue in Cambodia relies relatively little on progressive income sources such as the personal income tax (PIT), income and capital gains, or property taxation. Revenue from personal income taxation and capital income and capital gains only make up 4.2 percent of GDP in Cambodia in 2019 which is the lowest among peers in ASEAN. Similarly, revenue from property taxation accounts for only 0.1 percent of GDP, which is also comparatively very low. This is despite the progressive profile of property taxation, which is predominantly levied on richer households in the urban area. Cambodian authorities already initiated and introduced the next Revenue Mobilization Strategy (RMS) covering 2019-2023 targeting modernization of tax and customs administration and policy.

b. Expenditure Composition

Although total spending remains contained, a rapid expansion of the wage bill put pressure on the fiscal consolidation effort. The public sector wage bill was increased to 8.6 percent of GDP in 2018. This represented a tripling of civil servants' minimum wage, compared to the level in 2013. In this context, it would be relevant to mention that there is a need to accelerate the critical

Introduction

tasks on public administration reforms to improve public service delivery. This is also crucial to underpin private sector development role in driving growth and reducing poverty.

On the other hand, capital expenditure data was reported at KHR590.440 billion in March 2020. This recorded an increase from the previous number of KHR382. 180 billion for February 2020. Capital expenditure data is updated monthly, averaging KHR324.816 billion from January 2007 to March 2020. The data reached an all-time high of KHR 1,685.660 billion in December 2019 and a record low of KHR 92.260 billion in January 2016.

It is worth noting that a series of efforts has been made to improve spending efficiency and results. For instance, introduction full program budgeting pilots at 10 key ministries and the introduction of the Financial Management Information System (FMIS).

c. Fiscal Balance

As mentioned above, the export and construction sectors are the main sources of direct revenues and indirect (and international trade) revenues, respectively. The agriculture sector is tax exempt. It is highly likely, as world bank observed in its May 2020 Cambodia Economic Update, that revenue collection in 2020 would be significantly below the budget target. The overall fiscal deficit (including grants) is therefore projected to widen to 9.0 percent of GDP in 2020. The shortfall in domestic revenue collection will require the authorities to dip into government savings. In 2019, government savings stood at 20.2 percent of GDP (or 22.2 trillion riels) after several years of accumulation. While buoyant revenue collection continues, the fiscal deficit (including grants) stood at 1.4 percent in 2019, compared to 1.9 percent in 2018, 1.6 percent in 2017, 1.6 percent of GDP in 2015, and 0.3 percent of GDP in 2014, due to rising current expenditure. The fiscal deficit, however, remained to be fully financed by external funds until 2019. Fiscal expansion in 2019 served as a stimulus, partly underpinning robust consumption growth. Government expenditure to have increased to

24.96 percent of GDP in 2019, up from 24.62 percent in 2018. Despite the authorities' fiscal expansion in 2019, governments' overall fiscal position remained strong. After years of fiscal consolidation, Cambodian government has accumulated substantial deposits at the central bank. The deposits, which stood at 14.9 percent of GDP, could be used as a fiscal buffer, given that the monetary policy continues to be constrained by Cambodia's highly dollarized economy.

According to official data, by end-2019, Cambodia had a total public debt outstanding of USD7.0 billion (or 28.6 percent of GDP) of which 0.04 percent was public domestic debt. Overall, the borrowing terms remained highly concessional, with a (weighted average) interest rate of 1.37 percent, a maturity of 25.5 years, and a grace period of 8 years. By major currencies, outstanding debt in US dollar, Special Drawing Rights (SDR) and Chinese Yuan were 43.2 percent, 28.1 percent and 16.1 percent respectively.

SUMMARY OBSERVATIONS

Key Issues At A Glance

Cambodia's economy has been hit hard by the global covid-19 outbreak. The outbreak caused sharp deceleration in most of Cambodia's main engines of growth in the first eight months of 2020, including weakened tourism and construction activity. The economy is projected to contract 1.3 percent in 2020 under the baseline scenario. Downside risks include a prolonged decline in tourist arrivals, and real estate market correction.

As predicted by World Bank in its September 2020 report, Cambodia's economy is set to regain considerable strength in 2021. Further waves of the virus globally pose a downside risk. The tourism sector has been hit hardest by the outbreak. Similarly, the garment industry is facing a global demand shock as well as partial withdrawal of the EU's 'Everything But Arms' (EBA) trade preferential treatment. Spillovers to the construction and real estate sector, one of Cambodia's growth

Introduction

drivers, amid financial market turmoil could potentially be detrimental to growth. Rebounds in economic activities in China and major markets in 2021 will improve Cambodia's growth outlook.

Poverty reduction is expected to continue but at a slower pace. Given the agriculture sector provides livelihoods for most of the poor, efforts to diversify the agriculture sector and rural households' incomes as well as to promote agro-processing are expected to help in the medium term. Downside risks to Cambodia's near-term growth outlook include continued decline in tourist arrivals due to lingering global outbreak, slow recovery in global economic activity that would further decelerate Cambodia's industrial sector due to extended demand shock to garment exports, and drastic slowdown in FDI due to prolonged financial market turmoil whereby construction activity does not pick up. Big correction in the Real Estate market and high outstanding credit are additional vulnerabilities.

Several measures under a newly introduced fiscal stimulus in the 2020 budget have been announced to mitigate the negative impact. Depending on their effectiveness, measures supporting the hardest hit industries with tax relief and retraining and upskilling programs for laid-off workers may help. Additional capital injection for the Rural Development Bank to support agro-processing firms and trade facilitation improvements will enhance longer-term competitiveness. Other initiatives include supporting small and medium sized enterprises alongside co-financing and risk-sharing initiatives with commercial banks and micro-finance institutions to improve access to finance. Measures to address key aspects underpinning the ease of doing business will also need to be considered. Improvements in fiscal and public investment management should continue to ensure effectiveness of the stimulus.

CHAPTER-TWO
HISTORY OF CAMBODIA AND A CHRONOLOGY OF EVOLUTION

Contemporary Cambodia, an enigmatic kingdom, with a history both inspiring and depressing, delivers an admirable present. The Cambodian people, popularly known as Khmers, have been hell and back, struggling through years of bloodshed, poverty and political instability. However, they have prevailed with their smiles intact. Credit goes to the Cambodian people's unbreakable and intoxicating spirit and infectious optimism.

Archaeological evidences indicate that the present-day country of Kingdom of Cambodia was inhabited at least since the 5th millennium BC. If we dwell into the history of Cambodia, we find that the country went through the following periods of political, social, and economic transformation:

(a) pre-history and early history;

(b) Funan Kingdom (1st century AD – 550);

(c) Chenla Kingdom (6th century – 802);

(d) Khmer Empire (802 – 1431);

(e) Dark ages of Cambodia (1431 –1863);

(f) French Colonial period (1863 – 1953);

(g) Administration of Sihanouk or Kingdom of Cambodia (1953-1970);

(h) Khmer Republic (1970 – 1975);

(i) Democratic Kampuchea (1975 – 1979);

(j) Vietnamese occupation and the People's Republic of Kampuchea (1979- 1989) and later renamed as 'The State of Cambodia' (1989 – 1993) ;

(k) Kingdom of Cambodia, also can be called Modern Cambodia (1993 – present).

1. EARLY HISTORY OF CAMBODIA

Archaeological evidence revealed stone tools from 6000 – 7000 BC, and pottery from 4200 BC in north-west Cambodia. Skulls and human bones found at Samrong Sen date from 1500 BC. Scholars traced the first cultivation of rice and the first bronze making in south-east Asia to these people. By the first century AD, the 2spoke languages very much related to the Cambodian or Khmer of the present-day. In the 1st century AD, the culture and technical skills of Cambodian or Khmer people far surpassed the primitive stage. Several evidences indicate that the most advanced groups of people lived along the coast and in the lower Mekong River Valley and delta regions in houses constructed on stilts where they cultivated rice, fished and kept domesticated animals. Recent research also unlocked the discovery of artificial circular earthworks dating to Cambodia's Neolithic era.

The Khmer people were among the first inhabitants of south-east Asia. They were also among the first in south-east Asia to adopt religious ideas and political institutions from India and to establish centralized Kingdoms comprising large territories. The earliest known kingdom in the area, Funan, flourished from around the 1st to the 6th century. This was succeeded by Chenla, which controlled large parts of modern Cambodia, Vietnam, Laos, and Thailand.

2. FUNAN KINGDOM (1st century AD – 550)

The Funanese Empire rose to eminence from its affluent and powerful home city of Oc Eo (in present day Vietnam), known in the Roman Empire as Kattigara, meaning the Renowned City. Contacts with the distant Roman Empire are evidenced by the fact that Roman coins have been found at archaeological sites dating from the 2nd and 3rd centuries. However, most of the foreign trade of the Funan Empire was carried on much closer to home with India, especially the Bengal area of India. Trade with India commenced well before 500BC. Trade with China began after the southward expansion of the Han Dynasty around the 2nd century BC. With the Indian trade came the Indianization of the Culture of Funan and the religion of Hinduism. Hinduism produced a syncretism phenomenon with other previous religions and beliefs already present in the Khmer culture. Funan and its succeeding societies which occupied this section of south-east Asia remained mainly Hindu in religion for about 900 years. Some cultural features and customs of Hinduism continue to exist within the current society.

The Funanese Empire reached its greatest extent under the rule of Fan Shih-man in the early 3rd century, extending as far south as Malaysia and as far west as Burma. The Funanese established a strong system of mercantilism and commercial monopolies that had become a pattern for empires in the region. Exports from the Funan Empire were largely forest products and precious metals -- including accessories such as gold, ivory, rhinoceros horn, wild spices like cardamom, lacquer hides and aromatic wood.

3. CHENLA KINGDOM (6th century – 802)

The Khmers, vassals of Funan, reached the Mekong river from the northern Menam river via the Mun river valley. Chenla, their first independent state developed out of Funanese influence.

Ancient Chinese records mention two Kings, Shrutavarman and Shreshthavarman who ruled at the capital Shreshthapura located in modern day southern Laos. The immense influence on the identity of Cambodia to come was wrought by the Khmer Kingdom of Bhavapura, in the modern-day Cambodian city of Kampong Thom. Its legacy was its most important sovereign, Ishanavarman who completely conquered the Kingdom of Funan during 612 – 628. He choose his new capital at the Sambor Prei Kuk, naming it Ishanapura.

After the death of Jayavarman 1 in 681, turmoil came upon the Kingdom and at the start of the 8th century, the Kingdom broke up into many principalities. Pushkaraksha, the ruler of Shambhupura announced himself as king of the entire Kambuja. Chinese Chronicles proclaim that, in the 8th century, Chenla was split into Land Chenla and Water Chenla. During this time, Shambhuvarman, son of Pushkaraksha controlled most of Water Chenla until the 8th century which the Malayans and Javanese dominated over many principalities.

4. KHMER EMPIRE (802 – 1431)

The golden age of Khmer civilization was the period from the 9th to the 13th centuries, when Khmer Empire, which gave Kampuchea, or Cambodia, its name, ruled large territories from its capital in the region of Angkor in Western Cambodia.

Jayavarman 11, King of the Khmers, first came to the Kuhlen hills, the future site of Angkor Wat in 802 AD. Later, under JayavarmanVII (1181-C.1218), Khmer reached its zenith of political power and cultural creativity. Jayavarman VII gained power and territory in a series of successful wars. Khmer conquests were almost unstoppable as they raised home cities of powerful seafaring Chams. However, territorial expansion stopped after a defeat by Dai Viet. The battle also witnessed Suryavarman VII's death. Following Jayavarman VII's death, Khmer experienced a gradual decline. Important factors were the aggressiveness of neighboring peoples (especially the THAI, or SIAMESE), chronic inter-dynastic strife, and the gradual deterioration of the complex irrigation system that had insured rice surpluses. The Angkorian monarchy survived until 1431, when the Thai captured Angkor Thom and the Cambodian King fled to the southern part of the country.

5. DARK AGES OF CAMBODIA (1431 – 1863)

The 15th to the 19th centuries were a period of continued decline and territorial loss. Cambodia enjoyed a brief period of prosperity during the 16th century because its Kings, who built their capitals in the region south-east of the Tonle' Sap along the Mekong river, promoted trade with other parts of Asia. This was the period when Spanish and Portuguese adventurers and missionaries first visited the country. It is known that the Portuguese visited Cambodia as early as 1555. However, the Thai conquest of the new capital at Lovek in 1594 marked a downturn in the Country's fortunes. Becoming a pawn in power struggles between its two increasingly powerful neighbors, Siam and Vietnam, Cambodia remained a protectorate of Siam. Vietnam's settlement of the Mekong Delta led to its annexation of that area at the end of the 17th century. Vietnam employed a strategy similar to those of North American pilgrims and pioneers: settle and claim. Such foreign encroachments continued through the first half of the 19th century. A successful invasion by Vietnam further limited Thai protectorship in Cambodia and established the Kingdom under full Vietnamese suzerainty.

6. FRENCH COLONIAL PERIOD (1863 – 1953)

In 1863, King Norodom signed an agreement with the French to establish a protectorate over his Kingdom. The state gradually came under French colonial rule. In 1940 – 41, during World War II, the Franco – Thai war left the French Indo-Chinese colonial authorities in a position of weakness. The Vichy government signed an agreement with Japan to allow the Japanese military transit through French Indo-China. Meanwhile, the Thai government, under the pro-Japanese leadership of Field

Marshal Plack Phibunsongkhram, took advantage of its position and invaded Cambodia's western provinces. At the end of the war, Cambodia's situation was chaotic. The Free French, under General Charles de Gaulle, were determined to recover Indochina, though they offered Cambodia and the other Indo-Chinese protectorates a carefully circumscribed measure of self-government. Convinced that they had a 'civilizing mission', they envisioned Indochina's participation in a French Union of former colonies that shared the common experience of French culture.

7. ADMINISTRATION OF SIHANOUK (1953 – 1970)

On 9th March, 1945, during the Japanese occupation of Cambodia, young King Norodom Sihanouk proclaimed an independent Kingdom of Kampuchea, following a formal request by the Japanese. Shortly thereafter, the Japanese government nominally ratified the independence of Cambodia and established a consulate in Phnom Penh. The new government did away with the Romanization of the Khmer language that the French colonial administration was beginning to enforce and officially reinstated the Khmer script. Since then, no government in Cambodia had tried to Romanize the Khmer language again. After Allied military units entered Cambodia, the Japanese military forces present in the country were disarmed and repatriated. The French were able to impose the colonial administration in Phnom Penh in October the same year i.e. 1945.

Sihanouk's 'royal crusade for independence' resulted in grudging French acquiescence to his demands for a transfer of sovereignty. A partial agreement was struck in October 1953. Sihanouk then declared that independence had been achieved and returned in triumph to Phnom Penh. As a result of the Geneva Conference on Indo-china, Cambodia was able to bring about the withdrawal of the Vietnamese troops from its territory and to withstand any residual impingement upon its sovereignty by external powers.

Neutrality was the central element of Cambodian foreign policy during the 1950s and 1960s. By the mid-1960s, parts of Cambodia's eastern provinces were serving as bases for North Vietnamese Army and National Liberation Front (NVA/ NLF) forces operating against South Vietnam, and the port of Sihanouk Ville was being used to supply them. As NVA activities grew, the United States and South Vietnam became concerned, and in 1969, the United States began a 14month long series of bombing raids targeted at NVA elements, contributing to destabilization. The bombing campaign took place no further than ten, and later twenty miles (32 km) inside the Cambodian border, areas where the Cambodian population had been evicted by the NVA. Prince Sihanouk, fearing that the conflict between communist North Vietnam and South Vietnam might spill over to Cambodia, publicly opposed the idea of a bombing campaign by the United States along the Vietnam-Cambodia border and inside Cambodian territory. In December 1967, Washington Post journalist Stanley Karnow was told by Sihanouk that if the US wanted to bomb the Vietnamese communist sanctuaries, he would not object, unless Cambodians were killed. The same message was conveyed to US President Johnson's emissary Chester Bowles in January 1968. So, the US had no real motivation to overthrow Sihanouk. However, Prince Sihanouk wanted Cambodia to stay out of North Vietnam – South Vietnam conflict and was very critical of the United States Government and its allies (the South Vietnamese Government). Prince Sihanouk, facing internal struggles of his own, due to the rise of the Khmer Rouge, did not want Cambodia to be involved in the conflict. Prince Sihanouk wanted the United States and its allies (South Vietnam) to keep the war away from the Cambodian border. Sihanouk did not allow the United States to use Cambodian air-space and airports for military purposes. This upset the United States greatly and contributed to their view that of Prince Sihanouk as a North Vietnamese sympathizer and a thorn on the United States. However, declassified documents indicated that, as late as March 1970, the Nixon administration was hoping to garner 'friendly relations' with Prince Sihanouk.

History of Cambodia and a Chronology of Evolution 33

Domestic Cambodian politics became polarized throughout the 1960s. Opposition to the government grew within the middle class and leftists including Paris-educated leaders like Son Sen, Leng Sary, and Saloth Sar (later known as Pol Pot), who led an insurgency under the Clandestine Communist Party of Kampuchea (CPK). Prince Sihanouk called these insurgents 'the Khmer Rouge', literally 'Red Khmer'. But the 1966 national assembly election showed a significant swing to the right, and General Lon Nol formed a new government, which lasted till 1967. During 1968 and 1969, the insurgency worsened. However, members of the government and army who resented Prince Sihanouk's ruling style as well as his tilt away from the United States, did have a motivation to overthrow him.

8. KHMER REPUBLIC (1970 – 1975)

While visiting Beijing in 1970, Prince Sihanouk was ousted by a military coup led by Prime Minister General Lon Nol and Prince Sisowath Sirik Matak in the early hours of March 18,1970. Despite Sihanouk's allegations, there was no evidence that this coup was planned by the United States Central Intelligence Agency. However, as early as March 12, 1970, the CIA Station Chief told Washington that based on communications from Sirik Matok, Sihanouk's cousin, that the Cambodian army was ready for a coup. Lon Nol assumed power after the military coup and immediately allied Cambodia with the United States. Son Ngor Thanh, an opponent of Pol Pot, announced his support for the new government. On October 9, 1970, the Cambodian monarchy was abolished, and the country was renamed the Khmer Republic. The new regime immediately demanded that the Vietnamese communists leave Cambodia.

Hanoi rejected the new republic's request for the withdrawal of NVA troops. In response, the United States moved to provide material assistance to the new government's armed forces which were engaged against both CPK insurgents and NVA forces. The North Vietnamese and Viet Cong forces, desperate to retain their sanctuaries and supply lines from North Vietnam, immediately launched armed attacks on the new government. The North Vietnamese quickly overran large parts of eastern Cambodia reaching to within 15 miles (24 kms.) of Phnom Penh. The North Vietnamese turned the newly won territories over to the Khmer Rouge. The King urged his followers to help in overthrowing this government, hastening the onset of civil war.

In April 1970, U.S. President Nixon announced to the American public that US and South Vietnamese ground forces had entered Cambodia in a campaign aimed at destroying NVA base areas in Cambodia. The US had already been bombing Vietnamese positions in Cambodia for well over a year by that point. Although a considerable quantity of equipment was seized or destroyed by US and South Vietnamese forces, containment of North Vietnamese forces proved elusive.

The Khmer Republic's leadership was plagued by disunity among its three principal figures: Lon Nol, Sihanouk's cousin Sirik Matak, and National Assembly leader In Tam. Lon Nol remained in power in part because none of the others were prepared to take his place. In 1972, a constitution was adopted and Lon Nol became President. But disunity, the problems of transforming a 30,000 men army into a national combat force of more than 200,000 men, and spreading corruption weakened the civilian administration and army.

The Khmer Rouge insurgency inside Cambodia continued to grow, aided by supplies and military support from North Vietnam. Pol Pot and Leng Sary asserted their dominance over the Vietnamese-trained communists, many of whom were purged. At the same time, the Khmer Rouge (CPK) forces became stronger and more independent of their Vietnamese patrons. By 1973, the CPK were fighting battles against government forces with little or no North Vietnamese troop support, and they controlled nearly 60 percent of Cambodia's territory and 25 percent of its population.

The government made three unsuccessful attempts to enter into negotiations with the insurgents, but by 1974, the CPK were operating openly as divisions, and some of the

NVA combat forces had moved into South Vietnam. Lon Nol's control was reduced to small enclaves around the cities and main transportation routes. More than 2 million refugees from the war lived in Phnom Penh and other cities.

On New-Year day 1975, Communist troops launched an offensive which, in 117 days of the hardest fighting of the war, collapsed the Khmer Republic. Simultaneous attacks around the perimeter of Phnom Penh pinned down Republican forces, while other CPK units overran five bases controlling the vital lower Mekong resupply route. A US-funded airlift of ammunition and rice ended when Congress refused additional aid for Cambodia. The Lon Nol government in Phnom Penh surrendered on April 17, 1975, just five days after the US mission evacuated Cambodia.

The relationship between the massive carpet bombing of Cambodia by the United States and the growth of the Khmer Rouge, in terms of recruitment and popular support, had always been a matter of interest to historians. Some historians cited the US intervention and bombing campaign (spanning 1965 – 1973) as a significant factor leading to increased support of the Khmer Rouge among the Cambodian peasantry. However, Pol Pot biographer David Chandler argued that the bombing 'had the effect the Americans wanted – it broke the Communist encirclement of Phnom Penh.' Peter Rodman and Michael Lind claimed that the US intervention saved Cambodia from collapse in 1970 and 1973. Craig Etcheson agreed that it was 'untenable' to assert that US intervention caused the Khmer Rouge victory while acknowledging that it might have played a small role in boosting recruitment for the insurgents. William Shawcross, however, wrote that the US bombing and ground incursion plunged Cambodia into the chaos Sihanouk had worked for years to avoid.

The Vietnamese intervention in Cambodia, launched at the request of the Khmer Rouge, had also been cited as a major factor in their eventual victory, including by Shawcross. Vietnam later admitted that it played 'a decisive role' in their seizure of power. China 'armed and trained' the Khmer Rouge during the civil war and continued to aid them years afterward.

9. DEMOCRATIC KAMPUCHEA (1975 -1979)

Immediately after its victory, the CPK ordered the evacuation of all cities and towns, sending the entire urban population into the countryside to work as farmers, as the CPK was trying to reshape society into a model that Pol Pot had conceived.

The new government sought to completely restructure Cambodian society. Remnants of the old society were abolished and religion was suppressed. Agriculture was collectivized, and the surviving part of the industrial base was abandoned or placed under state control. Cambodia had neither a currency nor a banking system.

Democratic Kampuchea's relations with Vietnam and Thailand worsened rapidly as a result of border clashes and ideological differences. While communist, the CPK was fiercely nationalistic, and most of its members who had lived in Vietnam were purged, Democratic Kampuchea established close ties with the Peoples' Republic of China, and the Cambodian-Vietnamese conflict became part of the Sino-Soviet rivalry, with Moscow backing Vietnam. Border clashes worsened when the Democratic Kampuchea's military attacked villages in Vietnam. The regime broke off relations with Hanoi in December 1977, protesting Vietnam's alleged attempt to create an Indo-China federation. In mid-1978, Vietnamese forces invaded Cambodia, advancing about 48 kilometers before the arrival of the rainy season.

The reasons for Chinese support of the CPK was to prevent a pan-Indochina movement, and maintain Chinese military superiority in the region. The Soviet Union supported a strong Vietnam to maintain a second front against China in case of hostilities and to prevent further Chinese expansion. Since Stalin's death, relations between Mao-controlled China and the

Soviet Union had been lukewarm at best. In February to March 1979, China and Vietnam fought a brief Sino-Vietnamese war over the issue.

In December 1978, Vietnam announced formation of the Kampuchean United Front for National Salvation (KUFNS) under Heng Samrin, a former DK division commander. It was composed of Khmer communists who had remained in Vietnam after 1975 and officials from the eastern sector – like Heng Samrin and Hun Sen – who had fled to Vietnam from Cambodia in 1978. In late December 1978, Vietnamese forces launched a full invasion of Cambodia, capturing Phnom Penh on January 7, 1979 and driving the remnants of Democratic Kampuchea's army westward toward Thailand.

Within the CPK, the Paris-educated leadership – Pol Pot, Leng Sary, Nuon Chea, and Son Sen – were in control. In 1976, a new constitution established Democratic Kampuchea as a Communist People's Republic, and a 250- member Assembly of the Representatives of the People of Kampuchea (PRA) was selected in March to choose the collective leadership of a state Presidium, the Chairman of which became the head of State.

Prince Sihanouk resigned as Head of State on April 4, 1976. On April 14, 1976, after its first session, the PRA announced that Khieu Samphan would chair the State Presidium for a five-year term. It also picked a 15-member cabinet headed by Pol Pot as Prime Minister. Prince Sihanouk was put under virtual house arrest.

Social and Cultural implications of the regime

Thousands starved or died of disease during the evacuation and its aftermath. Many of those forced to evacuate the cities were resettled in newly created villages which lacked food, agricultural implements, and medical care. Many who lived in cities had lost the skills necessary for survival in an agrarian environment. Thousands starved before the first harvest. Hunger and malnutrition, bordering on starvation, were constant during those years. Most military and civilian leaders of the former regime who failed to disguise their past were executed. Some of the ethnicities in Cambodia, such as the Cham suffered specific and targeted and violent persecutions. To the point of some international sources referring to it as the 'Cham genoside'. Entire families and towns were targeted and attacked with the goal of significantly diminishing their numbers and eventually eliminated them. Life in 'democratic Kampuchea' was strict and brutal. In many areas of the country, people were rounded up and executed for speaking a foreign language, wearing glasses, scavenging for food, and even for crying for dead loved ones. Former businessmen and bureaucrats were hunted down and killed along with their entire families; the Khmer Rouge feared that they held beliefs that could lead them to oppose their regime. A few Khmer Rouge loyalists were even killed for failing to find enough 'counter-revolutionaries' to execute.

Modern research located 20,000 mass graves from the Khmer Rouge era all over Cambodia. Various studies estimated the death toll at between 740,000 and 3,000,000, most commonly between 1.4 million and 2.2 million, with perhaps half of those deaths being due to executions, and the most from starvation and disease.

A US State Department funded Cambodian Genocide Project estimated approximately 1.7 million killings. R.J. Rummel, an analyst of historical political killings, gave a figure of 2 million.

A UN investigation reported 2 to 3 million dead, while UNICEF estimated 3 million had been killed. Demographic analysis by Patrick Heuveline suggested that between 1.17 and 3.42 million Cambodians were killed, while Marek Sliwinski estimated that 1.8 million was a conservative figure. Researcher Craig Etcheson of the Documentation Centre of Cambodia suggested that the death toll was between 2 and 2.5 million, with a 'most likely' figure of 2.2 million. After 5 years of researching grave sites, he concluded that 'these mass graves contain the remains of 1,386,734 victims of execution.

10. VIETNAMESE OCCUPATION AND THE PEOPLE'S REPUBLIC OF KAMPUCHEA (1979 – 1989) AND LATER RENAMED AS 'THE STATE OF CAMBODIA' (1989- 1993)

On January 10, 1979, after the Vietnamese army and the KUFNS invaded Cambodia, the new People's Republic of Kampuchea (PRK) was established with Heng Samrin as head of State. Pol Pot's Khmer Rouge forces retreated rapidly to the Thai border. The Khmer Rouge and the PRK began a costly struggle that played into the hands of the larger powers, namely, China, the United States and the Soviet Union.

A civil war was imposed on impoverished Cambodia that displaced 600,000 Cambodians to refugee camps along the border between Thailand and Cambodia. The new regime murdered tens of thousands of people.

Peace efforts began in Paris in 1989 under the State of Cambodia, culminating two years later in October 1991 in a comprehensive peace settlement. The United Nations was given a mandate to enforce a ceasefire, and deal with refugees and disarmament known as the United Nations Transitional Authority in Cambodia (UNTAC).

11. MODERN CAMBODIA (1993 – present)

On October 23, 1991, the Paris Conference reconvened to sign a comprehensive settlement giving the UN full authority to supervise a ceasefire, repatriate the displaced Khmer along the border with Thailand, disarm and demobilize the factional armies, and prepare the country for free and fair elections. Prince Sihanouk, President of the Supreme National Council of Cambodia (SNC), and other members of the SNC returned to Phnom Penh in November 1991, to begin the resettlement process in Cambodia. The UN Advance Mission for Cambodia (UNAMC) was deployed at the same time to maintain liaison among the factions and to begin demining operations to expedite the repatriation of approximately 370,000 Cambodians from Thailand.

On March 16,1992, the UN Transitional Authority in Cambodia (UNTAC) arrived in Phnom Penh to begin implementation of the UN Settlement Plan. The UN High Commissioner for Refugees began full-scale repatriation in March 1992. UNTAC grew into a 22,000-strong civilian and military peace-keeping force to conduct free and fair elections for a constitutional assembly.

Over 4 million Cambodians (about 90 percent of eligible voters) participated in the May 1993 elections, although the Khmer Rouge or Party of Democratic Kampuchea (PDK), whose forces were never actually disarmed or demobilized, barred some people from participating. Prince Ranariddh's royalist FUNCINPEC Party was the top vote recipient with 45.5 percent of the vote, followed by Hun Sen's Cambodian People's Party and the Buddhist Liberal Democratic Party, respectively. FUNCINPEC then entered into a coalition with the other parties that had participated in the election. The parties represented in the 120member assembly proceeded to draft and approve a new constitution, which was promulgated on September 24,1993. It established a multiparty liberal democracy in the framework of a constitutional monarchy, with the former Prince Sihanouk elevated to King. Prince Ranariddh and Hun Sen became First and Second Prime Ministers respectively, in the Royal Cambodian Government (RGC). But in 1997, Ranariddh was ousted by a coup and fled to Paris and was replaced with Ung Huot. Prince Ranariddh was tried in his absence and found guilty of arms smuggling, but was then pardoned by the King. Many FUNCINPEC leaders were forced to flee the country during and after the coup. However, FUNCINPEC leaders returned to Cambodia shortly before the 1998 National Assembly election. In 1998 election, the CPP received 41 percent of the vote, FUNCINPEC 32 percent, and the Sam Rainsy Party (SRP) 13 percent. The CPP and FUNCINPEC formed another coalition government, with CPP the senior partner. Hun Sen became Prime Minister, Ranariddh was President of the National Assembly.

Cambodia's first commune elections were held in February 2002. The election results of 1,621 commune (municipality) councils were largely acceptable to the major parties, though procedures for the new local councils were not being fully implemented. In July 2003, National Assembly election were held and the Cambodian People's Party of Prime Minister Hun Sen won a majority, but not enough to rule outright. The King then urged the two other parties, Sam Rainsy Party and FUNCINPEC, to accept the incumbent Hun Sen as prime minister. In mid-2004, a coalition government was formed by CPP and FUNCINPEC and Hun Sen became the Prime Minister.

On October 4, 2004, the Cambodian National Assembly ratified an agreement with the United Nations on the establishment of a tribunal to try senior leaders responsible for the atrocities committed by the Khmer Rouge. Donor countries pledged USD43 million international share of the three-year tribunal budget, while the Cambodian government's share of the budget was USD13.3 million. The Tribunal started trials of senior Khmer Rouge leaders in 2008. Cambodia also had been recovering from the land mines which were used heavily by the Khmer Rouge and Vietnamese fighters. By June, 2015, it was believed that all most all of the land mines had probably been removed from Cambodia. In July 2008 and July 2013 Parliamentary elections, Hun Sen's ruling CPP claimed victory. Similarly, in 2018 also, ruling CPP won the Parliamentary election.

CAMBODIA – A CHRONOLOGY OF EVOLUTION AT A GLANCE

1863: Cambodia became a protectorate of France. French colonial rule lasted for 90 years.

1941: Prince Norodom Sihanouk became King. Cambodia was occupied by Japan during World War 11.

1945: The Japanese occupation ended.

1946: France re-imposed its protectorate. A new Constitution permitted Cambodians to form political parties. Communist guerrillas began an armed campaign against the French.

1953: Cambodia won its independence from France. Under King Sihanouk, it became the Kingdom of Cambodia.

1955: Sihanouk abdicated to pursue a political career. His father became King and Sihanouk became prime minister.

1960: King Sihanouk died. Prime Minister Sihanouk became head of state.

1965: Cambodia broke off relations with the US and allowed North Vietnamese guerrillas to set up bases in Cambodia in pursuance of their campaign against the US-backed government in South Vietnam.

1969: The US began a secret bombing campaign against North Vietnamese forces on Cambodian soil.

1970: Prime Minister Lon Nol overthrew Sihanouk in coup. He proclaimed the Khmer Republic and sent the army to fight the North Vietnamese in Cambodia. Sihanouk -- in exile in China – formed a guerrilla movement. Over next few years, the Cambodian army lost territory against the North Vietnamese and communist Khmer Rouge guerrillas.

1975: Lon Nol was overthrown as the Khmer Rouge led by Pol Pot occupied Phnom Penh. Sihanouk briefly became head of state, the country was re-named Kampuchea.

All city-dwellers were forcibly moved to the countryside to become agricultural workers. Money became worthless, basic freedoms were curtailed and religion was banned. The Khmer Rouge coined the phrase 'year zero'.

Hundreds of thousands of the educated middle-classes were tortured and executed in special centers. Others starved, or died from diseases or exhaustion. The total death toll during the next years was estimated to be at least 1.7 million.

1976: The country was re-named Democratic Kampuchea. Sihanouk resigned; Khieu Samphan became head of state; Pol Pot became Prime Minister.

1977: Fighting broke out with Vietnam.

1978: Vietnamese forces invaded in a lightning assault.

1979: The Vietnamese took Phnom Penh. Pol Pot and Khmer Rouge forces fled to the border region with Thailand. The People's republic of Kampuchea was established.

1981: The pro-Vietnamese Kampuchean People's Revolutionary Party won parliamentary elections. The international community refused to recognize the new government.

The government–in-exile, which included the Khmer Rouge and Sihanouk, retained its seat at the United Nations.

1985: Hun Sen became Prime Minister. Cambodia was plagued by guerrilla warfare. Hundreds of thousands became refugees.

1989: Vietnamese troops withdrew. Hun Sen tried to attract foreign investment by abandoning socialism. The country was re-named the State of Cambodia. Buddhism was re-established as the state religion.

1991: A peace agreement was signed in Paris. A UN transitional authority shared power temporarily with representatives of the various factions in Cambodia. Sihanouk became head of state.

1993: General election saw the royalist FUNCINPEC party won the most seats followed by Hun Sen's Cambodian People's Party (CPP).

A three-party coalition was formed with FUNCINPEC's Prince Norodom Ranariddh as Prime Minister and Hun Sen as Deputy Prime Minister.

The monarchy was restored. Sihanouk became King again. The country was re-named the Kingdom of Cambodia. The government–in-exile lost its seat at the UN.

1994: Thousands of Khmer Rouge guerrillas surrendered in government amnesty.

1996: Deputy leader of Khmer Rouge Leng Sary formed a new party and was granted amnesty by Sihanouk.

1997: Hun Sen mounted a coup against the Prime Minister, Prince Ranariddh, and replaced him with Ung Huot. The coup attracted international condemnation. The Khmer Rouge put Pol Pot on trial and sentenced him to life imprisonment.

1998: Prince Ranariddh was tried in his absence and found guilty of arms smuggling, but was then pardoned by the King. Pol Pot died in his jungle hideout in April 1998. In July 1998, elections were won by Hun Sen's CPP, amid allegations of harassment. A coalition was formed between the CPP and FUNCINPEC. Hun Sen became Prime Minister. Ranariddh became President of the National Assembly.

2001: A law setting up a tribunal to bring genocide charges against Khmer Rouge leaders was passed. International donors, encouraged by reform efforts, pledged USD560 million in aid.

In June 2001, US-based Cambodian Freedom Fighter (CFF) members convicted of 2000 attack in Phnom Penh. Group pledged to continue campaign to overthrow Hun Sen.

In December 2001, first bridge across the Mekong River opened, linking east and west Cambodia.

2002: First multi-party local elections were held. Ruling Cambodian People's Party won in all but 23 out of 1,620 communes. Ranariddh's half-brother Prince Norodom Chakrapong set up his own Norodom Chakrapong Khmer Soul Party.

2003: Serious diplomatic upset with Thailand over comments attributed to a Thai TV star that the Angkor Wat temple complex was stolen from Thailand. Angry crowds attacked the Thai embassy in Phnom Penh. Hun Sen's Cambodian People's Party won general election but failed to secure sufficient majority to govern alone.

2004: After nearly a year of political deadlock, Prime Minister Hun Sen was re-elected after CPP struck a deal with the loyalist FUNCINPEC party. Parliament ratified Kingdom's entry into World Trade Organization (WTO). King Sihanouk abdicated and was succeeded by his son Norodom Sihamoni.

2005: In February 2005, opposition leader Sam Rainsy went abroad after parliament stripped him of immunity from prosecution, leaving him open to defamation charges brought by the ruling coalition.

In April 2005, Tribunal to try Khmer Rouge leaders received green light from UN after years of debate about funding.

In December 2005, Rainsy was convicted in absentia of defaming Hun Sen and was sentenced to 18 months in prison.

2006: In February 2006, Rainsy received a royal pardon and returned home.

In May 2006, Parliament voted to abolish prison terms for defamation.

In July 2006, Ta Mok, one of the top leaders of the Khmer Rouge regime, died aged 80.

In November 2006, FUNCINPEC party, a junior partner in the ruling coalition, dropped Prince Norodom Ranariddh as the leader.

2007: In March 2007, Ranariddh was sentenced in absentia to 18 months in prison for selling the FUNCINPEC party's headquarters – a charge he denied.

In July 2007, UN-backed tribunals began questioning Khmer Rouge suspects about allegations of genocide.

In September 2007, most senior surviving Khmer Rouge member, Nuon Chea – 'Brother Number Two' – was arrested and charged with crimes against humanity.

2008: In April 2008, US court convicted CFF leader Chhun Yasith of master-minding 2000 attack in Phnom Penh.

In July 2008, Hun Sen's ruling CPP claimed victory in parliamentary election criticized by EU monitors. Cambodia and Thailand moved troops to disputed land near Preah Vihear temple after decision to list it as UN World Heritage Site fanned nationalist sentiment on both sides.

In October 2008, two Cambodian soldiers died in an exchange of fire with Thai troops in the disputed area. One Thai soldier died later of wounds.

2009: Former Khmer Rouge leader Kaing Guck Eav known as Duch went on trial on charges of presiding over the murder and torture of thousands of people as head of the notorious Tuol Sleng prison camp.

Parliament again stripped opposition leader Sam Rainsy of immunity. He was charged but failed to appear in court.

Another row with Thailand, after Cambodia refused to extradite ex-Thai prime minister Thaksin Shinawatra and appointed him as an economic adviser instead.

2010: Comrade Duch was found guilty of crimes against humanity and was awarded 35- years prison sentence.

Diplomatic ties with Thailand resumed after Cambodian government announced resignation of Thaksin Shinawatra.

Exiled opposition leader Sam Rainsy was sentenced in absentia to 10-year in jail after being found guilty of manipulating a map to suggest Cambodia was losing land to Vietnam.

2011: Tensions rose as Cambodia charged two Thai citizens with spying after they were arrested for crossing the disputed border. Respective forces exchanged fire across the border. Hun Sen called UN peace keepers.

Three most senior surviving Khmer Rouge members, including leader Pol Pot's right-hand man, 'Brother Number Two' Nuon Chea, went on trial on charges of genocide and crimes against humanity.

Cambodia and Thailand agreed to withdraw troops from disputed area.

2012: In February 2012, Duch lost appeal against conviction at UN-backed tribunal and had sentence increased to life.

In March 2012, a second judge quit the tribunal. Swiss judge Laurent Kasper said that he was leaving because his Cambodian counterpart, You bunleng, had thwarted attempts to investigate some former members of the Khmer Rouge regime.

In April 2012, outspoken environmental activist Chut Wuthy was shot dead in a confrontation with police while travelling in a threatened forest region in the south-west.

In May 2012, government suspended the granting of land for development by private companies in a bid to curb evictions and illegal logging.

In July 2012, Cambodia and Thailand withdrew their troops from a disputed border area near the Preah Vihear temple in line with a ruling by the International Court of Justice which aimed to halt out-breaks of armed conflict in recent years.

In October 2012, former King Norodom Sihanouk, died of a heart attack. He was 89.

In November 2012, government approved the controversial Lower Sesan 2 hydroelectric dam project on a tributary of the Mekong.

2013: In February 2013, tens of thousands of people turned out in Phnom Penh for the cremation of the former king, Norodom Sihanouk.

In March 2013, former Khmer Rouge Foreign Minister Leng Sary died while awaiting trial for genocide, leaving only Nuon Chea and Khieu Samphan among prominent Khmer Rouge figures still alive and under arrest by the UN-backed tribunal.

In June 2013, Parliament passed a bill making it illegal to deny that atrocities were committed by the Khmer Rouge in the 1970s.

In July 2013, opposition leader Sam Rainsy returned from exile.

In September 2013, mass protests happened in Phnom Penh over contested election results. Parliament approved new five-year term for Hun Sen. Opposition boycotted the parliament.

2014: In January 2014, riot police cleared a two-week opposition protest camp held in Phnom Penh as part of a long-running campaign launched against the government after the disputed 2013 election.

In July 2014, more than 150,000 Cambodian workers returned home from neighboring Thailand after rumors circulated that the new military junta there would crack down on illegal migrants.

Opposition Cambodia National Rescue Party (CNRP) agreed to end its year-long boycott of parliament as part of an agreement with Prime Minister Hun Sen to break the dead lock over the disputed 2013 parliamentary election.

In August 2014, a UN-backed court in Cambodia sentenced two senior Khmer Rouge leaders to life in prison for their role in the terror that swept the country in the 1970s. The two, second-in-command Nuon Chea, and the former head of state Khieu Samphan, were the first top Khmer Rouge figures to be jailed.

2015: In January 2015, Prime Minister Hun Sen marked thirty years in power.

In March 2015, a UN-backed tribunal in Cambodia indicted two more former commanders of the Khmer Rouge, Im Cheam and Meas Muth, with crimes against humanity.

2016: In September, Prime Minister Hun Sen declared a political 'ceasefire' following a wave of prosecutions of opposition members ahead of elections in 2018.

In October 2016, opposition Cambodian National Rescue Party (CNRP) resumed it's months-long parliamentary boycott over alleged threats from the ruling party.

In November 2016, a UN-backed tribunal upheld the life sentences of former Khmer Rouge leaders Nuon Chea and Khieu Samphan after they appealed against their convictions for crimes against humanity.

In December 2016, exiled opposition leader Sam Rainsy was sentenced to five years in prison after a document was published on his Facebook page which the government said was a forgery. Mr. Rainsy was found guilty of posting an inaccurate post about a border treaty between Cambodia and Vietnam.

2017: In February, Sam Rainsy resigned as head of the Cambodian National Rescue Party (CNRP). He had been in self-imposed exile since 2005, when parliament stripped him of his immunity. Cambodian Parliament amended a law to bar anyone convicted of an offence from running for office. The legislation in effect banned main opposition politician Sam Rainsy from participating politics after he was found guilty of defamation.

In March 2017, human rights activist Kem Sokha was appointed as the new leader of the opposition Cambodia National Rescue Party (CNRP), replacing Sam Rainsy.

In September 2017, opposition leader Kem Sokha was charged with treason.

In November 2017, Cambodia's Supreme Court dissolved the Cambodia National Rescue Party, the country's only significant opposition party.

2018: In February, Cambodia introduced lese-majeste law, which made it a criminal offence to defame or insult the King.

In July 2018, Prime Minister Hun Sen's ruling CPP party won all 125 seats in the Parliamentary election.

2019: In August, Sam Rainsy of the banned Cambodia National Rescue Party expressed his plan to return to Cambodia from exile in November 9. He also vowed to 'liberate' Kem Sokha, a co-founder of the banned party, who has been under house arrest since 2017 on the charges of treason which is fabricated as explained by Rainsy. However, since Mr.Rainsy's return was announced in August, Cambodian authorities have launched a fresh crackdown on members of the outlawed party.

2020: In February, Cambodian Prime Minister Hun Sen met Chinese President Xi Jinping in Beijing in a show of solidarity amid the corona virus crisis. Hun Sen was the first foreign leader to visit China after the outbreak began, calling Cambodia and China 'steadfast friends' and criticizing other countries for restricting travel to China.

In July 2020, Cambodia concluded its FTA talks with Mainland China, as mentioned by the Cambodian Ministry of Commerce. According to Cambodian officials, the deal was expected to propel bilateral trade between Cambodia and People's Republic of China (PRC) to USD10 billion by 2023.

CHAPTER-THREE
RURAL DEVELOPMENT THROUGH RAPID TRANSFORMATION IN AGRICULTURE

Any discussion of Cambodian political and economic development without discussing rural Cambodia, will be incomplete. According to the World Bank collection of development indicators, compiled from officially recognized sources, 76.61 percent of Cambodia's population lives in rural villages in 2018. Agriculture continues to play an important role in Cambodia's economy, but it provides a livelihood for a smaller proportion of today's population than it did in the past. A study from the agriculture ministry released in June 2017 found that around 40 percent of the population work in farming, down from about 80 percent in 1993. Agriculture accounted for 22 percent of Cambodia's GDP in 2019. Rice is by far the most important product, making up around half of agricultural GDP and using around 3.3 million hectares of land in 2019. Fishing and fisheries make up another cornerstone of Cambodia's rural economy providing an estimated 80 percent of animal protein in the typical Cambodian diet.

The Cambodian government has prioritized agriculture as a key sector for development since the government first released its Rectangular Strategy. Version VIII of the strategy aims to push agricultural investment beyond strengthening rural incomes, into improved technology, research and development, crop diversification and promotion of commercial production and agro-industries.

The above policy decisions signaled a transition away from small-scale family farms to industrial farming. The trend is partly enabled by government lease of large land holdings to private companies as economic land concessions (ELC). Contract farming and private land leases are other vehicles through which industrial agriculture in Cambodia is expanding.

In terms of the history of rice production in Cambodia, rice has been cultivated by Khmer farm households in these lowlands of Cambodia for perhaps 3000 years and probably longer in the uplands (Helmers 1997; Higham 2014). The more intensive lowland rice techniques developed in southern China --- involving the use of the plough to prepare bunded rice fields into which seedlings are transplanted from a nursery – were introduced about 1500 years ago. The powerful kingdom of Angkor which dominated the region from the ninth to the fourteenth centuries was based on the appropriation of rice surpluses and the mass mobilization of rural labor through slavery. The capital of Angkor located near Siem Reap to the north of the Tonle Sap Lake was surrounded by rice paddies irrigated from large reservoirs through a system of canals, permitting multiple cropping (Higham 2014: 400-403). With the decline of Angkor, the centre of population moved to the South-Eastern part of present-day Cambodia, which is still the most densely populated part of the country. Rice farming in this period was probably sufficient for the needs of rural households, though it was still faced with threats from an unpredictable environment, state-imposed taxes and periodic conflicts. Nevertheless, over the centuries, farmers had adapted rice-growing to the different ecosystems and selected suitable varieties for local conditions; about 2000 traditional rice varieties have been identified as unique to Cambodia (Helmers 1997).

Under the French colonial regime, little was done to improve small-holder rice production; hence yields remained at a little over 1 ton per hectare. The growth of production was almost entirely due to the expansion of cultivated area. From 1900 to 1950, the area cultivated increased, in line with population growth, from about 400,000 hectares to 1,660,000 hectares, and total production increased from 560,000 tons to 1,580,000 tons, but the average yield declined from 1.4 tons per hectare to 1.0 tons per hectare (Slocomb 2010: 59). From 1900, the French administration pursued a policy of promoting agricultural exports, especially of rice and cattle, to supply French agro-processing and export businesses in Saigon (Helmers 1997). French settlers were given more than 16,000 hectare of land concessions to establish large rice estates on fertile soils in Battambang Province using hired labor. These estates were supported with infrastructure including irrigation works, research stations (focusing on varieties, fertilizers, and mechanization), and a railway line to Phnom Penh. In the pre-war decades, rice exports ranged from 50,000 to 200,000 tons of paddy per year, of which around 30,000 tons came from the Battambang plantations and the rest from smallholders. By 1940, Cambodia was the world's third largest rice-exporting country (Helmers 1997). Smallholders did reasonably well out of these sales when prices were high, such as in the 1920s, but scaled back cultivation to subsistence levels and sought relief from the rice tax when prices fell, as in the 1930s.

Under Prince Sihanouk's Sangkum government (1953 – 1970), there was investment in irrigation infrastructure in some provinces and six rice research stations were established for varietal trials and seed production. The government also took control of the French rice plantations in Battambang. By 1965, paddy production had grown to 2.75 million tons and exports to 500,000 tons, almost entirely due to further expansion in cultivated area; yields remained around 1.1 tons per hectare (Helmers 1997). A state corporation was established in 1962 with a monopoly over production inputs and rice exports. By the mid-1960s, the corporation sought to forcibly collect rice at low official prices, prompting the growth of black-market trade to Vietnam and armed rebellions in Battambang and elsewhere (Kiernan and Boua 1981).

A favorable season in 1969 meant that, in early 1970, the rice crop was a record 3.8 million tons. However, as the war situation escalated, including American carpet bombing in the east of the country, rice production was devastated. Under Lon Nol's Khmer Republic (1970-1975), total output fell by 84 percent (Helmers 1997; Slocomb 2010: 147-149). Exports were suspended in 1971 in an attempt to shore up domestic stocks. The Democratic Kampuchea (Khmer Rouge) regime that controlled Cambodia from 1975 to 1979 focused on developing rice production (Helmers 1997; Slocomb 2010), not just for subsistence but to provide the surplus to fund its revolutionary program for economic independence (or 'Super Great Leap Forward'). The regime brutally forced people to work in the paddy fields and construct irrigation systems throughout Cambodia as part of its ambitious plan to achieve two or three crops a year and raise yields to 3 tons per hectare. However, most of the irrigation schemes failed and the forced collectivization of labor left the country's agriculture in disarray. Rice was requisitioned to supply the army and to export in exchange for arms, while locals starved. When Vietnamese forces took over in 1979, they found that the countryside was devastated and famine was widespread.

The Vietnamese installed People's Republic of Kampuchea (PRK) (1979-1989) focused on rehabilitating rice farming, but with very limited resources. Farming was again organized on socialist lines, with all land collectivized and groups of 20-25 households constituted as the basic unit of production, though in practice it was common for individual households to manage their own plots within the village communal land and for the groups to merely share animals and equipment and to exchange labor. Vietnamese advisers introduced some International Rice Research Institute (IRRI) varieties such as IR36 and IR42 but there was no rice research service to test or promote these and other modern inputs. The Cambodia – IRRI – Australia Project (CIAP) was established in 1987 and began to build the country's rice research capacity, but the impact was not seen until the 1990s. During 1980 – 1989, the area cultivated increased by 31 percent from 1,441,000 hectares to 1,890,000 hectares, short of the PRK's target of 2.5 million hectares, and total production increased by 54 percent from 1,670,000 tons to 2,570,000 tons, below the target of 3 million tons (Slocomb 2010). Average yields increased only slightly from 1.2 to 1.4 tons per hectare. Nevertheless, by the end of the decade, Cambodia was almost self-sufficient in rice. In 1989, the PRK was renamed the State of Cambodia and crucial reforms were introduced (Helmers 1997; Slocomb 2010). Private land tenure was established, with the communal lands broken up and allocated to individual households based on the number of household members, and the market economy was legitimized, in recognition of its de facto reassertion in the preceding decade.

The Royal Government of Cambodia (RGC) was installed after the United Nations (UN) supervised elections in 1993, paving the way for increased foreign investment and aid directed to agricultural and rural development. At this point, farmers in the low lands were still largely dependent on conventional farming practices, low-yielding traditional varieties, very low rates of inorganic fertilizers, almost no use of agrochemical inputs, and little mechanization of land preparation or harvesting. They were subject to various pressures, including the seasonality and variability of rainfall, lack of irrigation, poor soil fertility, weed and pest problems, few farm resources, and limited access to inputs, credit, and markets. The average yield from rainfed lowland rice was only 1.5 tons per hectare, one of the lowest in Asia (Nesbitt 1997b; Javier 1997). Hence the majority of households were producing rice at subsistence levels. In addition, opportunities for productive employment of land and labor in the dry season were limited. Meanwhile population growth in the decade to 1993 had surged to between 2.9 and 3.9 percent. As mentioned earlier, agricultural research had resumed in the late 1980s under CIAP and this began to have an impact in the 1990s. The primary objective was to improve rice production to alleviate the country's chronic rice shortage. By 2006, 37 improved varieties had been developed and released, mainly for the rainfed lowlands, with a potential yield range of 2.5 tons to 4.5 tons per hectare (Sakhan et al. 2007). The program also covered rice agronomy, pest management, soil classification, and mechanization (Nesbitt 1997b). This research effort has had a significant impact on rice yields and production in Cambodia, providing the basis for the expansion of output and exports in recent decades.

AGRICULTURAL AND RURAL GROWTH SINCE 1993

After the war-time devastation of the 1970s and 1980s, the Cambodian economy experienced more than two decades of rapid growth, averaging 7.6 percent over the period 1994-2019 (World Bank 2019). GDP per capita also steadily increased from USD1,043 in 2013 to more than USD1,561 in 2018 and continued to increase to USD1,621 in 2019, giving Cambodia, in the process, the status of a lower middle-income country. This growth has been associated with a marked reduction in poverty, from 48 percent in 2007 to 14 percent in 2014 and then further reduced to 12.9 percent in 2018, though most families who escaped poverty remain 'near-poor' and economic inequality like everywhere in the world, is on the rise. With the growth of the industry and service sectors (particularly garment manufacture, construction, and tourism), agriculture's share of the economy has declined over the period. The average value added in the Agricultural sector as percent of GDP from 1993 to 2018 was 34.28 percent with a minimum of 22.01 percent in 2018 and a maximum of 47.72 percent in 1995. Agriculture as a proportion of gross domestic product (GDP) fell from 47.72 percent in 1995 to 28 percent in 2015. In 2018, the share of agriculture in Cambodia's gross domestic product was 22.01 percent. In 2019, the Cambodian economy remained on track and grew strongly despite a slower than anticipated rise in agricultural production. While industry and services had grown faster than agriculture, the agricultural sector also grew at a rapid rate. Gross Agricultural Production grew 8.7 percent during 2004 to 2012 and Agricultural Value Added at 5.3 percent (World Bank 2015). This rapid growth was driven by crop production, mainly the rice sector, the output of which has grown at 5 percent from 1990 to 2017. Reports from the Ministry of Agriculture, Forestry and Fisheries revealed that as of December 2019, paddy rice was cultivated on an area of 2.5 million hectares with an average yield of 3.1 tons per hectare. This was lower than the yield hectare of the neighboring countries, such as Thailand (3.5 tons per hectare), Laos (4.1 tons per hectare), and Vietnam (6.2 tons per hectare). In 2019, around 8 million tons of wet season rice production in Cambodia was reported by Khmer Times. About two-thirds of the reduction in poverty during the period was attributable to agricultural growth, where higher rice prices stimulated increased production and farm incomes as well as pushing up farm wages. According to a review of the agricultural sector by the World Bank (2015), Cambodian agriculture has benefited from a market-oriented policy, including (a) an open trade policy, enabling farmers to benefit from improved access to the international market as well as cross-border trade with Thailand and Vietnam; (b) wider availability of machinery services such as threshers and combine harvesters; (c) better access to rural finance, especially micro-finance; and (d) investment in rice milling.

The growth in rice production was due partly to an expansion of cultivated area (at a rate of 1.7 percent during 1990-2019), but more so to an increase in yields (at a rate of 3.5 percent in the same period). Moreover, the area expansion has levelled off while there is still potential for further yield growth. The national rice yield in Cambodia now averages 3.5 tons per hectare, compared with 1.1 tons per hectare in the 1960s and 1.5 tons per hectare in the 1990s (MAFF 2013; Helmers 1997; Nesbitt 1997b). The yield increase was mainly due to the adoption of improved varieties and increased use of fertilizer; only 8-9 percent of arable land is irrigated and the potential for expanding surface irrigation infrastructure is limited (Johnston et al. 2013). The more profitable Cambodian aromatic rice varieties, mainly grown in the western provinces such as Battambang, now account for 10 percent of the annual cultivated area and 30 percent of total production (World Bank 2019). The growth in production has generated a rice surplus above estimated domestic requirements (World Bank 2019). The notional surplus increased from 1.44 million tons of milled rice in 2008 to 2.38 million tons in 2013. With increasing liberalization of trade and explicit government encouragement -- especially with the 2010 Policy Paper on the Promotion of Paddy production and Rice Export, in which rice was designated as 'White Gold' – the export of rice has increased sharply (ADB 2014). In 2013, formal exports of rice were 378,850 tons, exported to over 50 countries, 91 percent of which were in the EU or Asia; half of these official exports were of high-quality fragrant rice. This was well below the target enunciated in the 2010 Policy Paper of 1 million tons of milled rice exports by 2015. However, in 2013, informal cross-border trade of rice and paddy (un-milled rice) to Vietnam and Thailand was estimated to be 1.5 million tons (in milled rice equivalent). Thus total exports of rice and paddy increased nearly 20-fold from 2008 to 2013, from just over 100,000 tons to 1.9 million tons (in milled equivalent). Though drying and milling capacity still remained a constraint and exports are still mainly in the form of paddy, capacity of the mills were being increased from 20 tons per hour in 2009, when there were only two large rice milling companies, to over 700 tons per hour in 2013. In 2018, official data indicated that milled rice exports had risen further to 626,225 tons. There was no corresponding figure for official and unofficial paddy exports, but the evidence is that these continue to exceed the exports of milled rice by a substantial margin. As Khmer Times reported, in 2019, Cambodia's milled rice were exported in 59 countries by 89 rice-exporting companies. As per Cambodia's Grain and Feed Annual Report published by USDA Foreign Agricultural Services, for marketing year 2018-2019, rice harvested area reduced to 3,190 thousand hectares owing to unfavorable weather conditions, but increased production to 9.23 million metric tons (MMT)as yield increased on the harvested acreage. As forecasted by them, in the marketing year 2019-2020, rice harvested area will not expand and production will increase modestly by one percent over marketing year 2018-2019, to 9.33 million metric tons on the basis of continued increasing yields. Also as per USDA report, reduced natural water supply resulting from El Nino would affect corn production in Cambodia where land for industrial crops is not sufficiently irrigated. However, in marketing year 2018-2019, harvested area and production were above USDA official numbers as farmers kept their expanded acreage from marketing year 2017 – 2018 in production.

Realizing the benefits of the growth at the farm household level depends on access to land, labor, water, finance, and markets. However, many rice-growing households in Cambodia, especially in the South-Eastern lowlands, have farms of less than one hectare. For Cambodia as a whole, the average size of rice farms increased from 1.9 hectare in 2008 to 2.1 hectare in 2012 (World Bank 2015), reflecting out-migration from the densely populated south-east and in-migration and area expansion in the north and north-west. However, this disguises an increase in inequality, with the average size of small farms decreasing during the period (from 1.0 hectare to 0.9 hectare) and the average size of medium and large farms increasing (from 1.6 hectare to 2.4 hectare and from 3.6 hectares to 7.0 hectares, respectively). At the same time, the unit profitability of rice farming has increased. Gross margins for wet season rice were estimated to be about USD250 per hectare and USD5.00 per day and for Dry season rice, USD300 per hectare and USD10 per day. However, for small firms using modern technology, the gross margin was USD522 per hectare in the wet season and USD276 per hectare in the dry season. The increasingly growth in profitability as well as the growth in population has increased the demand for land, as reflected in rising prices – the purchase price for rainfed lowland plots increased by 400 percent from 2005 to 2019 and for irrigated land by 820 percent.

Rice farming has also been undergoing rapid mechanization, following the trend in Thailand and Vietnam, with significant implications for labor requirements (World Bank 2019). Mechanization initially took the form of power tillers (two-wheeled tractors) for land preparation and small, moveable pumps for irrigation (whether from rivers, canals, receding floodwaters, farm ponds, or tube wells). These were attractive because they were affordable, multifunctional, and saved on labor, time, and costs. Contracted services of reapers and threshers were also widely taken up but are being overtaken by combine harvesters, the number of which is rapidly increasing. However, methods to save on planting labor such as drum seeders and rice planters have not been widely adopted. As a consequence of this mechanization process, the labor used in wet season rice production decreased during 2010-2019 and such decrease in labor utilization for dry season rice production was even more in the same period. There is further room and potential for these labor requirements to be reduced further.

Access to irrigation schemes, as noted earlier, has been limited and there are few suitable sites for further expansion of surface irrigation infrastructure. However, in recent decades, there has been an increase in the use of groundwater for irrigation, especially in the south-eastern lowlands. While groundwater has been used for domestic purposes for centuries, the availability of small, portable pumps has encouraged many farmers to sink tube wells in their rice fields and use this source for supplementary irrigation of wet season or dry season (recessional)rice, or for alternative, less water-demanding dry season crops. The sustainability of this use of groundwater is still a matter for research, with some evidence of long-term decline in Prey Veng and Svay RiengProvinces, though in Kandal and Takeo, closer to the main channel of the Mekong and Bassac Rivers, it seems that aquifers are readily recharged during each wet season. Access to this form of on-farm irrigation can have a significant impact on the productivity of rice-based cropping system.

Another trend affecting the capacity of small-scale rice farmers to increase production and incomes is the availability of credit. Before the 1990s, farmers only had access to short-term, high-interest loans from local money lenders. From 1993, there was a proliferation of non-government organizations (NGOs) involved in rural development, some of which offered micro-finance. One of these has grown into the Association of Cambodian Local Economic Development Agencies (ACLEDA) Bank, Cambodia's largest commercial bank with branches in Myanmar and Laos. From 2000 onwards, government reforms enabled many of these NGOs to become specialized micro-finance institutions (MFI), providing loans at commercial interest rates for use as working capital (to pay for seed, fertilizer, hired labor, and other inputs) and to purchase durable capital items such as pumps and two-wheeled tractors (and also land). By 2019, there were more than 80 MFIs registered with the National Bank of Cambodia (NBC) – and there are additional hundreds of smaller NGOs, rural credit operators and unlicensed moneylenders that also offer microloans. As reported by the Chairman of the Cambodia Microfinance Association (CMA) in October 21, 2019, that more than 2.1 million Cambodian families are benefitting from the services of MFIs, borrowing a combined more than USD6 billion. He also mentioned that about 90 percent of all villages in the Kingdom are enjoying access to micro-credit. He aimed to expand micro-finance services to every village in Cambodia so that people living in rural areas can access loans to expand their businesses and have better lives.

Apart from rice farming, a significant proportion of farm households throughout Cambodia now also depend on non-farm work opportunities for their livelihoods. The recent rapid developments of construction, light industry, and the services sector in urban centers, especially in and around Phnom Penh, has provided many job opportunities. Young household members frequently migrate to urban areas to seek non-farm employment to help support their families in the villages.

While these young wage earners have few skills and little future earning potential, their absence from the villages can severely constrain the farm labor force.

In line with the Rectangular Strategy, Cambodia's agriculture sector witnessed expanded diversification into other crops, such as corn, sugarcane, cashew nuts, rubber and cassava during the last decade. The land area of non-paddy crops grew from 210,000 hectares in 2008 to 770,000 hectares in 2012 and the area under rubber nearly doubled between 2008 and 2013, when it reached 307,854 hectares. By June 2017, 433,827 hectares were under cultivation for rubber. International investments in the sector are becoming more visible. For example, in April 2016, a USD360 million Chinese-owned sugar mill was officially opened in Preah Vihear province. The Plant has an annual production capacity of 360,000 tons of sugar, 50,000 litres of ethanol and 9 megawatts of electricity. While mentioning that Cambodia now produces a wide range of crops which are typical of a tropical country; it is noteworthy that given it's natural endowments, Cambodia has high potential to produce high-quality products. In addition, the kingdom has been relatively preserved from excessive use of chemicals so far. With a growing effort to enforce strict norms and standards, Cambodia should be able to gain an increasing share of the international markets for major crops.

The crop yield of subsidiary and industrial crops is increasing much faster than that of rice. Subsidiary crops enjoyed a 400 percent boom in production between 2006 and 2019. In addition to providing an alternative source of income, growing subsidiary and industrial crops offers higher returns to producers. To support this transformation, several programs assist farmers by providing them with market information, training, and technology as well as financing options. Collaborating with such projects could provide a market entry mechanism for prospective Dutch businesses aiming to supply Cambodian farmers with agricultural inputs. Such products are typically exempted from import tariffs and investments in this field are eligible for various incentives. Hence, given the expertise of Dutch companies, irrigation solutions, agricultural machinery, seed distribution and fertilizers could be considered as relevant opportunities. One more thing that Cambodia also lacks a developed food processing industry – only 10 percent of Cambodia's agricultural goods are processed. Likewise, much of Cambodia's agricultural exports are raw products (cashew nuts, mangoes, rubber, and cassava), headed to Thailand and Vietnam, where they are processed. This results in a significant loss of potential value add for Cambodia. Local industries for products like cassava starch, rubber products or processed fruits are still nascent but remain open to venture investors, and remain a mostly untapped market.

While referring to livestock and fisheries sectors of Cambodia, rising living standards, coupled with greater diversification of household food consumption has led to an increased demand for livestock and meat. Cambodia imported 54,149 tons of livestock and meat to meet domestic demand in 2019, according to a Ministry of Agriculture, Forestry and Fisheries report. According to the report, Cambodia, in 2019, produced a total of 231,283 tons of meat for domestic consumption, equivalent to 81 percent of total domestic demand. Cambodia's Ministry of Agriculture, Forestry and Fisheries also reported that the decline in family livestock raising operations and a growing demand for food has forced the kingdom to import meat from foreign countries to fill the shortages. However, the Ministry, as reported, is currently focusing on promoting domestic rearing. The Ministry expressed their hope that for the year 2020 and the next coming years, Cambodia's meat imports will be reduced. The Ministry has a policy of boosting domestic rearing by at least three percent annually. It is also reported that the commercial animal rearing in Cambodia is gradually showing positive sign of growth. In 2019, Cambodia also exported animals for meat to foreign markets. According to the UN's Food and Agriculture Organization, the average Cambodian eats 17.6 kg of meat per year – including 5kg of beef, 9.29kg of pork, 3.3kg of poultry and 0.01kg miscellaneous meats.

The fisheries sector covers freshwater fishing, maritime fishing and aquaculture, all of which are present in Cambodia. Aquaculture in particular follows a promising trend (+139 percent growth in 2019 compared to 2010). Following this development, it could be possible for companies to target Cambodian aqua-firms as a potential market for fish seeds and feed.

In terms of future strategy and assistance program for Cambodia, Asian Development Bank's (ADB) sector strategy will continue to support four key areas: agricultural productivity enhancement, diversification, commercialization and connectivity, and sustainable natural resources management. ADB's strategy is deliberately selective in pursuit of these ends.

Enhancing agricultural productivity involves measures to make on-farm practices more efficient, based on the improved use of natural resources (e.g., soils and water) and non-exploitation of ecologically sensitive areas. Given that the Cambodia's government regards rice development as a flagship priority, ADB's approach will be to replicate some of the productivity-oriented components of the Tonle Sap Poverty Reduction and Smallholder Development Project (e.g., improved access to quality seeds, markets, and agricultural extension through innovative rural information and communication technology) and the Climate-Resilient Rice Commercialization Sector Development Program (e.g., land use zoning and planning ecosystem mapping and soil classification, improved land management, seed production and distribution, technical extension materials production). ADB is also committed to extend coverage into other provinces around the Tonle Sap Basin. This includes irrigation systems enhancement, mainly to improve the efficiency of water management through land leveling (and to accommodate increasing peak flows), and to maintain operational sustainability (e.g., through farmer water user committees). This scheme includes basic research and extension capacity development within the Ministry of Agriculture, Forestry and Fisheries.

Enhancing scope for future productivity growth in Cambodia's agriculture requires a greater orientation toward higher-value outputs, especially non-commodity outputs capable of value-added transformation. Promoting diversification involves better rationalization of the production resource base to allow more specialization within rice cultivation. This includes higher value and internationally competitive varieties, and promoting the cultivation of higher-value non-rice crops. Higher-value rice includes glutinous rice, aromatic rice (many of which have historically been quite area-specific in their cultivation), and rice grown under organic production systems. Non-rice crops are typically fruits and vegetables in lowland and irrigated areas, but also include flowers, bamboo, pulses, maize, cassava, and tree crops in upland areas, as well as livestock (in the east) and aquaculture. Although many crops and primary outputs with such value-adding potential are already known in Cambodia, areas are small, cultivation and management history is short, and agronomic and economic data are largely absent. Accordingly, ADB commits support for research and development of rice varieties and non-rice crops with market potential. This includes the development of environmentally friendly input regimes and management practices (e.g., by better managing input applications) to replace those that are potentially damaging to soils, water, and wider ecosystems. Such regimes include the system of Rice Intensification, 'drought escape', precision or drip irrigation, small-scale intercropping, zero or minimum tillage, and bare and degraded lands planting.

Commercialization is going to support by a range of national and regional measures that use to (1) make agriculture more market-oriented; and (2)better link primary producers to product markets, Cambodia's urban areas, and regional demand. This scheme will incorporate support for (a) filling critical parts of the country's rural infrastructure deficit through the expansion of post-harvest facilities (for transport, cleaning, drying, grading, and storage); (b) improving rice milling efficiency (i.e., by providing access to credit and technical capacity building to reduce Cambodia's high milling costs); (c) promoting access to farm development credit, market information, technology transfer, and other farm business services (including weather-related crop insurance, soil testing, and equipment provision and servicing); and (d) improvements in rice marketing, focusing on non-rice crops that have market potential. Investment designs will explore innovative ways of partnering with the private sector, based on experiences gained in Cambodia and elsewhere. Options for the private sector to bid for supply and manage services, such as information and extension, on behalf of government to be explored.

Support for sustainable natural resources management includes (a) mapping ecosystem functions and conducting assessments of ecosystem services as inputs into land-use planning processes; (b) strengthening and supporting natural resource institutions and processes; (c) improving the biodiversity monitoring system to maintain ecosystem integrity; (d) strengthening community organizations in forestry and fishery protected areas to manage common property resources; (e) supporting innovations for developing community livelihoods based on conservation; and (f) supporting forest and fishery resources policing (i.e., training and increasing numbers of rangers and community-based forest patrollers).

Toward gender development, a large number of women work in agriculture, but are under-remunerated for their efforts because they are mainly engaged in subsistence production. In the proposed pipeline, gender mainstreaming will continue to be emphasized to help the government achieve gender targets stated in the National Strategic Development Plan. ADB projects and programs aim to (1) support women's participation in local planning and decision-making forums, such as those related to irrigation infrastructure investments and water user groups; (2) improve women's access to training and new technologies to increase productivity and support a shift to higher value, market oriented production; and (3) increase women's access to markets and financial services.

As a very recent endeavor, toward Cambodia's rural economic development in general and agricultural sector development in particular as well as to modernize Cambodia's agriculture, the Agriculture Sector Master Plan 2030 (ASMP 2030) is a promising plan. The Department of Planning and Statistic (DPS) of the Ministry of Agriculture, Forestry and Fisheries (MAFF) and the Food and Agriculture Organization of the United Nations (FAO) organized a consultative workshop on 14th February 2020 in Phnom Penh where around one hundred representatives from government ministries, development partners, civil society and NGOs gathered and conveyed their inputs. It was the first national workshop of this kind, which was held to collect inputs from all relevant stakeholders for ASMP 2030 which envisaged a competitive, inclusive, resilient and sustainable modern agriculture sector in Cambodia in the next ten years. For Cambodia, the said MAFF led event was also recognized as a formal national level consultation that gathered all relevant government ministries and development partners (DPs), who would be able to provide substantive inputs to the 35th UN FAO Regional Conference for Asia and Pacific (APRC) to be convened in 2020. The ASMP 2030 will be the main reference document from which MAFF will base it's contribution to APRC.

As summarized by the Secretary General of MAFF, the ASMP 2030 discussed challenges facing Cambodia's agriculture sector, from main crops, animal production to fisheries and forestry, and a growing local and international demand for high quality agricultural produce for food. The Secretary General also emphasized the significant decline of natural resources, including water scarcity and the severe change of climate, causing irregular weather pattern and drought. These are also some of the key themes to be covered at the FAO 35th APRC, the highest governing body of the Organization at Regional level, a forum for government ministers and delegates from more than 40 countries in the region, with other institutions, civil society and the private sector as observers, to meet and debate challenges related to food and agriculture. It's main outcomes are recommendations which will ensure FAO's effective work and priorities in the region for the following two years.

Agriculture remains one of the Cambodia's key economic drivers and is a source of employment for about 42 per cent of the population, the World Bank reported in 2017. The RGC recognized that agriculture has important roles in contributing to the attainment of the Sustainable Development Goals (SDGs) as indicated in a number of country's strategies and policies, such as the Rectangular Strategy IV, the National Strategic Development Plan (NSDP) 2019-2023, and the Zero Hunger Action Plan, 2016-2025. Secretary of State of MAFF said during his opening remarks that ASMP 2030 will help improve farmers' livelihood and food security for Cambodia as the Master Plan looks not only at boosting agricultural production, but to enhance agricultural commercialization, processing and an inclusive value chain for exports. ASMP 2030 is set to achieve at least three percent rise in the total valued added in the sector annually while bringing annual agricultural labor productivity up to USD4,625 by 2030 from about USD1,839 in 2018. In order to reach the set indicators, strategic objectives and actions, the plan must be centred on increasing competitiveness, inclusive agricultural growth, high quality, safe and nutritious products for farmers and Cambodian population while ensuring the sustainable use of land, fisheries and forestry resource management. In other words, this long-term strategic plan is required to support the country to strengthen a vibrant agricultural sector that benefits Cambodian farmers and the population everywhere. By ensuring safe and quality and nutritious foods for people, a larger scale of quality products can enter regional and international markets, maximizing the country's agricultural markets and trade.

Participants of the Workshop were actively engaged in the discussion and shared their comments on each indicator, together with suggested constructive strategic actions to reach the target. FAO representative in Cambodia indicated the high importance of the AMSP to guide the development of the sector

Rural Development through Rapid Transformation in Agriculture

until 2030. He also added that the revitalization of the sector is critical for economic development and for the livelihoods of the very large percentage of the population, as they continue to rely on agriculture, animal production, fisheries and forestry as main source of income. Diversification of production, development of value chains and value adding are all recognized as essential aspects for the modernization of agriculture and for meeting the challenges of the future. He continued that rapid rate of urbanization in Cambodia has important implications for patterns of food production and consumption. Achieving the country's Zero Hunger challenge Action Plan by 2025 and the Cambodian SDGs of a 'world with zero hunger' by 2030 will require more productive, efficient and sustainable food production and systems in the country. This will require an urgent transformation of the current agri-food system, and a better awareness of the importance of nutrition.

Secretary of State of MAFF, at his closing remarks, thanked all stakeholders and partners and ensured that MAFF's policy formulation team will take into consideration all inputs from all stakeholders and partners and work closely with relevant ministries to revise the concerned indicators.

CHAPTER-FOUR
THE FACT-SHEETS OF INDUSTRIAL PERFORMANCE AND DEVELOPMENT-A REVIEW

A. CONTEXT OF THE CAMBODIAN ECONOMY

Over the last 62 years since its independence in 1953, Cambodia has experienced a number of very different political ideologies which strongly influenced its industrial policy of the time. The main regimes were : (1) The Sihanouk Regime (1953 – 1970), which attempted to foster industrial development through a mixed approach of encouraging private capital and enterprises coupled with State investments; (2) The Khmer Republic (1970 – 1975), which adopted a laissez faire approach but was ravaged by civil war; (3) Democratic Kampuchea (1975 – 1979), which saw the rise to power of the Khmer Rouge leading to nationalization, de-industrialization, genocide, and the destruction of all private capital; (4) the People's Republic of Kampuchea (PRK) (1979 – 1989), a socialist regime with a focus on agriculture that remained closed to the world economy; (5) the State of Cambodia and the UN Period (1989 – 1993), a transition period to a market economy; and (6) the Kingdom of Cambodia (1993 to present day), a market economy mainly based on foreign investment and foreign markets.

Since the 1993 election, overseen by the United Nations (UN), Cambodia has been in transition to a full market economy, following decades of war and isolation from international markets by a socialist regime. It is since then that an expansion of industry has been observed. Accordingly, since 1993, the industrial sector has played important role in the Cambodian economy. Its share in GDP increased from a mere 12.6 percent to 26.2 percent in 2006. The industrial sector suffered a short decline and remained steady at 22 percent due to the change in international trade regime and the global economic crisis. In 2013, the sector's share in GDP rebounded to around 24 percent. The average annual growth rate spread over the past 15 years (1998 – 2013) was estimated at 12.4 percent compared to 4.7 percent and 8.5 percent for the agriculture and the service sector respectively. In that light, the industrial sector is the best performer in term of achieving the highest growth.

The industrial sector is also the main provider of jobs. In 1993, about 72 percent of the total labor force was in the agriculture as compared only to about 5 percent in the industrial sector. However, according to the 2008 population census, jobs in the industrial sector accounted to nearly 600,000 or an equivalent of 8.6 percent of the total jobs. Again, according to the 2012 Socio-Economic survey, the number jumped to some 1.4 million jobs or an equivalent of 18.6 percent of the total jobs. It would be relevant to note, however, that these jobs are seasonally adjusted. Based on the labor force survey for the dry season of the year 2012, there were some 1.8 million jobs or an equivalent of 25.2 percent of the total jobs.

Cambodia's current economic growth does not rely much on investment, which signifies that there is still room for more investment. An analysis on the contribution of expenditure to GDP indicates that the source of growth of over 70 percent of GDP depends on private consumption, 12 percent in public expenditure of the government and other organizations, leaving export and investment covering the rest. By the standard of developing countries, the contribution rate of investment should be between 30 percent and 40 percent or possibly higher in order to boost the economy to jump to the next level of development. As it stands, Cambodia's economic growth relies heavily on the garment, tourism, construction and rice sectors, implying there is a need to invest more to prop up new economic growth.

Interestingly, the growth in some major sectors still rely primarily on external environment as the country's economic policies are totally market driven. In general, core sectors of the economy are determined by international trade activities. For example, the garment sector grew in response to the quota system of the US and the EU trade preferences; the rice export growth has witnessed a sharp increase, thanks to the EU trading scheme. Furthermore, the tourism sector growth, which is linked to Cambodia's cultural heritage and nature, depends on the growth of income. Cambodia requires to utilize these opportunities to create the necessary economic base for modernizing its industrial sector, and to capture other emerging opportunities to propel its industrial development to a higher level.

As a whole, the industrial sector requires to play a crucial role once again in the growth strategy as a driving force for supporting medium to long-term growth, a potential sector for job creation specifically for youth and a new enforcement for the economy to absorb additional investment besides agriculture and tourism.

B. EVOLUTION OF INDUSTRY: A HISTORICAL PERSPECTIVE

a. Sihanouk Regime (1953 – 1970)

Cambodia gained full independence from France in 1953. During the French Colonial era (1863 – 1953), emphasis was placed on agriculture and as such the newly independent Cambodian economy began with a low industrial base. The colonial administration focused on house-hold based rice cultivation, the development of large rubber plantations and the integration of the economy of Cambodia to the French economy. Some factories were established to supply the domestic market including textiles, paper and foundries, but had to rely on imports of raw materials which were foreign-owned or owned by the elite Chinese ethnic group.

The focus of the newly independent Cambodian State that emerged in 1953 was on building Cambodia's industrial base. It was attempted to achieve this through a policy of modernization which was the trend in the newly independent states in Asia and Africa at that time. The Two –Year Plan (1956 – 1957) also known as the ' Plan of Study, reflection and experimentation ' and the first Five- Year Plan (1960 - !964) were introduced . The Two – year plan (1956 – '57) concentrated on developing infrastructure, while the Five – Year Plan (1960 – '64) focused more on building factories. During Sihanouk regime, Cambodia largely accepted economic co-existence with foreign interests, hiring foreign personnel to fill the posts formally staffed by the French administration during the French colonial era and accepting foreign capital investments. The economy could best be described as a mixed economy which merged individual capital and enterprise with state capital and supervision. The State created enterprises to break the monopoly of local Chinese merchants in purchasing agricultural products and selling them to villages. State co-operatives in the country-side also operated their own credit programs which historically were monopolized by the Chinese. The following Table shows a significant increase in the number of factories between 1955 and 1968, from none to 28 State-owned factories and 29 Joint-venture factories (private and public ownership) while small and medium private factories increased dramatically from 650 in 1965 to 3,700 in 1968.

TABLE : 4.1 The Number and Classification of Factories between 1955 and 1968

	1955	1968
State-owned factories Joint-Venture factories	0	28
(private and public ownership)	0	29
Small and medium Private factories	650	3,700

Source: Working paper entitled 'Economic history of industrialization in Cambodia' by Sokty Chhair and Luyna Ung.

In Cambodia, the first railway was built in 1922 by France, connecting the north-eastern part of the country, known as the rice bowl of Cambodia, to Phnom Penh, the Capital city. The purpose of the railway was to integrate Cambodia's economy to the world, rather than to promote development within Cambodia. In 1939, as mentioned by Khieu (1959), 80 percent of the volume of products transported by the railway were destined for abroad. Only remaining 20 percent were shipped to the rest of the country.

During the cold war period, Cambodia experienced significant investment in infrastructure largely financed by donor interests. As a peaceful island surrounded by war-torn countries in Indo-China, it was a strategically important location from a military perspective, particularly given the neutral foreign policy adopted by Prince Sihanouk during the 1960s. As a result, Cambodia saw it's foreign assistance increase from donors on both sides of the cold war. With this heavy assistance, several megaprojects were built: the highway linking the capital Phnom Penh and the port city of Sihanouk Ville was built with American aid and the port itself with French funding; French and Germany jointly funded railway construction connecting Phnom Penh to Sihanouk Ville; a 10,000 kilowatts Kirirom hydro-electric plant was constructed with a loan from Yugoslavia; while a plywood factory was built with Chinese aid (Slocomb 2010). In addition, the Chinese built a 5,000 tons paper mill, a textile factory, and a large cement factory. Three other factories were built by the Czech; a palm sugar refinery in Kampong Spen, a tire factory at Takhmau in Kandal, and a tractor assembly plant in Sihanouk Ville. In the Five-Year economic plan (January 1960 to December 1964), only 2 percent of the budget was contributed by Cambodia, 57 percent of the contribution was from the USA, 23 percent from China, and 17 percent from France.

While infrastructure improved, along with the number of enterprises, there was little by way of structural change evident in the aggregate figures. As narrated in the following Table:

4.2, manufacturing accounted for 8.6 percent of GDP in 1962, increased to 10.5 percent in 1966, and 12 percent (including mining) in 1968. Cambodia's exports overwhelmingly depended on primary products. Rice and rubber were by far the largest exports, accounted for more than half of total exports.

The removal of protective tariffs at the end of 1969 heavily hit small enterprises, which accounted for 90 percent of firms at that time. Due to the protective industrial policies, many firms could not compete when being exposed to foreign markets. Only a handful of large investors benefited from the policy change but they too were affected by inflation and rising labor costs. Efforts were made to industrialize further through a policy of import-substitution but this had little success due to the prevailing inefficiencies of state-owned enterprises. The survival of these enterprises had mainly been sustained by heavily protected tariffs. By the end of this era, the economic structure of Cambodia appeared similar to the economy of the newly independent economy in 1953.

TABLE: 4.2 Sector Share of GDP at 1966 Prices, in % 1962-1966

Agriculture	30.7	30.3
Animal Husbandry	4.3	4.9
Fishing	2.4	2.3
Forestry	3.9	3.5
Salt mining	0.1	--
Manufacturing	8.6	10.5
Energy and Water supply	0.9	1.1
Construction	6.8	5.3
Transportation	2.0	2.1
Commerce	23.8	22.2
Public administration, Defence, and Financial Institutions	13.1	14.4
Other services	3.4	3.4

Source : Ministry of Planning (1966) cited in Slocomb (2010)

TABLE: 4.3 Sector Share of GDP in Cambodia, 1968

ECONOMIC ACTIVITY IN 1968	
Agriculture	41%
Commerce	23%
Mines and Industries	12%
Construction	5%
Transportation	2%
Other services	17%

Source: Based on Chantrabot (1993) cited in Ear (2009:49)

b. Khmer Republic (1970 – 1975)

From 1970, Cambodia was plunged into a civil war with each side supported by either China or the USA. However, even before the regime change in 1970, the leaders of the coup, General Lon Nol and Sisowath Sirik Matak, who would be the new leaders in the new regime, led the national salvation government from August,1969 charged with the responsibility of reviving the stagnant economy which emerged from the Sihanouk regime.

The new policy, which embraced laissez faire, involved devaluing the currency, removing state controls on foreign trade and banking, and reducing state involvement in enterprise. In other words, the most significant change to industrial policy was the disengagement of the public sector and the emphasis on private enterprises as the mechanism for commercial and industrial development (Slocomb 2010). Rice and maize production were liberalized with the dissolution of state monopoly over the export of grains and cereals. The state only remained the monopoly power in the production and distribution of electricity above 500 kilowatts, military-related sectors, railway, postal services, and telecommunication services.

These policies were, however, short-lived and their implementations were interrupted by the civil war. The price of necessities was fixed and controlled by the State and the State kept it's exclusive monopoly over all main primary products such as rice, maize, rubber, and precious or semi-precious stones. The war-time economy depended solely on foreign assistance, mostly from the USA, for survival.

Table 4.4 highlights the impact that the civil war had on the agricultural production for rice, rubber, and corn leading to significantly lower yields. The manufacturing index which had been 100 in 1960 fell to 73 in 1972.

TABLE : 4.4 Agricultural Production in Hundreds of Thousands of Metric Tons, 1968–1974

	1968-69	1969-70	1970-71	1971-72	1972-73	1973-74
Rice	2,503	3,814	2,732	2,138	953	762
Rubber (tons)	51	52	13	1	15	12
Corn	117	137	121	80	73	---
Palm Sugar	---	34	23	---	---	---

Source : Based on Ear (1995)

c. Closed Economy (1975 – 1989)

The period spanning 1975 and 1989 consisted of two rival regimes both of which followed a Marxist ideology. Slocomb (2010) described Cambodia during this period as a revolutionary economy. Both regimes closed the door to foreign investment and markets and their priority sector was agriculture with industry playing only a supporting role in supplying agricultural implements and processing agricultural products. The extent to which the two regimes adopted Marxism was their main distinction. The former was more harsher and dogmatic while the later was more pragmatic and responsive to local conditions.

d. Democratic Kampuchea (1975 – 1979)

The Khmer Rouge came to power influenced heavily by Maoist ideology. The ambition was to make the transition to communism in Cambodia in the shortest possible time period.

The economic policy was to demolish capitalists, enslave the labor force and focus on the rapid development of agriculture. To achieve this, the regime completely and immediately collectivized agriculture, nationalized all sectors of the economy, and adopted a policy of self-reliance. All assets were owned by the state and all international involvements were removed. This new policy completely reversed the economic policy adopted by the previous regime which represented a shift from one extreme pole of economic ideology to the other. Phnom Penh and other provincial cities were emptied and the urbanites were forced to work as collective farmers in the country-side. Private ownership was completely banned and money was eliminated. From 1975 to 1979, the bourgeoisie class was considered an enemy of the state and entrepreneurship disappeared. The regime also banned all international trade leaving only very limited trade with a few allied communist countries.

e. People's Republic of Kampuchea (1979–1989)

After the liberation of Cambodia from the Khmer Rouge Regime, the new regime, the PRK left with little to restore was the Cambodian economy. The economy was dominated by subsistence agriculture with little or no industry. During the period of PRK regime, only 63 out of 85 enterprises in Cambodia were potentially operational but only 12 factories were functioning producing textiles, tires, plastics, and iron tools with raw materials supplied by international non-governmental aid agencies (Slocomb 2010:215). The first task of the PRK was to restore food and self-sufficiency in an economy where human and physical infrastructure had been destroyed. A guerrilla war with the Khmer Rouge, who were still at large along Cambodia's border with Thailand, persisted. Engineers, skilled workers, and other human resources had either fled to other countries as war refugees or fell victims of genocide. From 1979 to 1989, economic policy focused on food security and the eradication of hunger throughout the country. State-owned enterprises were re-established, which included tobacco, cotton, and electricity companies, a mechanical workshop, spare parts, beverage and glass-ware factory, and a tire factory, all with the aim of providing basic consumer goods and public utilities. State enterprises frequently sold products at subsidized prices and/or offered them as rations for government officials. The State subsidized prices for some basic commodities such as kerosene, cigarettes, soap, rice, sugar, and condensed milk. During the 1980s, informal trade and smuggling were widespread.

According to Vickery (1986: 128-29), there were three economic organizations that co-existed in the economic system adopted by the PRK. First, there was the state which controlled large industry, finance, transport, official foreign commerce, and some large agricultural plantations. Second, there were the collectives, called solidarity groups, which controlled agricultural production such as land and agricultural equipment. Third, there was the family which involved small trade, handicraft, and side agricultural works which households could engage in once they finished their obligations to the solidarity group. In 1986, ninety-seven percent of the rural population were in the collective sector which was composed of more than 100,000 solidarity groups each of which consisted of seven to fifteen families. This was not enough, however, to feed the population of Cambodia and immediate food relief was provided by Vietnam, the soviet-bloc countries and international humanitarian aid organizations.

In 1988, the total value of industrial production, including handicraft was only USD20 million but it was dominated by state-owned enterprises (Slocomb 2010:215). The share of industry in GDP was only 5 percent in 1985 compared to 19 percent in 1969, while the share of agriculture in GDP increased to 90 percent in 1985. Until 1985, only about half of the pre-war plants had re-opened and the ones that did produced far below full capacity due to frequent electricity power cuts and a lack of spare parts and raw materials. In 1988, the share of state-owned manufacturing output was around two-thirds of all manufacturing output.

d. State of Cambodia and The UN Period (1989–1993)

With the fall of the Soviet Union and the Eastern Bloc, the reform was the beginning of the gradual process of economic transformation. The process of reform toward becoming a market economy was compounded by the signing of the Paris Peace Accord in October 1991. As part of the peace agreement, the government of Cambodia relinquished its role in certain areas during the rehabilitation phase. This included the provision of basic needs such as food, security, health, housing, training, education, public utilities, and basic transport infrastructure. During the reconstruction phase, entrepreneurship and private sector development was also promoted to prepare for entry into a free market economy.

The International Committee on the Reconstruction of Cambodia, a consultative body which included the government, donors, and other involved parties, monitored the process of transition. This body, which later evolved into the consultative group, met annually to provide loans and grants for development, on the condition of reforms being implemented by the government. Through these reforms, Cambodia's political and economic development moved from a command to a laissez faire capitalist economy, from a large to a small bureaucracy, and from domestic to export-oriented production (Slocomb 2010:289). In the mid-1980, Cambodia introduced private property leading to the gradual privatization of state-owned companies and the de-collectivization of agriculture.

Table 4.5 illustrates some of the successes of this period with GDP experiencing strong growth in 1988 at 9.8 percent, a slowdown in 1989 and 1990, and a recovery thereafter largely driven by the build-up of the UN operation. Agriculture contributed slightly over half of GDP during this time while the service sector accounted for around 33 percent of output and industry 15 percent.

TABLE: 4.5 Real GDP Growth Rate and Share of GDP, 1988-'92

	1988	1989	1990	1991	1992
GDP	9.8	3.5	1.2	7.6	6.9
AGRICULTURE	5.9	7.1	1.2	6.7	4.8
INDUSTRY	15	1.8	-2.1	8.9	8.4
SERVICES	13.6	--1.1	2.7	8.4	9.5

GDP BY SECTOR					
AGRICULTURE	50.5	52.2	52.3	51.8	50.8
INDUSTRY	15.7	15.4	14.9	15.1	15.3
SERVICES	33.8	32.4	32.8	33.1	33.9

Source : Based on Irvin (1993)

These successes and market reforms were, however, undermined by macroeconomic imbalances caused by declining state revenue due to the increased unit cost of goods and services procured for operations and investments, the removal of humanitarian aid and credit from the Soviet Union, and high inflation caused by monetary financing of the budget deficit (Royal Government of Cambodia 2009). As a result, the inflation rate accelerated from 70 percent in 1989 to 200 percent in 1992 (Table 4.6). Inflation was stabilized in 1993 through reductions in the government deficit (Irvin 1993) but the high inflation rate of the previous years led to a decline in public confidence in the national currency and the permanent dollarization of the economy.

TABLE: 4.6 Inflation Rate, 1989-1992 :

GDP BY SECTOR				
YEAR	1989	1990	1991	1992
RATE (%)	70	157	121	200

Source: Based on Ear(1995).

e. Kingdom of Cambodia (1993 – Present)

After the first general election in 1993, the government prepared and implemented a comprehensive macro-economic policy and structural reform program with efforts to integrate Cambodia's economy into the region and the world. In the late 1980s, Cambodia began the process of market liberalization. The state monopoly to foreign trade was abolished in 1987, and the foreign investment law was brought into force in 1989, enabling private companies to engage in foreign trade. In the early 1990s, trade policies were further liberalized, largely removing restrictions on firms and individuals engaged in international trade. Most quantitative restrictions and the licensing of imports were eliminated. In the late 1990s, there was a more deliberate phase of positive steps toward a highly liberal trade regime.

To promote industrial development, the government provided generous incentives to attract foreign direct investment (FDI) and at the same time strived to find export markets for FDI-manufactured products. Tax exemptions were provided on imported intermediate goods and on the exporting of finished goods. Cambodia became a member of the ASEAN Free Trade Area in 1999 and eventually the World Trade Organization (WTO) in 2003. Membership of these organizations placed further requirements on Cambodia to liberalize trade in goods and services and foreign capital ownership. FDI played a significant role in creating production bases, especially to exploit trade opportunities in advanced economies. The inflow of FDI increased from just USD124 million in 1993 to USD520 million in 2009 and to over USD1.5 billion in 2012 and to over nearly

USD3.6 billion in 2019, up 12 percent year-on-year, from 2018 (based on database of the Ministry of Economy and Finance).

Many state-owned activities have been terminated and only economically viable enterprises are allowed to continue. Public enterprises compete with the private sector in the area of utilities, education, and transportation and most only survive due to geographical constraints to regional and world competition. As per data and information provided by Economic Census (EC2011) conducted by the National Institute of Statistics (NIS) and the Ministry of Planning in March 2011, private establishments accounted for 96 percent of the total number of establishments and 90 percent of the number of persons engaged in 2011, while state-owned establishments accounted for less than 3 percent of the total number of establishments and 8 percent of the number of persons engaged.

Cambodia's growth performance ranked 6th. across all countries in the world and has higher exports per capita than other countries at Cambodia's level of economic development (World Bank 2019).

As mentioned, Cambodia's economy is predominantly private. There are fewer state-owned enterprises than in many neighboring countries. In 2018, agriculture accounted for around 22.01 percent of GDP, industry contributed approximately 32.29 percent and the services sector contributed about 39.49 percent to Cambodia's total GDP. Despite significant growth in manufacturing and services, the majority of people (78 percent) still live in rural areas in 2019. Annual population growth fell from 1.5 percent over the period 1998-2008 to 1.2 percent between 2008 and 2019.

The Cambodian economy has undergone a significant transition. While garments and tourism are two of the most important industries, other manufacturing and service industries have also emerged in recent years. The economy is more diversified in 2019 than it was in 2008 when 80 percent of exports were garments and 55 percent were to the United States.

In 2014, 69 percent of exports were garments and 17 percent to the United States. In 2019, 68 percent of total exports were garment, textile and footwear products and approximately 20 percent of Cambodia's total exports going to the United States. However, there is potential for more growth and diversification.

Like many developing countries, the majority of businesses in Cambodia are very small (74 percent engage only one or two people). In addition, most are informal (98.8 percent of businesses with less than 10 employees are not registered). While these businesses form a significant part of the economy and provide work for many people, they tend to be less productive than larger businesses. Smaller and informal businesses also are less likely to have access to finance, pay less (or no) taxes, and typically do not provide training for their workers or comply with labor laws and other regulations. Most Cambodians (6.2 million persons) worked in rural areas in 2014, and 57 percent of these worked directly in agriculture. In 2019, nearly 12 million people were living in rural areas and around 65 percent of the rural working Cambodians relied on agriculture, fisheries, and forestry for their livelihoods. Around 58 percent of total employed persons worked in agriculture in 2009, and than reduced to around 45 percent in 2014, and further reduced to around 32.3 percent in 2019. The proportion of workers in industry increased from 16 percent in 2009, to 24 percent in 2014 and to 29 percent in 2019, reflecting growth in light manufacturing as well as construction and other activities. Cambodia has significant potential to make more productive use of its people.

Key risk factors for Cambodia's economic development include its dependence on a few key sectors such as garments, agro-processing, tourism, and construction, which are vulnerable to international markets, coupled with the fact that technological spillovers and economic linkages from foreign firms to other sectors of economy are low. The government in recent years has begun to promote local micro, small, and medium enterprises, and also to increase the value addition of the production chain.

C. PRESENT STATUS OF THE INDUSTRIAL SECTOR IN CAMBODIA

As mentioned earlier, it was not until the early 1990s that industrial development was given prominence in economic policy in Cambodia. The growth of industry can be categorized into four different phases. The first phase, 1993-1998, saw an increase in the share of manufacturing to GDP from 12 to 16 percent. The second phase was from 1999-2003, when Cambodia had achieved full peace in 1998 and successfully integrated into ASEAN in 1999. At the end of 2004, growth in the garment sector, the driver of the manufacturing sector, faced uncertainty due to the expiration of the multi-fibre arrangement (MFA). The third phase of manufacturing development during 2004-2007 began when Cambodia became a member of the WTO. During this phase, the share of the manufacturing sector in the economy reached its peak of more than 25 percent of GDP. During the fourth and recent phase, from 2008 to 2019, Cambodia witnessed steady industrial growth, despite some hindrances due to global financial crisis, and industry related major policy decisions.

Cambodia's industrial sector has been dominated by manufacturing and construction during the last ten years. Food, beverages, and tobacco (FBT) and textile, wearing apparel, and footwear (TWF) together account for 80 percent of value added of the manufacturing sector. The number of enterprises in Cambodia has been increasing gradually during the last two decades. The labor force participation rate always keeps itself high at around 82 percent, while employment continues to increase according to the World Bank collection of development indicators. World Bank data also indicated, the number of employed people (15-64) increased from 6.8 million in 2007 to about 8.6 million in 2016, and to 8.88 million in 2019. This corresponds to the average growth rate of 2.7 percent during 2007-2019. By sector, agriculture employment registered a negative growth rate of 10.7 percent, while the employment in the service sector increased by 79.5 percent; and in the industrial sector grew the highest rate of 182.7 percent. Similar to the case of GDP, the share of total employment in agriculture has declined while it increased in industry. Particularly, between 2007 and 2019, the share of employment in agriculture decreased from 57.7 percent in 2007 to 36.4 percent in 2016, and to 32.3 percent in 2019. At the same time, employment in industry increased from 15.5 percent in 2007 to 26.6 percent in 2016, and to 29 percent in 2019. It is evident that there is a certain movement of workforce from agriculture to other sectors, particularly to industry. As per official data compiled from authorized sources, between 2007 and 2019, the economy created more than 2.9 million non-farm jobs, most of them were in export-oriented garment sectors, of which around one-third were filled by workers shifted out from agriculture. As National Employment Agency (NEA) of Cambodia reported based on CSES data, the annual employment growth rates were -3 percent, 4.5 percent, and 5.2 percent for agriculture, industry and services respectively, and the overall annual employment growth rate was 1.6 percent during 2014 and 2019. The major increases in employment (in terms of absolute number) happened in trade (around 65,000), garments (around 56, 000), hotel and restaurant (around 55,000), construction (around 37,000), other manufacturing (around 15,000), and transport and communication (around 14,000) during 2014-2019. As per survey conducted by the National Employment Agency of Cambodia in 2018, there were 4,571 of total establishments, accounted for about 962,972 employments as of 2017. Briefly by sector, there were ten sectors that underwent the survey, such as accommodation; construction; education; finance and insurance; food and beverage; garment, footwear and apparel; health; ICT; logistic; warehousing and transportation; and rubber and plastics.

Based on GDP, the industrial sector consists of three important activities, namely: garment production, construction and food and beverage processing. Other sectors have yet to make significant inroad while wood and paper processing and publishing has even seen a decline. The garment sector plays an important role in the industrial sector with its share jumping from a mere 8.2 percent in 1993 to 51.8 percent in 2004, the year of its highest growth. Subsequently, it witnessed a slight decline down to 42.4 percent in 2013. The number of garment and footwear factories registered for exports in Cambodia over 2019 jumped 24 percent compared with the year earlier, according to new data from the Ministry of Commerce. The Cambodian Ministry of commerce's annual report, cited by The Phnom Penh Post, says it granted export rights under the preferential trading system to 78 garments, footwears and bag factories in the first eleven months of 2019. The report adds that Cambodia's exports to international markets reached more than USD10 billion in the first ten months of 2019, mainly from the garment, textile, footwear and travel products sectors. Garments exports were worth USD8.2 billion, textiles USD40 million and footwear USD905 million. The garment sector continues to be one key engine of growth, providing on average 635,000 jobs in 2018 at 643 factories. Around 90 percent of the workforce is female. Cambodia is the second largest beneficiary of Everything but Arms (EBA) trade preferences, accounting for over 18 percent of all imports coming into the EU market under the EBA scheme in 2018. EU imports from Cambodia totaled Euro5.3 billion in 2018, 95 percent of which took advantage of EBA preferences. Clothing and textiles accounted for around three-quarters of EU imports from Cambodia at Euro 4billion. However, in February 2019, the EU Commission started the process that could lead to a temporary suspension of Cambodia's preferential tariff arrangements under the EBA trade scheme. EBA preferences can be removed if beneficiary countries fail to respect core human rights and labor rights, and the EU has for some time been concerned about human rights violations in Cambodia. The decision if imposed by the Commission would come into effect by 1st September, 2020. Such suspension would lead to a permanent decline in garment sector output and employment in the long run, the report noted.

As mentioned earlier, European Union was the largest importer (46 percent) of Cambodia's garment sector and the

United States was the second (24 percent) in 2019. However, exports to other markets have been growing strongly. Canada took just 0.5 percent of Cambodia's garments exports in 2010, but more than 9 percent in 2018; Japan took just 2.7 percent in 2010, but nearly 11 percent in 2018. Currently (in 2020), the unit labor cost for manufacturing a cotton shirt in Cambodia is estimated at USD0.33, compared to USD7.00 in the United States. This advantage may be lost with the further development of robotics in the garment industry. The ADB quoted observers saying that robots could drop the US production cost to around USD0.40.

Better Factories Cambodia (BFC – a partnership between the International Labor Organization and the International Finance Corporation, a member of the World Bank Group) was established in Cambodia in 2001, largely to improve working conditions and competitiveness. A memorandum of understanding between BFC, the government and the Garment Manufacturers' Association has been renewed six times since then, the current agreement was renewed on 20th December, 2019.

The construction sector, which represents 30 percent share of the industrial sector in 1993 has dramatically declined to its lowest level of 20.2 percent in 1998, but has since rebounded back to 30.1 percent in 2013. In 2019, Cambodia's construction sector attracted a total investment of US D9.35 billion, up 79 percent from USD5.22 billion in 2018, according to official report released by the Ministry of Land Management, Urban Planning and Construction (MLMUPC). The report also mentioned that the ministry had granted licenses to 4,446 construction projects in 2019, up 55 percent from 2,867 projects in 2018. Key investors in the Kingdom's construction and real estate are from China, South Korea and Japan. MLMUPC's secretary of state said that Cambodia currently had 1,624 high-rise buildings (between 5 and 54 floors) and 298 locations of new towns and residential complexes in 2019. However, most of the high-rise buildings and new towns are located in Phnom Penh, capital of Cambodia.

According to the MLMUPC's report, some 1,081 construction and home design companies are operating in the country in 2019, generating approximately 150,000 jobs.

Despite the strong performance of the garment, and construction / real estate sectors, Cambodia remains an agrarian country. Food and agro-processing industries are growing in Cambodia. By 2019, the country started to export processed food and agricultural products in greater volume after producing them mostly for local consumption in the past. According to the Ministry of Agriculture, in 2018, Cambodia exported 4.26 million tons of agricultural goods, 200 tons of which were vegetables. The Cambodian processed food and beverage market significantly developed in recent years, thus making the investments from regional and international brands possible. The growing economic conditions, urbanization, and tourism in top cities, like Siem Reap and Phnom Penh, are driving the processed vegetables and fruits market in Cambodia. Owing to the ongoing industrial developments and government support, foreign players are also looking forward to establishing fruit processing industries in the country. For example, Coconut Palm Group Co. Ltd., a leading tropical fruit juice manufacturer, plans to invest in coconut plantations and set up a factory in Cambodia to produce fruit juice in 2020. Thus, the growing food processing industries, government support for the food processing industries, and export demand for fruit juices will certainly stimulate the growth of the food processing industry in Cambodia.

Overall, most of Cambodia's enterprises are in retail and food establishments. Of some 510,000 enterprises, only 70,000 or 14 percent are in manufacturing, in which 45 percent are in food and beverage processing while the remaining 35 percent are garment and textile enterprises. It is note-worthy that 80 percent of large industrial enterprises are in garment, textile and foot-wear. The manufacturing structure is still relatively underdeveloped because garment and textile production and food processing are industries with low value added and less sophisticated. The production of construction materials, electronics, engines and machineries, chemical products, motorbike and car assemblies, plastic products and other consumption materials are still mostly at their early stage, and their productions are used very minimally as import substitution.

Looking at the labor allocation in the industrial sector, about 50 percent of the workers are employed in the garments sector, 25 percent in the construction sector, close to 10 percent in the food/ beverage processing sector and 13 percent in other manufacturing segments as indicated by Cambodia Government's latest Socio- Economic Survey. The structure of labor allocation is similar to that of the value-added structure. As per International Labor Organization Bulletin in December 2018, Garment, Textile and footwear (GTF) sector in Cambodia directly generates employment for more than one million workers, nearly 80 percent of whom are women. Based on their survey data, ILO reported that more than 90 percent of the sector's total workforce are engaged in regular, formal employment. The GTF sector is comprised of three sub-sectors: Garment, textile and footwear. Of these, in 2019, a overwhelming majority (almost 88 percent) of all GTF workers worked in the garment sub-sector. Footwear accounted for 7.7 percent of the GTF workforce in Cambodia, followed by textiles, at 4.5 percent.

In terms of export structure, over the 2000 – 2008 period, export of textile and foot-wear, and export of woods/wooden products accounted for 75.6 percent and 22 percent of total export, respectively. However, between 2009 and 2013, export of woods and wooden products had increased tremendously by around 30 percent per annum, whereas export of textile and footwear declined to just around 58 percent. In 2018, garments and textiles were the largest export industry in Cambodia, shipped USD13.1 billion worth of goods, accounted for 63 percent of the country's total exports. The primary markets for these exports, which also include accessories such as buttons, Velcro and zippers, were the European Union (40 percent), United States (30 percent) and Canada (9 percent). Most of the country's garment and textile factories are foreign-owned, with Taiwan (28 percent), Mainland China (19 percent), Hong Kong (17 percent) and South Korea (13 percent) leading the pack.

Footwear and headwear are collectively Cambodia's second-largest export. In 2018, the industry shipped products valued at USD2.3 billion, or 11 percent of Cambodia's total exports. The primary destination of these exports were the European Union (46 percent), the United States (17 percent) and Japan (12 percent).

Food and beverage is the third largest export industry in Cambodia. Cereals, vegetables, roots and fruits and nuts make up the bulk of the sector's USD1.5 billion (7.2 percent) in exports. There is confidence within the industry that the food and beverage sector is on the road of major growth, based on the increase of middle-class population in the country and growing investments from foreign, regional F&B companies.

Moreover, there is an improvement in export of light manufactured items, including bicycles, electrical wires, electronic motors, circuits, television parts, toys, furniture, spring and screws and bolts, etc. in the recent years. In 2017, Cambodia exported bicycles worth of USD355 million. Electrical and vehicle parts exports together reached USD430 million in 2017, but these are often assembled or subject to further processing overseas. In 2017, Cambodia became the European Union's number one supplier of bicycles. Cambodia's light manufacturing assembly sector, located primarily, but not exclusively in special economic zones, covers principally labor-intensive operations.

The manufacturing sector accounted for 31 percent of Cambodia's economy in 2016. The country's growth rate for value added in industry is the highest in South east Asia. The Asian Development Bank has forecast the country's manufacturing to continue to grow by around 9.6 percent, with a slowdown in garments and footwear off set by stronger growth in emerging industries: electrical parts, automobile components, bicycles, milled rice and rubber.

There were 1,528 factories in Cambodia at the end of 2018 according to figures from the Ministry of Industry and Handicraft, with 922, almost two-thirds operated by weaving, bag, garment, and footwear manufacturers. 178 new factories opened in 2018, compared to 150 in 2017. Total income from production of both domestic and export products was about USD13.17 billion in 2018, an increase of 23 percent over 2017.

As a whole, by end-2019, the manufacturing sector still remained comparatively concentrated and narrow based, as reflected in the ratio of the number of industrial enterprises over the total number of enterprises. To witness substantial growth in the manufacturing sector of Cambodia, it is crucially important to focus on expanding the production base and diversifying export products.

The Economic Census Survey (ECS) and the Cambodia Inter-censal Economic Survey (CIES) 2014, published by the National Institute of Statistics (NIS) of the Ministry of Planning, with the support of Japan International Co-operation Agency (JICA), are the two most comprehensive and latest sources of data on Cambodia's SME sector. According to the CIES data, in 2014, there were 513,759 enterprises in Cambodia. Of these, 97.6 percent were micro-enterprises. The SME sector, therefore, was very small, accounted for a little over 2 percent of the overall number of businesses. These figures suggest that the existence of a 'missing middle' in the country's production structure, a common feature in the ASEAN region and beyond. In terms of their contribution to the economy, SMEs accounted 14 percent of the annual sales for the industry in 2014, whereas large and micro-enterprises accounted for 50 percent and 36 percent respectively.

The ASEAN SME policy Index 2018 recognized Cambodia's efforts in implementing good regulatory practices and creating an environment conducive to SME development. But, it pointed out that the country is still in the early stages of policy implementation due to inherent institutional challenges, namely, lack of budget and qualified personnel. At present, the majority of government efforts to support SMEs are focused on networking and advocacy as well as short-term workshops and trainings in key areas such as book-keeping, business planning and human resource management. In December 2017, Prime Minister Hun Sen announced that the government would be developing an SME bank in order to facilitate SME access to finance. Based on discussion with stake-holders, it has been confirmed that the government has set aside USD100million as capital of the proposed financial institution. Though the bank will be managed by the Ministry of Economy and Finance, it is not yet known whether the bank will involve private shareholders or if it will be fully owned by the government. The bank is expected to start operation in 2020 and will be based on the Rural Development Bank model.

One noteworthy observation that emerged from the survey conducted by the National Employment Agency of Cambodia in 2018, was the positive employment growth between 2016 and 2017 and its forecasts for 2018 and 2019. Between 2016 and 2017, the total employment level of ten sectors, namely, accommodation; construction; education; finance and insurance; food and beverage; garment, footwear, and apparel; health; ICT; Logistic, warehousing, and transportation; and rubber and plastics, increased by a positive growth rate of 1.5 percent, approximately by 14,123 additional jobs annually. Between 2017 and 2019, annual creation of additional jobs were 21,546 with an annual growth rate of 2.2 percent. Of course, the growth was different among sectors. Between 2017 and 2019, fastest annual growth rate was in food and beverage sector (7.5 percent), followed by finance and insurance (5.7 percent), and ICT sector (5.7 percent). The garment, footwear and apparel sector, with the largest share of employment also witnessed a positive annual growth rate of 1.5 percent between 2017 and 2019. The largest contribution to employment growth between 2017 and 2019 came from the garment, footwear and apparel sector (52.6 percent), followed by finance and insurance (21.5 percent), and food and accommodation (6.9 percent).

Phnom Penh, Takeo, and Kampong Cham have the most industrial establishments of all provinces, a figure that correlates with the provincial population density. Kampong Cham Province (located 156 kilometers north-east of Phnom Penh) has a medium level of industrial development. It is observed that larger industries tend to locate in Phnom Penh and Kandal (which circles Phnom Penh). This is probably due to the availability of good infrastructure and public services. Kampong Cham is rich with tobacco and rice millers while Battambang is a rice basket of Cambodia. As mentioned, kandal benefits from its proximity to the capital. Svay Rieng, Sihanouk Ville, and Koh Kong are new production bases for medium and large industrial enterprises due to the establishment of special economic zones in these provinces.

From the view of official registration, the Ministry reported that, from January to November 2018, business registration increased in Cambodia by 138 percent compared to the same period in 2017. The number of foreign businesses that got registered with the Ministry grew by 63 percent, reaching a total of 142 companies in 2018. Local registration expanded by a whopping 132 percent, from 4,812 firms in 2017 to 11,188 in 2018. Registration of sole proprietorships increased by 166 percent, from 1,209 in 2017 to 3,222 in 2018, as the report mentioned. Meanwhile, dissolutions also increased during 2018. 142 businesses filed for a certificate of dissolution in 2018, while only 58 did so in 2017. World Bank senior country economist in Cambodia remarked at an event organized by Cambodia's Central Bank in December 2018 that the process of registering a business in the Kingdom is still cumbersome and expensive, particularly when compared to neighbors Thailand and Vietnam. He pointed out that Cambodia slipped in the World Bank's ease of doing business index, going from the 131st in 2017 to 138th spot in 2018.

In terms of 'weak entrepreneurship and urban-centered establishment' as a key characteristic of Cambodia's industrial structure, it would be note-worthy that weak entrepreneurship is reflected by the structure of ownership and the fact that they are still in their early stage. As per data provided by the official authority, by end-2019, more than half of the total enterprises that are currently operating in Cambodia were just established since 2008, and even with the counting going back to 2003, the number of newly established enterprises have reached more than 75 percent. Similar situation applies in each industrial sub-sector.

About 70 percent of large enterprises and 40 percent of medium enterprises are in the form of foreign direct investment, whereas the majority of micro and small enterprises are Cambodian owned, accounting for nearly 99 percent and 95 percent respectively, as per data from the Investment Climate Assessment of Cambodia ,2018.

In terms of 'Low value addition and low level of technology application' as a key characteristic of Cambodia's industrial structure, it would be relevant to note that the Cambodian industry is labor-based focusing on certain labor-intensive and unsophisticated production chain. For example, in the garment and textile industry, about 60 percent of factories are operating in Cut, Make, and Trim (CMT), whereas only one-fourth of them are engaged in down-stream production like embroidery, washing, packaging, and eventually exporting finished products. This situation also applies to the packaging industry which has recently witnessed some investment. In other sub-sectors, the production chain is quite similar that it consists of cutting, making, labeling, and assembling. In the assembly plants, there are only low skilled and low value-added jobs such as assembling of key component parts and screwing.

The majority of domestic enterprises focuses only with generally low level of technology usage. For instance, in the rice processing sector, prior to the launch of the Policy Document on the Promotion of Paddy Rice Production and Export of Milled Rice 2010, Cambodia had only a small number of international standard rice mills. But the situation has been changing in the last ten years. Likewise, other manufacturing sectors are also gradually adopting comparatively better technology than they used earlier in order to increase the productivity, thereby increasing its competitiveness. For example, the production of bricks, tiles or pots employed earlier poor technology and hence was unable to produce a variety of products. But, now domestic enterprises are also slowly changing to survive in the competitive market.

D. MAJOR CHALLENGES OF INDUSTRIAL DEVELOPMENT IN CAMBODIA

a. Intensive Co-Ordination and Effective Decision Making

Intensive co-ordination is required for industrial development in every aspect and level, be it at the policy, institutional, regulatory, and managerial level, and in term of infrastructure development, financial services, technical and technological capacity as well as private sector participation. These elements are inextricably inter-twined and their co-ordination needs to be well communicated so as to provide effective support to concrete industrial activities. Ensuring good co-ordination will, in addition, contribute to improving the investment climate, gaining more confidence from investor and promoting reputation of the country as a major investment destination in the region.

In term of regulatory framework, coherent co-ordination efforts are needed to be placed with regard to the issues of investment incentives, taxation, system, trade regime, transport, and other relevant regulatory aspects. Such type of lack of co-ordination creates unwanted difficulties for the industrial growth and undermines the government efforts to mobilize resources to achieve its industrial development goals.

Access to clear and transparent relevant information is the pre-requisite for sound investment decision-making. For optimum industrial development, it is necessary to establish a clear mechanism to facilitate access to investment information that could reduce searching cost as well as to encourage broader participation. It will also ensure smooth functioning of a more competitive and sustainable industrial development.

The government's various roles in orienting, leading, coordinating and supporting the private sector is also very crucial for industrial growth. Industrial development necessitates both an effective leadership and coordination whereby the lead institutions play an active professional role in ensuring close co-operation between relevant institutions in order to successfully implement the various initiatives and policy measures.

b. Skills-Base and Technical Knowledge

In order to advance the manufacturing sector development agenda, it is indispensable to create a critical mass and skill mix of workers, technicians, engineers and scientists. It is obvious that the limited pool of trained skill workers, technicians and engineers will prohibit the country from absorbing and utilizing modern sciences and technology for industrial development while resorting to hiring costly expertise from overseas. Cambodia needs to develop a proper human resource capacity to support its investment policy, the lack of which would seriously undermine the competitiveness of its industrial sector. Skills training still remains inadequate to service Cambodia's industrial sector, which suffers from low productivity as a result. Also, the system regulating the recruitment process should be reviewed and improved. Thus the worker recruitment procedures for the industrial sector, provision of their training, nurturing their working habit and discipline as well as expectation about the sector would entail a major change in the labor market.

With the high rate of student drop-out still prevalent, the Cambodian industry is stuck in a labor intensive and low productivity industry mode. To posses the basic foundation to learn technical skills, workers should have completed at least grade 9, which is a pre-requisite for moving to learning technology. In term of productivity, a very low level of education in the workforce will lead to loss in productivity in the long term as workers are not able to acquire new skills and have no choice but to accept low paying jobs. In this regard, the government requires to design the policy in such a way as to open up opportunities for workers to continue learning and acquiring new skills.

More attention is required to be paid to the development of metrology and standards, which in fact provide the technological backbone to instill consumer trust and confidence in manufacturing production, be they at the large factories, enterprises or handicraft level. It is evident that the use of proper metrology and standards add enormous value to the production process by way of cost reduction, better confidence and trust in the market in terms of quantity, price, quality, and safety of products. The promotion of metrology and standards is undoubtedly key to attracting investors to develop the industrial sector.

c. Linking Key Infrastructures and Coordination

Despite an enormous effort in building physical infrastructure for the last two decades, it is still inadequate, especially for the purpose of driving the country to the next stage of development. The recent attempt to export of one million tons of rice has highlighted the need for infrastructure improvement to ensure reliable and timely supply chains. The major national road networks are congested, leading to transportation delay and even adding more pressure on the existing road structure. As such, the need for better supporting infrastructure and a highly effective logistic system is to be fulfilled with the drive for industrial development and the expansion of export, particularly in targeted industrial areas and export gateways.

Lack of stable electricity supply at a competitive price is a key challenge for industrial development. The country still suffer from adequate electricity supply despite the government's effort to promote investment in the electricity sector. Electricity demand is estimated to increase potentially from 142 to 182 megawatts on average per annum until 2025. Attracting more investment in the electricity sector is crucial to ensure a reliable electricity supply. As much as the supply issue is an urgent priority for the manufacturing sector, ensuring a lower and competitive price is also as important in light of the country's relatively current high price vis-a-vis to its neighboring countries.

Other important issue related to physical infrastructure such as clean water supply and sewage system must be reconsidered in a new dimension. Demand of clean water is estimated to increase potentially from 10,000m^3/day to 14,000m^3/day annually, and by 2021, such a demand can reach around 140,000m^3/Day. Moreover, the sewage discharge may possibly require a capacity of around 120,000m^3/day. It should be noted that certain SEZs still do not have adequate clean water supply and sewage system. Therefore, the provision of such necessary infrastructure must be taken into consideration and be well planned in advance, especially for the targeted industrial zones.

Proper planning of location for manufacturing facilities is extremely crucial. By 2021, it is estimated that the demand for the areas needed for new factories could increase from 3,400 ha to 4,500 ha. Presently, out of the approved 22 SEZs, which encompass around 9,000 ha, only some 280 ha are under operation. As such, it is utterly important to link the provision of adequate physical infrastructure, such as transportation and other public utilities to the new planned economic zones.

As for priority industries, Cambodia does not have lead institutions to drive and coordinate relevant institutions particularly in initiating intervention, monitoring progress and providing trouble-shooting solution to address operational concerns. There is a need to have in place a monitoring mechanism to exert additional pressure on the responsible institutions to take measures and solve the said problems.

d. Financing or Financial Market Solution

The banking sector development, including the microfinance sector, has been vigorous for the last decade in supporting sustainable growth, though it has yet to be responsive to the needs of investment capital. Financial deepening is still limited when compared to other regional countries. Financing for investment projects is far from enough, especially for large development projects. Unless there is a flexible financing mechanism in place, investment projects would be hard to materialize. A financing mechanism for specific activities should be developed to drive industrial activities along with the strengthening of domestic saving mechanism such as insurance and pension plan to ensure sufficient source of credit with low interest rate. As such, the ability to integrate private savings into one system will offer various financing options for industrial projects.

Securities market is also an avenue for mobilizing capital and can serve as a mechanism to mobilize financing for long-term investment and sustainable business project development. In the context of industrial development, it could be seen as a complementary financing options to foster the sector. For example, if SEZs are qualified for listing in the stock market, the additional capital to be raised from the securities market can be utilized to speed up the development and expansion of infrastructure or to strengthen professional management so as to attract more investment.

To review the possibility of issuance of government bond is another option, especially when Cambodia is no longer able to obtain concessional financing along with the strengthening of revenue collection and domestic savings. Last but not the least is the use of public-private sector partnership or under a tri-lateral partnership- framework of government, development partners and private sector to leverage investment in concrete priority sectors.

e. Labor Market and Industrial Relations

Industrial relations is still a major challenge for industrial development not only in Cambodia but also in almost all countries going through a transition from agriculture/rural to industry/urban setting. A proper management of such transition can lay the foundation for attracting investments in the future, especially to ensure better working conditions, high productivity and reasonable wage for the workforce.

According to a survey conducted by the Japan External Trade Organization (JETRO), in 2019, the average annual salary of manufacturing workers is about USD2,920 in Cambodia, a level which is still competitive as compared with its regional peers, like USD3,810 in Vietnam. In recent years, the monthly minimum wage has risen rapidly from USD100 in 2014 to USD182 in 2019. The duty-free export access to major developed countries, including the EU, US and Japan, under the Generalized System of Preferences (GSP) schemes, is one of the key advantages of export-oriented manufacturing in Cambodia. In January 2019, the US senators introduced the 'Cambodian Trade Act of 2019', which would require the US government to review the preferential trade privileges given to Cambodia under the General System of Preferences (GSP). Also in February 2019, the EU started the official review process that could lead to a temporary withdrawal of Cambodia's preferential trade access under the 'Everything But Arms (EBA)' scheme. However, in this regard, it is noteworthy that in 2019, Cambodia also launched the 'Cambodia Independence Policy' which aims to reduce its reliance on the preferential trade status, through improving trade policies and customs efficiency.

E. ROYAL GOVERNMENT OF CAMBODIA'S INDUSTRIAL DEVELOPMENT POLICY: 2015 – 2025

INDUSTRIAL POLICY

Cambodia's industrial policy is built upon seven main points:

1. Developing labor-intensive industries;
2. Promoting the development of agri-business;
3. Developing industries which are based on the use of basic natural resources;
4. Promoting SMEs, micro-enterprises, and handicrafts;
5. Encouraging technology transfer and export product diversification;
6. Establishing industrial and export processing zones;
7. Increasing production of goods for import substitution.

At the core of this industrial policy is the focus on attracting investment into sectors where Cambodia has comparative advantages for export promotion. As such, a key component of industrial policy has involved reductions in barriers to exports and the import of business inputs. This is one of the main aspects of policy that is considered to have been effective.

The Cambodia Industrial Development Policy (2015-2025) has a clear vision to maintain sustainable and inclusive high growth and transform and modernize Cambodia's industrial structure from labor-intensive industry to skill-driven industry by 2015 (RGC 2015). Targets for 2015-25 include: (a) economic diversification by increasing the share of industry in GDP from 24.1 percent to 30 percent and GDP's share of manufacturing from 15.5 percent to 20 percent; (b) export diversification by increasing exports of non-garment and footwear from 1 percent to 15 percent, processed agricultural products from 7.9 percent to 12 percent, and decreasing exporting of garment and footwear from 77 percent to 50 percent; (c) promotion of SMEs by registering SMEs and ensuring that 50 percent of small enterprises and 70 percent of medium enterprises have proper financial records and balance sheets.

MACRO-ECONOMIC POLICY

Cambodia's macro-economic policy stance is largely consistent with its key objectives of attracting foreign investment and export promotion. As a largely dollarized economy, Cambodia relies mainly on a conservative fiscal policy to prevent inflationary pressures. Monetary policy has allowed financial sector. Current and capital accounts are open and there is no restriction on the exchange rate. The main medium to long-term goals of the National Bank of Cambodia (NBC), as set out in the National Strategic Development Plan (NSDP) (2009-2013) (RGC 2009,2013) are to: (a) maintain price stability with an inflation target of under 5 percent; (b)ensure the continued soundness of the financial sector; (c)continue to manage a floating exchange rate regime with a target of around KHR4,100 per USD; (d) maintain foreign reserves to finance at least three months of import. International reserves increased from USD500 million in 2000 to USD6.027 billion in 2015, to USD12.715 billion in November 2019, excluding gold and special drawing rights (SDR). In the first quarter ended 2020, Cambodia's gold reserve was 12.4 tons.

In order to strengthen micro-economic stability, the government sets out the following priorities: (a) implementing a flexible fiscal policy to be consistent with monetary policy; (b) diversifying the export base; (c) keeping public debt at a manageable level; (d) strengthening institutional co-ordination; (e) enhancing private sector development; (f) promoting labor market development; (g)encouraging investment in key sectors and ensuring an increase in international reserves; (g) continuing to implement a managed floating exchange rate regime to maintain stability of the Riel; (h) strengthening public and investor confidence in the local currency to promote its greater use; and (i) strengthening the supervision and management of liquidity, credit, and market risks in compliance with international standards.

TRADE POLICY

A key feature of industrial policy in Cambodia is its emphasis on trade. The domestic market has been too small to support long-term growth, and so export-oriented investment is crucial. Cambodia has capitalized on the intra-regional complementarity that stems from differences in labor costs, the availability of natural resource endowments, and trading regulations.

Cambodia joined ASEAN in 1999 and the WTO in 2003. This marked the final step into the major regional and international organizations that govern international economic relations. For the garment industry the accession presented not only a challenge to become more competitive, but also opportunities for expansion because of the removal of the quotas for Cambodian exports to the 147 WTO members.

LABOR MARKET POLICIES

Cambodia's labor market remains free and open in practice, though labor laws have been in place since 1992. The emergence of the garment sector led to new labor laws in 1997, which focused on freedom, the establishment of unions, and rights for demonstration. The 1997 law applies only to the garment sector and its related sectors. There were a total of 989 strikes between 2003 and 2014, averaging 1.6 per week (GMAC 2015b).

Minimum wages are a key feature. The legal minimum wage in Cambodian factories was USD40 per month in 1997 for regular employees and it took thirteen years to increase to USD61 in 2010 (GMAC 2015b). However, it has increased steadily from USD80 in 2013 to USD117 in 2014 and USD145 in 2015. Effected from 1st January 2019, the minimum wage for workers in the textile, garment and footwear sector of Cambodia was set at USD182 per month (increase of 7 percent plus USD5 over previous year). The minimum wage for probationary workers was set at USD177 per month (rising to USD182 after the probationary period). The latest development was on 20th September 2019 when Cambodia's Labor minister issued a directive raising legal minimum wage for workers in its crucial garments, textiles and footwear industry to USD190 per month, effective from 1st January 2020, an increase of 4.4 percent over previous year. President of the Cambodian tourism and Services Workers federation reported that tourism and service workers received base wages of USD80 to USD130 a month in 2019, rates which were determined by employers.

The 'better factory program' was introduced in 2010 in Cambodia. The basic objective of the program is to improve working conditions in Cambodia's textile and apparel sector, particularly through an independent monitoring system of working conditions in garment factories. The program resulted from USA – Cambodia trade negotiations in exchange for market access to the USA.

THE INSTITUTIONAL AND REGULATORY FRAMEWORK

The government of Cambodia regards the private sector as the main impetus for the country's economic growth, and initiated the Government-Private Sector Forum. The Council for the Development of Cambodia (CDC) also facilitates investment applications and decisions. The length of investment application procedures was reduced to a maximum of forty-five days. This law provides a clear and more liberal investment regime, with attractive incentives for FDI. According to CDC, to improve the business and investment climate and to comply with WTO regulations, the Royal Government of Cambodia has recently placed emphasis on updating and adopting new laws and regulations on investment, trade, and business.

SECTOR SPECIFIC POLICIES

Garment Sector

The garment sector is now one of Cambodia's fastest-growing for private investment. This is mainly the result of normalized trade relationship (NTR) agreements, first signed with the

European Union in 1996 and then with the USA in 1997. The agreements were the result of Cambodia being granted most favored nation (MFN) status and status under the generalized system preference (GSP) agreement. Between 1994 and 1999, Cambodia's garment exports grew by more than 100 percent, from USD495 million to USD1,102 million, with about 90 percent of garment shipments going to the USA. This strong performance prompted the USA to introduce quotas on twelve categories of Cambodian garment exports in 1999, but this measure did not significantly affect the expansion of the industry, whose exports continued to rise to almost USD3 billion in 2008, to USD5.785 billion in 2014. In 2019, a report from General Department of Customs and Excise of the Ministry of Economy and Finance said, Cambodia exported more than USD7.97 billion worth of garment, textile and footwear (GTF) products in the fist nine months of the year, up 13.18 percent year-on-year from USD7.044 billion.

Rapid development in the garment industry, combined with the country's democratization process, has resulted in the accelerated growth of unions. In 1998, the Clinton administration developed the US-Cambodian Trade Agreement on Textiles and Apparel (1999-2004) which linked market access to labor standards. The International Labor Organization (ILO)'s Better Factories Cambodia was instituted in 2010 for independent monitoring.

TOURISM

The policies for tourism are based on three basic principles of sustainability and poverty reduction, active promotion, and lengthening the average stay (RGC 2009). From 2009 to 2013, the government prioritized completing tourism plans, marketing studies, and tourism campaigns to raise regional and international awareness of Cambodia's tour programs. The Tourism Strategic Development Plan (2012-2020) and Cambodia Tourism Marketing Strategy (2015-2020) have a target of attracting 7 million foreign tourists in 2020. However, despite reporting fewer coronavirus cases than most of its neighbors, Cambodia could be among the region's biggest Covid-19 losers due to economic and financial contagion effects.

Cambodia's tourism industry, which usually contributes around one-third of gross domestic product (GDP) has been facing virtual halt since the pandemic first emerged in China in January 2020 and thereafter spread worldwide. Air passenger number in Cambodia fell by more than 90 percent in April, according to the State Secretariat of Civil Aviation, while ticket sales at Cambodia's world famous Angkor Wat temples fell by 99.5 percent.

F. KEY MEASURES TO PROMOTE THE IMPLEMENTAION OF THE

Industrial Development Policy

Besides the policy measures and action plans, the Royal Government of Cambodia also initiated to implement four key concrete measures to be fully complied by the end of 2018. These measures were of great significance as they enabled the Royal Government to monitor the efforts and progress of the implementation of the IDP. The four key measures were also served as an indispensable basis and pre-conditions for determining the success in ensuring that the vision, objectives and goals of the policy are getting realized by 2025. Those four key measures were:

a) Prepare and implement a plan to reduce electricity tariffs for industrial and commercial purposes including strengthening reliability and expanding coverage of electricity supply.

b) Develop and implement a master plan for transport and logistic system development with the aim of creating an integrated and highly effective multimodal transport and logistics system, focusing on connecting the major economic poles and the three economic corridors, Phnom Penh-

Sihanouk Ville, Phnom Penh – Bavet, and Phnom Penh – Poipet to become key national economic corridors through the construction of internationally standards highways and the set up of an effective logistics system.

c) Further strengthening labor market mechanisms and skills training development to ensure stability of the labor supply, increase productivity and improve living standard of workers by promoting skills training programs, strengthening the mechanism for setting minimum wage and enhancing harmony in industrial relations based on the principles of positive union and the kindness of employers towards their employees. This can be done through existing mechanisms, including the Labor advisory Committee and the Cambodia Productivity Committee.

d) Develop and transform Sihanouk Ville Province into a model multi-purposed Special Economic Zone, following the concept of Special Administrative Region. Under this concept, a master plan, legal and regulatory framework and other administrative arrangements are being developed and designed to provide full authority and jurisdiction for mobilization of resources, talents, investments and businesses to develop the province to become an economic pole and industrial, trade and tourist hub in line with sustainable and environmentally sound development concepts in order to recognize it as the ASEAN Green Industry and Metropolitan City.

In addition to the above efforts, the Royal Government also foresees a number of major risks that need to be attended to and to be resolved: (1) risks related to regional and global environment changes; (2) risks related to management of macro-economic issues; (3) risks related to political instability; and (4) risks related to governance, institutions and coordination. Mindful of these major risks, the Cambodia government is fully committed to drive the implementation of the adopted policies, strategies and measures to achieve its intended objectives.

G. CONCLUDING OBSERVATION

The Cambodian economy is at a crucial transformation stage after sustaining high growth over the last decade. The country is moving toward becoming a middle-income country, which requires comprehensive structural reforms aimed at strengthening economic diversification and competitiveness to ensure sustainable economic growth with equitable redistribution of wealth. This requires consideration for a new development approach vis-à-vis expanding development opportunities and investment in new growth sectors by way of improving the necessary socio-economic infrastructure, supply of energy, expansion of transport infrastructure and development of logistics, promotion of technical and sciences education, and institutional strengthening.

In this regard, The Cambodia government has decided to adopt the IDP in order to provide a policy framework and a specific mechanism for driving economic growth and creating jobs with focus on the manufacturing sector, agro-industrial sector and SMEs. In pursuance of this policy, Cambodia will succeed in its economic structural transformation by moving from an agricultural based economy toward a manufacturing and agro-industry based economy, and subsequently in the final phase toward diversification in other sectors especially those that use technology and innovation. The Cambodian Government has been working with bilateral and multilateral donors, including the Asian Development Bank, the World Bank and IMF, to address the country's many pressing needs. More than 30 percent of the government budget comes from donor assistance. A major economic challenge for Cambodia over the next decade will be fashioning an economic environment in which Cambodia's industrial sector can create enough jobs to handle it's demographic imbalance.

CHAPTER-FIVE
ACHIEVEMENTS AND FUTURE DIRECTION IN SUSTAINABLE INCLUSIVE DEVELOPMENT

A. INTRODUCTION

Over the last two decades, Cambodia has demonstrated strong economic performance, making great strides towards sustained, rapid and broad-based economic development. Cambodia has also maintained an average GDP growth rate of over 7 percent per year ensuring strong macroeconomic stability and an open economy. During the period, real GDP per capita growth in Cambodia has averaged 6 percent, well above the ASEAN average of 4 percent. This has resulted in higher average incomes, remarkable reduction in poverty, more employment opportunities and decline in overall inequality, and it reflects through the faster growth of consumption among the bottom 40 percent of the population.

Cambodia's rapid development has been a catalyst for the transformation of it's economy. Government's policies that prioritize industrialization and modernization in the country have resulted in a declining share of the agricultural sector in

GDP. Yet the agricultural sector still remains an important pillar of the economy and a major source of employment. Cambodia is one of the world's top ten rice exporters, doubling its exports of milled rice during 2013-2019. Cambodia is an open economy with an increasingly attractive investment climate. Cambodia exported goods worth more than 60 percent of it's GDP to 147 countries in 2019. Besides manufacturing sector, the service sector has also seen strong annual growth especially through better performance in domestic trade and transportation. Tourism, retail/wholesale, and real estate sectors continue robust growth in recent years. Progress on social indicators, notably in health and education, has also been strong during the last decade. Public health has improved, including a notable reduction in maternal, child and infant mortality rates and significantly reduced malaria incidence. Education reforms have enhanced the opportunities for youth and created an improved supply of quality human resources and skills to the job market.

Despite remarkable progress, obstacles to growth still persist and income inequality between regions remains a concern. Infrastructure gaps in Cambodia are substantial. At the same time, income disparities between regions are considerable. On average, household income in rural regions, representing nearly 80 percent of the population, is only 60 percent of that in urban area.

B. INEQUALITY IN CAMBODIA

From 1997 to 2019, inequality in consumption and income declined in Cambodia. According to data from the Standardized World Income Inequality Database (SWIID), the Gini coefficient for consumption fell from 40.4 percent in 1997 to 29 percent in 2012. At the same time, the Gini coefficient for disposable income declined from 36.7 percent in 1997 to 33.9 in 2012. Gini index measures the extent to which the distribution of income or consumption expenditure among individuals or households within an economy deviates from a perfectly equal distribution.

Thus a Gini index of 0 represents perfect equality, while an index of 100 implies perfect inequality. From 2012 to 2015, the inequality in consumption appeared to had been broadly unchanged, while the inequality in income had risen somewhat. Migration was one potential driver behind this decline with urban population increasing from 17 percent in 1994 to 23 percent in 2017. The reduction in inequality coincided with a substantial decline in absolute poverty. As International Monetary Fund reported in it's Working Paper of September 2019, in Cambodia, inequality in income was larger than in consumption. Average income is 12 percent larger than average consumption. At the same time, income is less evenly distributed with less density around the mean and more in the tails. This is consistent with the understanding that the propensity to consume tends to fall with income, which implies that inequality generally will be larger in income than consumption. One probable reason is hedging behavior, which causes households with high income to save to insulate themselves from income shocks. Access to lending can also help households smoothen income shocks. Gaps in income and consumption remain, especially between urban and rural households. As per National Institute of Statistics data and World Bank Report 2018, household income, on average, in the rural areas accounted for around 80 percent of the population is only 60 percent of that in the urban area. At the same time, average rural consumption was only 70 percent of that in the urban area. The consumption gap between urban and rural households was seen across all product groups except health. Gaps in consumption between the urban and rural sectors are prevalent in housing-related spending, transportation, food and non-food consumption. Health-related expenditure are higher among rural households. As World Bank observed, this is likely related to generally worse health conditions in rural areas, inter alia caused by larger gaps in sanitation facilities and nutrition. Regarding rural-urban income gap, it is mainly driven by differences in income sources. While the average rural household derives the largest share of income from self-employment, the average urban household derives it's largest from salary. The average salary in the urban area is almost double that in the rural sector. Similarly, income from self-employment is on average 1.13 times larger in the urban area. Rural households rely relatively more on net income transfers than urban households.

While taking further stock of the current state of human development of Cambodia, it would be meaningful to re-iterate 'People are the real wealth of a nation. The basic objective of development is to create an enabling environment for people to enjoy long, healthy and creative lives.' --- as mentioned in the opening of the first global Human Development Report, published in 1990. Contemporary human development thinking places particular emphasis on ensuring universal access to health care, education and basic services, and affirmative action to address structural inequalities. These types of actions are now hardwired in the 17 Sustainable Development Goals (SDGs) adopted by the global community in 2015 to provide ambitious targets for people, planet and prosperity through 2030.

A hallmark of Cambodia's development has been macroeconomic stability, with low levels of inflation and balance of payments equilibrium, despite instability in the global economy. Progressive economic liberalization and ongoing public and private investment, have transformed a country once ravaged by a decade of domestic conflict, preceded by the desperate years of Khmer Rouge rule. As of end-2019, government borrowing has remained in check, and revenues have grown strongly in recent years, with domestic taxes now accounting for over 20 percent of GDP. The economy is highly open and has few capital controls, and as a result trade and foreign investment have flourished. Cambodia's economy remains highly dollarized, with around 80 percent of transactions by value conducted in the US currency. As mentioned earlier, Cambodia's economy has also witnessed ongoing structural changes. Nevertheless, there are questions about the extent and quality of these changes, and the degree of underlying improvements in productivity. Employment has lagged structural shifts. Workers displaced from agriculture have largely been absorbed by the new economy, specifically by the garment and construction industries.

Cambodia's population had grown to nearly 16.5 million by 2019, and although the rate of increase has slowed, the population continues to expand at 1.65 percent per year. Cambodia has 25 provinces, including Phnom Penh municipality, with varying population distribution and socio-economic conditions. Provinces in the far north-east (Ratanakiri, Mondulkiri, Preah Vihear and Stung Treng) and south-west (Koh Kong) are remote, and either forested or mountainous. Most people live along two major river systems, the Mekong and Tonle Sap. Cambodia's primary economic corridor runs from the far south-east to the midpoint of the western border with Thailand. Phnom Penh and its neighboring core provinces are the most economically vibrant areas by some margin. Provinces with high trade potential and an ability to benefit from Cambodia's laissez faire economy, such as those on the south-east Vietnamese border, those close to the Sihanouk Ville port and others on the Thai border, have also grown rapidly in recent years. The government has responded to regional disparities with a regional economic policy rooted in the creation of around 30 special economic zones, where businesses enjoy more favorable operating conditions. The zones enable the development of industrial clusters, and in turn, new and better-quality employment opportunities for local populations. Cambodia has also experienced and is experiencing growing internal migration, predominantly to its economic core. Against a favorable economic backdrop, Cambodia has achieved steady advances in human development as measured by the human development indices (HDI). On the 2019 global HDI, Cambodia ranked 146 out of 189 reporting countries, placing it in the medium human development category. From 1990 to 2019, Cambodia achieved the seventh fastest rate of improvement in HDI globally, and the second fastest in Asia. Progress in Cambodia was strongest between 2000 and 2010, tapering off before accelerating again from 2016. Cambodia's human development performance is now well-ahead of the average for the least developed group. The main driver of Cambodia's striking rate of improvement has been dramatic rises in life expectancy, especially in remote and highly challenged areas. Rising income has also contributed, reflecting ongoing economic growth. Education has seen continued improvements but weaker relative and absolute performance.

Inequality in human development has declined somewhat in Cambodia, mirroring changes in income distribution. Losses in human development due to inequality, given by the divergence between the HDI and the inequality-adjusted index, fell from close to 29 percent in 1990 to less than 19 percent in 2019. This was due mainly to a more equitable distribution of income, but also to wider access to health and education. Cambodia's performance toward removing inequality in human development is converging on that of Indonesia and its positive trajectory suggests that it's position will improve further. Also as per Global Gender gap index compiled by the World Economic forum, in 2017, Cambodia gained 13 places to rank at 99 out of 144 countries. Underpinning this change were women's rising shares in decision-making and executive positions, and higher levels of participation in higher education.

Trends in human development measures of inequality have been very positive, but again Cambodia still lags neighboring countries. Efforts are still needed to ensure outcomes match strong performance on income inequality. All sections of society need to benefit from the expansion of human development. This depends greatly on improved public service provision, specifically access to decent quality schooling and health care, but additionally, comprehensive social protection and improved public infrastructure are important. A similar case can be made for gender equality and women's empowerment, where despite long-term improvements, Cambodia still need vigorous action to tackle disparities.

C. POLICIES AND STRATEGIES OF CAMBODIAN GOVERNMENT

The Royal Government of Cambodia (RGC) embraced the United Nations' 2030 Agenda for Sustainable Development and its associated 17 Sustainable Development Goals (SDGs) with a strong commitment to their achievement. The Cambodian SDGs (CSDGs) framework 2016-2030 also added one additional goal, related to clearance of land mines and explosive remnants of war, reflecting the national priority of de-mining Cambodia's territory. This resulted in a final version comprising 18 CSDGs, 88 nationally relevant targets, and 148 (global and locally defined) indicators including 96 national indicators. The Royal Government of Cambodia partnered with United Nations agencies in developing two preliminary analyses – (1) the Rapid Integrated Assessment (RIA) (2016) and (2) the SDG Assessment (2017). The RIA mapped Cambodia's National Strategic Development Plan (NSDP) and other principal strategies to identify areas of alignment between the SDGs and Cambodia's policy agenda, while the SDG assessment focused on the indicators and availability of reliable data sources. The RGC then fully adapted the SDGs to fit with the Cambodian context to include national needs, challenges, and aspirations. The CSDGs Framework, alongside the Political Platform of the RGC set out in the Rectangular Strategy Phase IV (RS-IV) provides the basis for the new cycle of the National Strategic Development Plan (NSDP) 2019-2023. The RGC prepared and endorsed the RS-IV after the last national elections in July 2018. At the national level, the core framework of the RS-IV specified four policy rectangles: (1) Human Resource Development; (2) Economic Diversification; (3) Private sector and market development; and (4) Sustainable and inclusive development. At the sub-national level, the planning processes addresses 4 challenges including (1) economy, (2) social development, (3) natural resources, environment, and climate change adaptation, and (4) security. The RGC accepts that the economic development, sustainability and inclusion are the keys to overall development in Cambodia and that the CSDGs still need to be matrixed to these sub-national processes, which have started in 2019.

D. PROGRESS ON GOALS AND TARGETS

The following are the in-depth review of 6 global prioritized goals, specifically CSDGs covering (1) Quality Education, (2) Decent Work and Economic Growth, (3) reduced Inequality, (4) climate Action, (5) Peace, Justice and Strong Institutions, and (6) Partnerships for the Goals, toward empowering people and ensuring inclusion, equality, and sustainability in Cambodia. It includes progress to date, challenges, and policy actions.

1. In the area of education and promotion of lifelong learning opportunities for all, available data suggest that Cambodia achieved significant progress during the last decade. The completion rate at primary and secondary levels, and the proportion of grade 1 students who passed through all ECE programs had increased from 80 percent, 39 percent, and 62 percent in 2015 to 86.1 percent, 47.6 percent and 72 percent respectively in 2018. Similarly, Cambodia achieved gender parity in education sector, and is beginning to tilt in the favor of girls in recent years. The gender parity index of gross enrollment rate at both lower secondary education and upper secondary education increased from 1.1 in 2015 to 1.2 in 2018. Adult literacy rate also increased from 78 percent to 82.5 percent over 2015-2018. Comparing to targets set in CSDG framework, the figures suggest that targets were being attained or in some cases exceeded through the implementation of the Education Strategic Plan 2014-2018. The New National Education 2030 Roadmap for CSDG4 will build on these achievements.

In terms of challenges, while continuing with the impressive progress, a number of challenges remain to be addressed including: (i) equitable and inclusive access for children to all levels of education and training; (ii) transition from primary to lower-secondary and high drop-out rates at the lower-secondary levels; (iii) quality issues from pre-primary to tertiary educators; and (iv) life-long learning, which is key to life-long employment and allows adoption of skills and knowledge to the structural change of the economy, is still a new concept for many people.

Regarding key policies and/or accelerating strategies, Cambodia's Ministry of Education, Youth and Sports (MOEYS) has developed and adopted the National Education 2030 Roadmap for CSDG4, which provides the overarching framework for a long-term holistic sector-wide approach for the development and delivery of education services and sets priorities and strategies on how Cambodia will achieve these targets. CSDG4 (Quality Education goal) is well aligned with the Governments priorities in the RS-IV. Improved general education, vocational and competence skills, entrepreneurship, creativity and innovation, and a healthy lifestyle are core components in Rectangle 1 of the RS-IV. Side 1 of the Rectangle 1 is the strengthening of the quality of education, science and technology with the objective of 'quality, equitable and inclusive education system'. Side 2 touches on technical training with an aim to ensure that 'each individual youth specializes in at least one skill in life'. Side 3 touches on enhancement of Public Health and Nutrition. Side 4 is on gender equity and social protection to enhance socio-economic situation and to strengthen the role of women.

2. In an attempt to attain inclusive and sustainable economic growth, full and productive employment and decent work for all, Cambodia achieved high average economic growth of around 7.0 percent per annum during the last two decades and attained lower middle-income status in 2015 in terms of GDP per capita, which reached USD1,620.64 in 2019. The percentage of Cambodians living under the national poverty line fell around 1 percent per year on average, down to about 10 percent in 2019 from 35 percent in 2005. The direct contribution of travel and tourism to GDP in 2019 almost touched the percentage set in the target. The growth rate of online business registration and growth rate of issuing certificate of origin through the automation system in 2019 was much higher than targeted while the growth rate of online trademark registration was a little bit

below the target. With substantial ongoing investment by both public and private sector, Cambodia's economy is forecasted to continue growing robustly, with further structural change in favor of industrial development, from 27.7 percent of GDP in 2015 to 32.8 percent in 2018 and 38.2 percent in 2022, with pause in 2020 because of COVID-19 world-wide pandemic. Financial services and the banking sector have been growing sharply during 2009-2019 and more soundly during 2015-2019, as high credit growth was brought under control. There has been a boom in the construction and real estate sectors in the past few years. However, it is unlikely to be sustainable due to the speculative nature of business in those sectors.

Challenges are there despite such considerable progresses. First, Cambodia needs to diversify and expand its manufacturing base by moving away from labor-intensive industries to those that demand a more skilled workforce, more advanced technologies, and higher value added. Second, although there has been a remarkable increase in the number of registered companies, some companies or enterprises are still unregistered and some have not provided update on their status. Related to Intellectual Property (IP), there is still lack of skilled officials who can process and respond to such matter quickly. Public awareness about IP is also still limited. Third, industrial development has been hampered by the lack of electricity, skills, and logistics, among other constraints. The Industrial Development Policy (IDP) 2015-2025 provides many good interventions and about 100 measures; however, limited progress has been made in that direction in the past few years. Fourth, as far as One Village One Product (OVOP) is concerned, challenges include (i) limited support from the subnational authority in promoting the OVOP movement; (ii) limited co-operation and co-ordination; (iii) insufficient human resources; (iv) limited budget for the promotion of OVOP movement; (v) limited co-operation between SMEs and the general secretariat of the OVOP in the promotion of Khmer products; and (vi) significant gap in competitiveness between Khmer and Foreign products in the capital/provinces/cities/districts' product exhibitions. Fifth, the development of greater potential for tourism is constrained by the lack of infrastructure to support the sector growth and diversification, and low quality of services and products that support the sector.

Regarding Key Policies toward fulfilling the goal of Decent Work and Economic Growth, the Royal Government of Cambodia (RGC) already introduced a number of policies to ensure that the growth is inclusive through productive employment, decent work for all, and environmental safeguarding. In 2015, the National Employment Policy (NEP) 2015-2025 was developed with the key elements of the policy strongly connected with the decent work agenda. At the same time, the Industrial Development Policy (2015-2025) was also prepared and adopted as a guide to promote the country's industrial development that will help maintain sustainable and inclusive high economic growth through economic diversification, strengthening competitiveness and promoting productivity.

The RGC also made a move to set up a Skills Development Fund (SDF) to stimulate pragmatic public-private partnership projects in bridging the skills gaps in the economy. It is expected to attract higher value -added investments and generate decent jobs. In 2018, the RGC issued a Sub-Decree to provide tax break to SMEs for up to 5 years. In addition, SME Bank and Entrepreneurship Development Fund and Entrepreneurship Promotion Centre have been created by the Ministry of Economy of finance and up for running since 2019. In early 2019, the RGC formed a working group to formulate a 'digital economy policy framework' with an aim to instigate and facilitate the growth of technologies in the Cambodian economy.

By end-2019, seventeen reform measures including the above were introduced at the Government Private Sector Forum with an aim to improve Cambodia's competitiveness by reducing logistic costs and attracting foreign direct investment.

3. In the area of CSDG toward reducing inequality within and among countries, based on Cambodian Socio-Economic Survey consumption data, inequality in Cambodia began to increase between 2004 and 2007 but has declined since then. The share of total consumption of the poorest 20 percent of households increased slightly from 7.5 percent in 2007 to 8.5 percent in 2009 and 9.3 percent in 2012, whereas the share of total consumption of the richest 20 percent of households decreased from 46 percent in 2007 to 41 percent in 2009. By 2019, the Gini coefficient of inequality was 0.27, which is the lowest one in the region.

Progress has also been made in issuing land titles to Cambodian citizens. As per Government data, by end of 2018, the RGC provided 5,127,819 land titles equivalent to 73.25 percent of the 7 million quotation mark. Registration of land of indigenous communities reached 24 communities equivalent to 2,558 families. The RGC has adopted the National Policy on Housing and Policy on Incentives and Establishment of the National Program for Affordable Housing Development in order to provide affordable houses to the deserving households, especially to the families of deceased soldiers, veterans with disability who are living in poverty without land/houses. Through social land concession programs, the RGC provided, by 2019, land to a total population of 78,545 households equaling 140,765.47 hectares.

The RGC also introduced a number of policies to reduce inequality in Cambodia. First, the RGC has formulated Cambodian Health Equity Fund (HEF) in order to provide access to free health care to those people who are categorized as poor having IDPoor status. Second, the National Ageing Policy 2017-2030 was produced by taking into account the projected demographic changes and the need to mainstream ageing into the development planning process. Third, a broad National Social Protection Policy Framework 2016-2025 was developed to create a strategic plan to ensure income security and reduce economic and financial vulnerability of its citizens. It will increase people's well-being and solidarity in the society and aims at reducing poverty to a maximum extent.

In terms of challenges, although a lot of efforts were being already made by the RGC, there is still a gap between the households in urban areas and those in rural areas. Inequality, especially the development gap between urban and rural areas in the country, led to a flow of internal and cross-border labor migration. The number of internal migrant workers is about one million and the number of cross-border migrant workers has hit more than one million by early 2019.

There is a limited coverage of social services. There is still a lack of capacity to assess disabilities. Social protection reforms hold much promise for keeping inequality in check, and promoting redistribution alongside a safety net to support economic activity.

The labor market also has been key to the inclusiveness of the economy in Cambodia, with strikingly high levels of participants regardless of gender.

Despite government efforts to accelerate international trade, strengthening and increasing trade integration into the world through trade agreements have met some challenges including, (i) limited types and quantities of products into the international market; (ii) quality control and standard requirement are not broad yet; (iii) export prices are still comparatively high (high production costs); and (iv) non-tariff barriers on Cambodia's products.

The Key Policies/Strategies are, as per Royal Government of Cambodia's Voluntary National Review 2019, that the RGC will continue to focus on pro-poor rural development in order to reduce inequality. According to a study by the Asian Development Bank, the main rural development issues consist insecurity in land tenure, low productivity in land and human capital, market failures and coordination issues, and limited financing for rural development.

Government is focused and committed toward inclusive education and health-care with increased public investment as these two are the most important sectors in rural development. The RGC has also expressed its commitment of strengthening social protection, including social safety nets and social insurance policies.

The RGC, as expressed in its voluntary review 2019, will also strengthen and increase relationship and trade agreements to speed up the trade integration into the region and the world in term of equality and equity.

4. In the area of Climate Action to combat climate change and its impacts, it is to be noted that Cambodia is one of the most vulnerable countries to climate change in the region and is among the top 10 countries globally. If we discuss the progress in this area, we observe that the National Council for Sustainable Development has been coordinating the implementation of CSDG of Climate Action. A dedicated Climate Change Technical Working Group (CCTWG) has been established including all concerned ministries and agencies, as well as provincial authorities. Climate Change has also been integrated in the Rectangular Strategy IV 2018-2023, and in the National Strategic Development Plan (NSDP) 2019-2023. Key achievements by end of 2019 include increasing annual public expenditure for climate change, improved integration of climate change in national and sectoral plans, and initial progress on reduction of Green House Gases (GHGs) emission. Cambodia has also ratified the Paris Agreement on Climate Change and submitted its Nationally Determined Contribution (NDC) to the United Nations Framework Convention on Climate Change (UNFCC).

In line with the NDC, the RGC implemented a number of actions to make Cambodia resilient to climate change, including:

i) Management and development of water resources, including the development of irrigation systems;

ii) Management of flood, salted water and drought;

iii) Protection and conservation of water resources;
iv) Management of information on water resource and meteorology;
v) Enhancement of sub-national climate change planning and execution of priority actions; and
vi) Promotion of public awareness and capacity building for climate response.

There are 14 ministries and agencies which developed and implemented Climate Change Action Plan (CCAP) 2014-2018 in their sectors

The CSDG of Climate Action implementation faces the following challenges:

i) Technological and human resources capacities to implement adaptation and mitigation solutions remain limited. Technology transfers should be promoted further;
ii) Despite recent improvements, for example with the climate change vulnerability index for communes and the 2019 Green House Gas (GHG) inventory, data availability remains a challenge, and capacities of sectors to analyze vulnerabilities and track climate change adaptation and mitigation need to be strengthened;
iii) Better evidence and research on how climate change impacts various vulnerable groups is required to improve the design and targeting of climate change programs;
iv) Financial support from developed countries for climate change priorities identified by Cambodia is insufficient. Better alignment of international assistance with national priorities is required;
v) Access to finance for climate-smart investments is still limited for the private sector; and
vi) Adequate financing instruments should be developed, linked with awareness campaigns and dissemination of climate-smart technologies.

Regarding Key Policies/Strategies, the Royal Government of Cambodia (RGC) is committed to continue to mainstream environment and natural resources sustainability into the national development planning through the National Council for Sustainable Development (NCSD), which is an inter-ministerial institution with the Prime Minister as its Honorary Chair and Minister of Environment as its Chair.

The RGC is also determined to implement the development and implementation of National Environment Strategy and Action Plan (NESAP) 2016-2023 complementing the existing national strategies, action plan and programs. To implement the Cambodia Climate Change Strategic Plan (CCCSP) 2014-2023, which is in line with the commitment made at the Rio+20 Conference on Sustainable Development, contributing to the achievement of CSDGs, CCCSP is allowing the integration of climate change into national and sub-national level planning and particularly into the National Strategic Development Plan (NSDP) and sector development plans of all relevant ministries. The Ministry of Water Resources and Meteorology will continue to ensure the sustainability of water resources for agriculture, urban and rural supply, hydropower, fishery, transportation and tourism. The Ministry has developed the Strategy and Action Plan for Water Resources and Meteorology 2019-2023 to implement the National strategic Development Plan 2019-2023 and RS-IV.

5. In the area of CSDG of Peace, Justice and Institutions, in terms of Progress, the RGC has been striving to consolidate peace, political stability and social order as the fundamental foundation to strengthen good governance, the rule of law and respect for human rights in accordance with national laws and regulations. Good governance continues to be at the core of national development priorities and progress continues on the implementation of all major reforms entitled (i) the fight against corruption, (ii) the Public Administration Reform, (3) the Legal and Judicial Reform, (iv) the Reform of the Royal Cambodian Armed Forces, (v) the Public Financial Management Reform, and (vi) the Decentralization and De-concentration reforms. The engagement of all relevant stakeholders through the creation of Technical Working Groups (TWGs) has also been ensured.

The RGC has also strived to ensure justice for all. In order to ensure a wider access to social justice, the RGC in February 2019 ordered the establishment of volunteer group of lawyers to defend poor women, who cannot afford to pay for representation. The establishment of the new legal team would not use the national budget, but an initial funding of USD500,000 will come from the Prime Minister's personal budget and will cover living and food expenses, with additional money for lawyers on missions in rural areas. Progress in this area includes key efforts made to improve legal and judicial systems. Some necessary legal frameworks were introduced in order to enhance the competence, independence, and impartiality of judiciary which is crucial for strengthening the rule of law. Major laws, including the Penal Code, Criminal procedure Code, the Civil Procedure Code, the Juvenile Justice Law (with a 3 year Strategic Operational Plan for its implementation) and other laws and regulations related to political, economic, social, and cultural life were promulgated to contribute to the realization of human rights and fundamental freedoms. Additionally, rotation of judges and prosecutors from one area to another is deemed as a notable strategy in fighting corruption within the judicial system.

The RGC, globally, has made sustained contribution to UN Peacekeeping, stands out as an example to the world and carries the same universal values of peace, security and friendship at its heart. In the 1990s, Cambodia benefited from the support of UN peacekeepers to bring peace. After some years, having regained political stability, starting from 2006, Cambodia has dispatched troops to peacekeeping operations across the globe to fulfill their important role in restoring and promoting peace and stability to conflicting nation states, and every peacekeeper has made priceless sacrifice. As Royal Cambodian Government expressed that Cambodia is proud to have contributed 315 women out of total 6,268 peacekeeping troops since 2006 to

2019, to the UN Peacekeeping Operations serving missions in Sudan, South Sudan, Chad, Lebanon, Mali, Central African Republic, Syria, and Cyprus. Cambodia is one of the largest contributors of blue helmets in the ASEAN region. The RGC has officially established the Law on Access to Information, which the Ministry of Information has led in collaboration with the Swedish Embassy and UNESCO through the establishment of a Joint Technical Working Group. The draft law has been finalized at the technical working group level in 2019, and it has proceeded to ensure legality and comprehensiveness in compliance with the international standards and the socio-economic situation of Cambodia.

The RGC has strongly committed to promoting partnership with Civil Society Organizations (CSOs) in all aspects of development and a series of initiatives have been taken by the RGC's ministries to remove certain administrative requirements and have held regular consultative fora with CSOs and establishing an inter-ministerial working group to address their requests and concerns. The Royal Government of Cambodia also took concrete actions to : (a)strengthen education to avoid corruption through the inclusion of anti-corruption lessons in the general education curriculum from grades 4 to 12; disseminate information on anti-corruption laws at public institutions, and via private sector, academia and media avenues; and organize public events and competitions on anti-corruption to encourage public participation. (b) Prevent corruption through monitoring the implementation of public services and produce other anti-corruption materials; issue warnings letters to those suspected of corruption; and stricter monitoring of examinations at all levels, from high school to public servant recruitment examinations; and ensure effective oversight of processes for procurement, and asset and liability declarations. (c) Enforce the law through the establishment and implementation of a convenient corruption complaint mechanism; enable investigation of cases where there is solid evidence and formulate cases and take perpetrators of corruption to court.

It is also noteworthy that the proportion of female government officials in ministries/agencies has been raised by 1 percent, increasing from 40 percent in 2016 to 41 percent in 2018. The RGC has also been providing civil registration with the issuance of free birth certificates and free legal assistance available for the poor. In addition, one-window service has been rolled out in 2018 as an effective governance mechanism to simplify administrative processes and ensure timely delivery of public services to all citizens, including businessmen, and small entrepreneurs.

If we look at the Challenges, one of the key challenges in fighting corruption is the lack of budget to enforce existing laws. Understanding of laws and its procedures of enforcement need to be further promoted to the public. The means of dissemination of laws and regulations from national to sub-national levels will be made more innovative in order to deliver the changes of steps more effectively.

Regarding Key Policies/Strategies, the RGC seeks to maintain peace, political stability, security and social order, improve living standards and people's welfare, promote and protect the fundamental rights and human dignity. The RGC expressed their commitment to ensure that no one in Cambodia is left behind in enjoying their rights and freedoms regardless of race, color, sex, language, religious belief, birth origin, social status, wealth or other statuses. The RGC will continue to reform legal and judicial systems by designing a legal framework with sustainability at its center to gain the public's trust. The RGC is also committed to continue to strengthen the implementation of existing laws to be more effective by increasing the dissemination of information, training programs for law enforcement officials. The RGC will continue to take actions to combat corruption by strengthening accountability and institutional capacity building, with support and participation from the public, participation from private sector and by strengthening law enforcement.

6. In the area of CSDG of Partnerships for the Goals to strengthen the means of implementation and revitalize the global partnership for sustainable development, in terms of Progress, the RGC so far achieved substantial success in strengthening partnership with development partners through continuous improvement and implementation of key policies and mechanisms, especially the preparation and implementation of the Development Co-operation and Partnership Strategy (DCPS) 2014-2018 and its successor for the period 2019-2023. The RGC has been able to mobilize resources for national development and considers co-operation financing crucial for social development as well as the development of the country's economy. In the period of 2015-2018, the volume of Official Development Assistance (ODA) accounted for around USD1.4 billion per annum. The ODA grant contribution leveled off at approximately USD800 million. The ODA / GDP ratio has fallen from 7.5 percent in 2015 to 5.7 percent in 2018. The overall volume of support to either sector or sub-sector seemed to be slightly higher than baseline and planned figures as set out in CSDGs targets within Cambodian Rehabilitation and Development Board / Council for Development of Cambodia (CRDB / CDC's) coverage.

The Development Co-operation and Partnership Strategy (2014-2018) had been developed and effectively implemented in line with Cambodia's evolved development context as an LMIC. It provided a comprehensive framework for promoting development partnerships in Cambodia articulated in the RGC's RS-IV. The strategy is also aligned with global initiatives on development effectiveness focusing on effective institutions, inclusive partnerships and development results. As a whole, there has been good progress in establishing and managing partnership mechanisms. The bilateral consultation mechanism between the RGC and Development Partners (DPs) continues to provide opportunity to jointly review development programs and discuss development issues and opportunity. These mechanisms, together with all other global partnership commitments, are regularly monitored, with the most recent survey feeding into the formulation of the Development Cooperation and Partnership Strategy for 2019-2023. A revised Technical Working Group (TWG) Guideline and a revised set of Joint Monitoring Indicators (JMIs) for 2019-2023 provide mechanisms for consultation and monitoring to further integrate the CSDGs in the work of different ministries and priority sectors as well as to build broad-based and inclusive partnerships. The RGC increased the national budget for national surveys and for conducting of the 2019 the General Population Census of Cambodia in line with the international recommendations and standards, in order to build capacity for the effective use of such data to monitor the progress against the targets and indicators of CSDGs aiming at improving the delivery of public services for all people.

In term of Challenges in this CSDG area, it is to be noted that achieving national development objectives and the CSDGs requires the mobilization of a significantly increased level of resourcing and will require more complex and comprehensive financial management structure for both private and public sources. Cambodia's strong record of economic growth, poverty reduction and Rectangular Strategy implementation means that the country has now surpassed the Human Assets Index threshold for LDC graduation. Continued effort and further actions toward lowering the Economic Vulnerability Index are required. Graduating from LDC status would reduce Cambodia's access a wide range of International Special Measures under various UN supported initiatives, mainly in the areas of trade, development, and technical assistances. Likewise, development partners also are likely to review their support, increase their requirements for cost-sharing, counterpart funding or transition to loan financing. Thus, new development partnerships and resources must be mobilized to ensure continued CSDG progress.

Regarding Key Policies/Strategies, the RGC's lead coordination and resource mobilization agency, Cambodian Rehabilitation and Development Board/Council for

Development of Cambodia (CRDB / CDC) will continue to ensure the strategic management of Official Development Assistance (ODA). The CSDG Framework complements the national development framework and provides a mechanism for effective partnering. To succeed in supporting the implementation of CSDGs, the Development Co-operation and Partnership Strategy (DCPS) 2019-2023 has been developed at a time when Cambodia's own development priorities and control are evolving. In this regard, the RGC recognizes that ODA remains particularly important for its national socio-economic development agenda, and will serve as a catalyst in leveraging other sources of development finance, both private and public, to further promote inclusive growth and sustainable economic development of Cambodia. The RGC is fully committed to continue working in partnership to secure successful implementation of its policy agendas including CSDGs, National Strategic Development Plan (NSDP), sector plans, and major governance reforms. The RGC's DCPS makes an important contribution to development partnerships efforts by establishing principles, setting objectives and identifying tools to promote effective co-operation.

The remaining twelve Cambodian Sustainable Developmental Goals are: (1) No Poverty in order to end poverty in all its forms everywhere; (2) Zero Hunger in order to end hunger, achieve food security and improved nutrition and promote sustainable agriculture; (3) Good Health and Well-being in order to ensure healthy lives and promote well-being for all ages; (4) Gender Equality in order to achieve gender equality and empower all women and girls; (5) Clean Water and sanitation to ensure availability and sustainable management of water and sanitation for all; (6) Affordable and Clean energy to ensure access to affordable, reliable, sustainable, and modern energy for all; (7) Industry, Innovation and Infrastructure in order to build resilient infrastructure, promote inclusive and sustainable industrialization and foster innovation; (8) Sustainable Cities and Communities to make cities, and human settlements inclusive, safe, resilient and sustainable; (9) Responsible Consumption and Production to ensure sustainable consumption and production patterns; (10) Life Below Water to conserve and sustainably use the oceans, seas and marine resources for sustainable development; (11) Life on Land to protect, restore and promote sustainable use of terrestrial ecosystems, sustainably manage forests, combat desertification, and halt and reverse land degradation and halt biodiversity loss; and (12) Cambodia Mine / ERW Free to end the negative impact of mine /ERW and promote victim assistance. All these remaining twelve Cambodian Sustainable Development Goals, in summary form, are on progress to date (as of end-2019) in a satisfactory manner against their respective baseline. Goals, targets and indicators are mostly on track as indicated by the Royal Government of Cambodia in their National Review 2019.

Conclusion

The Cambodian economy is at a crucial transformation stage after sustaining high growth over the last decade. The country is moving toward becoming a middle-income country, which requires comprehensive structural reforms aimed at strengthening economic diversification and competitiveness to ensure sustainable economic growth with equitable redistribution of wealth. This requires consideration for a new development approach vis-a-vis expanding development opportunities and investment in new growth sectors by way of improving the necessary socio-economic infrastructure, supply of energy, expansion of transport infrastructure and development of logistics, promotion of technical and sciences education, and institutional strengthening.

In this regard, the Royal Government has decided to adopt the Industrial Development Policy (IDP) in order to provide a policy framework and a specific mechanism for driving economic growth and creating jobs with focus on the manufacturing sector, agro-industrial sector and SMEs. In pursuance of this policy, Cambodia will succeed in its economic structural transformation by moving from an agricultural-based economy

Achievements and Future Direction in Sustainable Development

toward a manufacturing and agro-industry based economy, and subsequently in the final phase toward diversification in other sectors especially those that use technology and innovation.

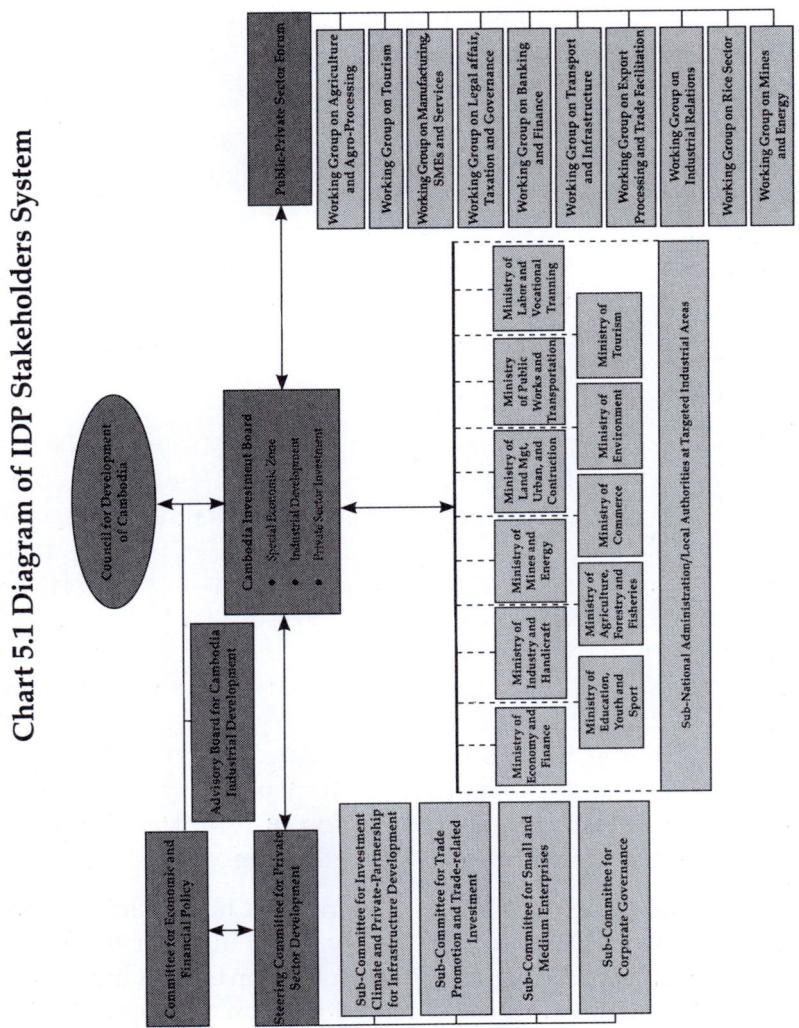

Chart 5.1 Diagram of IDP Stakeholders System

Chart 5.2
Organization Chart of Cambodia Rehabilitation Development Board and Cambodia Investment Board

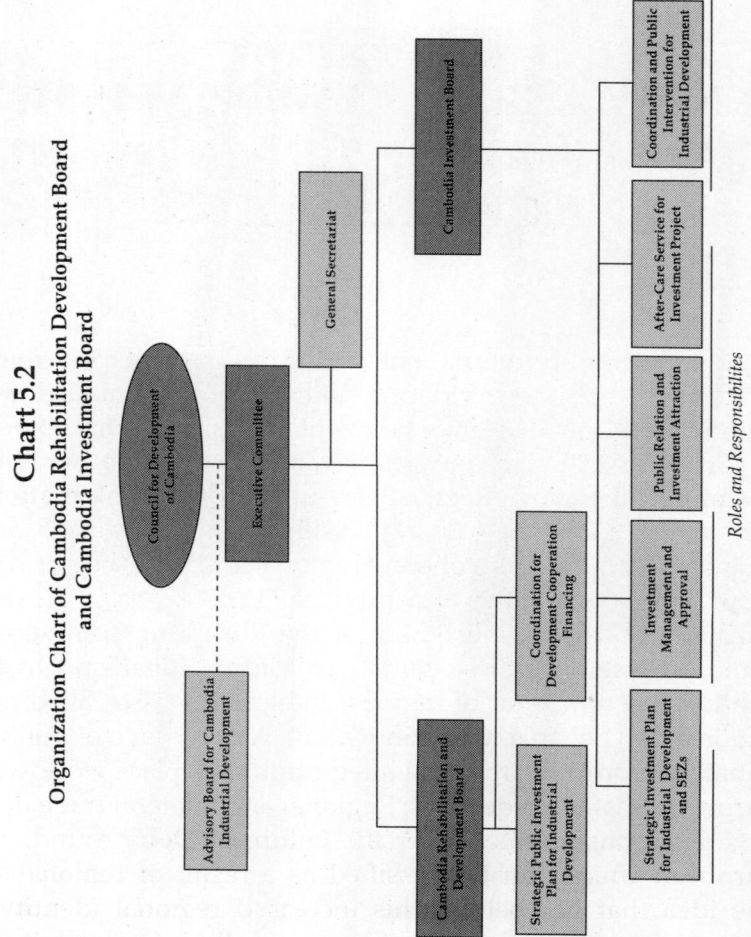

Roles and Responsibilites

CHAPTER-SIX
NEW ASEAN REGIONALISM: CAUSES, ACHIEVEMENTS AND CHALLENGES

Regionalism, in international relations, is the expression of a common sense of identity and purpose combined with the creation and implementation of institutions that express a particular identity and shape collective action within a geographical region. Regionalism is one of the international commercial system (along with multilateralism and unilateralism). The first coherent regional initiatives began in the 1950s and 1960s, but they accomplished little, except in Western Europe with the establishment of the European Community. Some analysts call these initiatives 'old regionalism'. In the late 1980s, a new bout of regional integration (also called new regionalism) began and continues still. A new wave of political initiative prompting regional integration took place worldwide during the last three decades. Regional and bilateral trade deals have also mushroomed after the failure of Doha round. The European Union can be classified as a result of regionalism. The idea that lies behind this increased regional identity is that as a region becomes more economically integrated, it will necessarily become politically integrated as well.

The Association of Southeast Asian Nations (ASEAN) is a regional grouping that promotes economic, political, and security co-operation among its ten members: Brunei, Cambodia, Indonesia, Laos, Malaysia, Myanmar, the Philippines,

Singapore, Thailand, and Vietnam. ASEAN countries have a total population of 650 million people and a combined gross domestic product (GDP) of USD2.8 trillion. The group has been playing a central role in Asian economic integration, signing six free-trade agreements with other regional economies and helping spearhead negotiations for what could be the world's largest free trade pact. However, some experts say that ASEAN's impact is limited by a lack of strategic vision, diverging priorities among member states, and weak leadership. According to them, the bloc's biggest challenge is developing a unified approach to China, particularly in response to Beijing's claims in the South China Sea, which overlap with claims of several ASEAN members.

ASEAN is chaired by an annually rotating presidency assisted by a secretariat based in Jakarta, Indonesia. Important decisions are usually reached through consultation and consensus guided by the principles of noninterference in internal affairs and peaceful resolution of conflicts. Some experts see this approach to decision- making as a chief drawback for the organization. Joshua Kurlantzick of Council on Foreign Relations (CFR) observed that 'these norms of consensus and noninterference have increasingly become outdated, and they have hindered ASEAN's influence on issues ranging from dealing with China and crises in particular ASEAN states. 'Other experts observe that ASEAN has contributed to regional stability by developing much-needed norms and fostering a neutral environment to address shared challenges. As Murray Hiebert, a senior associate of the Southeast Asia Program at the Washington-based Center for Strategic and International Studies (CSIS) observed that 'In Asia, talking and relationship building is half the challenge to solving problems'.

Formed in 1967 (the Year 2020 marks the 53rd anniversary of the establishment) ASEAN united Indonesia, Malaysia, the Philippines, Singapore, and Thailand, which sought to create a common front against the spread of communism and promote political, economic, and social stability amid rising tensions in the Asia Pacific. In 1976, the members signed the Treaty of Amity and Co-operation in Southeast Asia, which emphasizes mutual respect and non-interference in other countries' affairs. Membership doubled by the end of the 1990s. The resolution of Cambodia's civil war in 1991, the end of the Cold War, and the normalization of relations between the United States and Vietnam in 1995 brought relative peace to mainland Southeast Asia, paving the way for more states to join ASEAN. With the addition of Brunei (1984), Vietnam (1995), Laos and Myanmar (1997), and Cambodia (1999), the group started to launch initiatives to boost regionalism. The members signed a treaty in 1995, for example, to refrain from developing, acquiring, or possessing nuclear weapons. Faced with the 1997 Asian financial Crisis, which started in Thailand, ASEAN members pushed to further integrate their economies. The ASEAN Plus Three cooperation mechanism was established in the late 1990s when ASEAN countries decided to enhance cooperation with other major economies of Asia against the backdrop of economic globalization. The first ASEAN Plus Three summit was held in Malaysia in 1997, a time when countries in the region were facing an economic setback. The financial crisis was regarded as having provided the impetus for this summit. A number of dialogue mechanisms at various levels have been established within the framework of ASEAN Plus Three, covering diplomacy, economy, finance, agriculture, labor, tourism, environment, fight against cross-border crime, health care, energy, telecommunications, social welfare and administration innovation. The Chiang Mai Initiative, for instance, was a currency swap arrangement first initiated in 2000 between ASEAN members, China, Japan, and South Korea to provide financial support to one another and fight currency speculation. In 2003, in Bali Summit, ASEAN Leaders adopted the Bali Concord II to consolidate ASEAN through three pillars, namely an ASEAN Security Community (ASC), an ASEAN Economic Community (AEC) and an ASEAN Socio-cultural Community (ASCC) among ASEAN member countries. The Regional Comprehensive Economic Partnership (RCEP) was formally launched in November 2012 at the ASEAN Summit in Cambodia. The RCEP is a proposed free trade agreement in the Indo-Pacific region between the ten member states of ASEAN, namely Brunei, Cambodia, Indonesia, Laos PDR, Malaysia, Myanmar, the Philippines, Singapore, Thailand, and Vietnam, and six of ASEAN's FTA partners – Australia, China, Japan, India, New Zealand, and South Korea. In 2018, the sixteen (16) negotiating parties accounted for about half of the world's population and 39 percent of the world's GDP. Putting it differently, RCEP potentially included more than 3 billion people or 45 percent of the world's population, and a combined GDP of about USD21.3 trillion, accounted for about 40 percent of world trade in 2018. Continued economic growth, particularly in China, India and Indonesia could see total GDP in RCEP grow to over USD100 trillion by 2050, roughly double the project size of Trans Pacific Partnership (TPP). On 23 January 2017, United States President Donald Trump signed a memorandum that stated withdrawal of USA from TPP, a move which was seen to improve the chances of success for RCEP. However, India opted out of RCEP on 4th November, 2019 in ASEAN Plus Three summit, citing the adverse impact the deal would have on its citizens, primarily due to concerns of a surge of imports, particularly from China, potentially affecting its own domestic industrial and farming sectors. India's decision to not join RCEP reduced the impact of RCEP significantly. Without India, the 15 negotiating parties account for around 30 percent of the world's population and just under 30 percent of the world's GDP. In light of India's departure, Japan and the PRC called on India to rejoin the partnership.

In terms of the achievements of ASEAN, followed by the Bali summit in 2003, the ten members adopted the ASEAN Charter in 2007, a constitutional document that provided the grouping with legal status and an institutional framework. The charter enshrines core principles and delineates requirements for membership. The charter laid out a blueprint for a community made up of three branches as mentioned above: the ASEAN Economic Community (AEC), the ASEAN Political Security Community, and the ASEAN Socio-Cultural Community.

ACHIEVEMENTS

ASEAN has made notable progress toward economic integration and free trade in the region. In 1992, members created the ASEAN Free Trade Area with the goals of creating a single market, increasing intra-ASEAN trade and investments, and attracting foreign investments. Intra-ASEAN trade as a share of the bloc's overall trade grew from about 19 percent in 1993 to 24.1 percent in 2019. Across the grouping, more than 90 percent of goods are traded with no tariffs. The bloc has prioritized eleven sectors for integration, including electronics, automotive, rubber-based products, textiles and apparels, agro-based products, and tourism.

Looking at the global economy, we can see that it entered a period of recovery after the crisis in 2008, and the global gross domestic product (GDP) expanded by 5.4 percent in 2010 before moderating within the 3.4 percent to 3.8 percent range from 2012 to 2018. The decade saw advanced and emerging economies implementing stimulus measures and adopting quarantine easing, followed by policy tightening and escalating trade tensions, amidst ongoing geo-political tensions. From 3.8 percent in 2017, global GDP growth moderated to 3.6 percent as growth momentum was dampened by the trade tensions. Growth in advanced economies slowed to 2.3 percent in 2018 following the softening of industrial production, political uncertainties, and natural disasters; while growth in emerging economies eased to 4.5 percent in 2018 from 4.8 percent in 2017 given the financial tightening and uncertain economic conditions (IMF 2019).

The ASEAN economy has consistently out performed the global economy. The region's GDP growth has remained close to 5.0 percent since 2011, while global GDP stayed below 4.0 percent over the same period. By 2018, ASEAN's share of global economy had expanded, in nominal terms, to 3.5 percent (up from 2.9 percent in 2010). ASEAN has risen to fifth place, in 2019, among the largest economies in the world, with nominal GDP estimated at USD3.0 trillion, an increase of more than

50 percent from its 2010 level. ASEAN trailed the US (24.2 percent), the EU (22.1 percent), China (15.8 percent), and Japan (5.9 percent). In PPP terms, the share of ASEAN's economy expanded from 5.5 percent of the global economy in 2010 to 6.5 percent in 2018, and was also ranked fifth in the world. Well embedded in global value chains, the region is also one of the largest globally in terms of trade in goods. In 2019, ASEAN had a 7.2 percent share in global trade in goods (ranked fourth after the EU, China, and the US) and a 6.8 percent share in global trade in services, and ranked fourth after the EU, the US, and China. ASEAN is also an attractive investment destination. In 2018, ASEAN received USD154.7 billion, or 11.9 percent of total global FDI inflows, the highest in its history, ranking third after the EU and the US. The region is also among the largest global investors, with outward investments amounted to USD69.6 billion – 6.9 percent of the world total.

Since the official launching of the AEC at the end of 2015, the ASEAN economic integration process continues to progress, guided by the AEC Blueprint 2025. Work is ongoing to achieve an AEC that, by 2025: is highly integrated and cohesive; is competitive, innovative, and dynamic; is resilient, inclusive, people-oriented, and people-centred; and is global, playing an active role in regional and global economic architectures.

1. TOWARD HIGHLY INTEGRATED AND COHESIVE ECONOMY

In term of trade in goods, the free flow of goods has long been an important aim of ASEAN economic integration. In fact, the creation of an ASEAN Free Trade Area (AFTA) in 1992 predated the launch of the AEC Blueprint 2015 in 2007. ASEAN and its individual member states have increasingly become stronger players in global trade. Collectively, ASEAN internally is the largest market for its total trade, at 23.0 percent in 2018; followed by China (17.2 percent), the EU (10.2 percent), and the US (9.3 percent). The shares of intra-ASEAN merchandise exports and imports in 2018 was 24.2 percent and 21.7 percent of ASEAN's total exports and imports, respectively. While the intra-ASEAN shares in total exports and imports did not change much between 2010 and 2018 (from 25.2 percent to 24.1 percent and from 25.0 percent to 21.8 percent, respectively) in absolute terms, intra-ASEAN exports increased by 30.6 percent over this period to reach USD345.2 billion in 2018, and intra-ASEAN imports by 26.8 percent to reach USD302.3 billion.

The establishment of the AEC has laid the foundation for a functioning single market and production base. Under the AEC Blueprint 2015, ASEAN has made strides in significantly eliminating intra-ASEAN tariffs. In addition, efforts are ongoing in implementing other commitments under the ASEAN Trade in Goods Agreement (ATIGA), which came into force in 2010, including trade facilitation measures. These have contributed to the freer flow of goods in the region. The Strategic Action Plan (SAP) 2016-2025 for Trade in Goods was endorsed at the 30th AFTA Council and the 48th ASEAN economic Ministers (AEM) Meeting in August 2016. The SAP 2016-2025 for Trade in Goods aims to guide ASEAN to achieve more integrated trade regimes, eliminate the remaining obstacles to regional trade, and promote a rules-based system to enable businesses to benefit the most from the ATIGA. The first strategic measure in the SAP 2016-2025 for Trade in Goods is to further strengthen the ATIGA. ASEAN has made significant progress in liberalizing tariffs under the ATIGA. As of May 2019, 99.3 percent of all tariffs have been eliminated by the ASEAN-6 (e.g. Brunei Darussalam, Indonesia, Malaysia, the Philippines, Singapore, and Thailand), while the corresponding figure for Cambodia, Lao PDR, Myanmar, Vietnam (CLMV) is 97.7 percent. Collectively, ASEAN has eliminated 98.6 percent of the total number of tariff lines in 2019. Efforts to liberalize tariffs under the ATIGA have effectively lowered the level of applied tariff rates in the region. In 2017, ASEAN's weighted average effective applied tariff rates reached 2.0 percent, with average tariff rates of 1.8 percent for the ASEAN-6, and 2.7 percent for the CLMV countries. The CLMV countries, in particular, have significantly reduced their applied tariff from an average of 5.1 percent in 2010 to 2.7 percent in 2017.

A country's participation in regional and international trade is affected by both tariffs and non-tariff measures (NTMs), which can be defined as policy measures other than tariffs that can affect cross-border trade. While many countries have made significant progress in reducing tariffs, there is a general trend of rising NTMs globally, along with the risks of these NTMs being used as protectionist regulations. In ASEAN, whereas the average tariff rates decreased from 8.9 percent in 2000 to 4.5 percent in 2015, the number of NTMs had increased from 1,634 measures to 5,975 measures over the same period. As per ASEAN Integration Report, 2019, as of 24th May,2019, ASEAN countries have a total of 5,886 NTMs based on official regulations. The prevalence of NTMs is not necessarily bad. The Plus six countries (Australia, China, India, Japan, ROK, and New Zealand), for instance, had a total of 16,025 NTMs based on official regulations that were in force as of 24th May 2019. In addition, a higher number of recorded NTMs may also signal more effective or compliant notification processes. Thus, what we seek to reduce, if not eliminate, is the restrictive or distortionary effects of NTMs on international trade. The ASEAN guidelines for the implementation of ASEAN commitments on Non Tariff Measures on Goods (hereafter referred to as the NTM Guidelines) was endorsed by the 32nd AFTA Council, which was convened on 29 August 2018 in Singapore. To further facilitate intra- ASEAN trade, a 'self-certification' scheme is also being initiated. This mechanism allows certified exporters to self-certify the origin of their exports to enjoy preferential tariffs under the ATIGA. The operationalization of the ASEAN-Wide Self-Certification Scheme (AWSC), which was first mooted in 2009, will minimize burdens associated with administrative compliance and decrease transaction costs.

Reducing trade costs is essential for countries to use trade effectively as an engine for growth and sustainable development. Over the past decade, many of the reduction in trade costs in ASEAN were achieved through the reduction of tariffs. In order to further reduce trade costs in the region, ASEAN has recently made strengthening of trade facilitation one of its key economic integration goals. A number of governance and planning instruments were adopted by ASEAN to further strengthen its trade facilitation agenda: (i) the ASEAN Trade Facilitation framework (ATFF); (ii) the Terms of reference of the ASEAN Trade Facilitation joint consultative Committee (ATF-JCC); and (iii) the ASEAN Trade Facilitation Strategic Action Plan (ATF-SAP). These governance and planning instruments will ultimately enhance ASEAN's trade and production networks, enabling it to better participate in global value chains. The measurable targets under the ATF-SAP include: (a) reduction in trade transaction costs in the AEC by 10 percent by 2020, (b) doubling of intra-ASEAN trade between 2017 and 2025; and (c) improved performance in global rankings / surveys (e.g. the World Economic forum's Global competitiveness Report and the World Bank's Ease of Doing Business).

The ASEAN Trade Repository (ATR) is one of the key initiatives in ASEAN's trade facilitation agenda, and is a commitment under the ATIGA. Launched in 2016, the facility provides a single point of access to all trade-related information of AMS. The ATR is an ASEAN-level IT interface linked to National Trade Repositories (NTRs), where national-level trade-related information is maintained by their respective governments. Another major trade facilitation initiative being undertaken is the ASEAN Seamless Trade Facilitation Indication (ASTFI), which were adopted at the 49th AEM Meeting in September 2017. The ASTFI were designed to measure and monitor the extent to which trade facilitation measures are implemented in the region through various ASEAN agreements, such as the ATIGA, the ASEAN Framework Agreement on Facilitation of Goods in Transit (AFAFGIT), as well as various sectoral work plans relevant to trade facilitation.

Another practical trade facilitation tool initiated by ASEAN is the ASEAN solutions for Investments, Services, and Trade (ASSIST), which is a non-binding and consultative mechanism for the expedited and effective solution of operational problems encountered by ASEAN-based enterprises on cross-border issues related to the implementation of ASEAN economic agreements, and, especially within the framework of the AEC. ASSIST aims at delivering practical solutions to specific trade problems within 40 to 60 working days, and allows the business sector to interact directly with AMS governments.

ASEAN Customs also plays an important role in facilitating the seamless movements of goods in the region. The customs integration agenda aims to simplify customs procedures in the region, a move that is expected to reduce trade transaction costs significantly. ASEAN's efforts on customs integration are guided by the Strategic Plans of Customs Development (SPCDs), which were endorsed by the 24th Meeting of ASEAN Customs Directors-General in May 2015. One of ASEAN's key achievements in this area is the ASEAN Customs Transit System (ACTS). A joint effort between Customs and Land Transport Authorities, ACTS enables free movement of trucked goods between participating countries without the need for a customs declaration at each border or a change of vehicle. The ASEAN Customs Administrations are also committed to develop a cooperation mechanism to promote the Authorized Economic Operator (AEO) status and its mutual recognition.

The ASEAN Single Window (ASW) enables electronic processing and exchange of data and information to accelerate customs clearance processes in the region. Apart from reducing unnecessary manual procedures, the ASW allows customs and relevant regulatory agencies to facilitate efficient and secure trade by; (i) eliminating human intervention both for endorsement and document validation; (ii) expediting the process of document validation/verification by enabling the usage of electronic information; and (iii) reducing time of document submission.

The ability to comply with relevant standards, technical regulations, and conformity assessment procedures (STRACAP) is imperative to securing access to international markets. Recognizing the importance of this issue, ASEAN's work in this area involves the harmonization of standards and technical regulations, improving quality and capability of conformity assessment, and enhancing information exchange on laws, rules, and regulatory regimes on standards and conformity assessment procedures. Established in October 1992, the ASEAN Consultative Committee for Standards and Quality (ACCSQ) is the lead ASEAN sectoral body in this area.

Considered a new engine for growth in ASEAN, services continues to be an important and growing economic sector in the region. The sector contributed 50.1 percent of the region's total GDP of USD3.0 trillion in 2018, which made it the largest component of ASEAN GDP. For many AMS, the services sector accounts for almost half of their real output, with some countries, such as Singapore, Thailand, the Philippines, and Malaysia recording even higher shares. At 60.7 percent, services also received the largest share of FDI flows into ASEAN in 2018, with the highest share contributed by financial and insurance activities. The services sector also provides good employment opportunity for women. Given that, in some AMS, such as Brunei Darussalam, Singapore, the Philippines, and Malaysia, this workforce makes up more than half of employment in these countries. ASEAN's trade in services consistently increased from 2010 to 2018, growing by 7.4 percent annually on average, or faster than trade in goods at 4.4 percent. In 2018, the region's services trade reached USD778.6 billion – an increase of 77.3 percent from USD439.2 billion in 2010. Meanwhile, intra-ASEAN services trade increased 50.7 percent from USD81.0 billion in 2010 to USD122.1 billion in 2018. Intra-ASEAN services exports grew at an average of 5.5 percent annually over the period, compared to 5 percent for services imports. ASEAN's services exports were valued at USD404.9 billion in 2018, an increase of 89.4 percent from USD213.8 billion in 2010, whereas its services imports reached USD373.8 billion in 2018, an increase of 65.8 percent from USD225.4 billion in 2010. Since 2016, ASEAN has been recording trade surpluses in its services trade, with its services exports growing higher than imports. In 2018, ASEAN's top three services exports were travel services (34.3 Percent), other business services (22.1 percent), and transportation services (18.6 percent). As for the top three service imports, these included transportation services (30.7 percent), other business services (24.1 percent), and travel services (21.1 percent). Travel services, other business services, and transportation services dominated both ASEAN services exports and imports in 2019 also like they did in the past decade.

ASEAN has also undertaken a number of initiatives to promote cross-border skills mobility, such as the Mutual Recognition Arrangements, ASEAN Agreement on Movement of Natural Persons, and ASEAN Qualifications Reference Framework. ASEAN Mutual Recognition Arrangements (MRAs) promote cross-border mobility of foreign professionals through mutual recognition of authorization, licensing, or certification of qualifications of professional service suppliers obtained in one country by another country participating in the arrangement. There are currently MRAs in force for eight professional services in ASEAN: (1) engineering services; (2) nursing services; (3) architectural services; (4) surveyors; (5) medical practitioners; (6) dental practitioners; (7) tourism professionals; and (8) accountancy services. These MRAs have different approaches. MRAs for engineering, architecture, and accountancy services provide ASEAN-wide certification for qualified professionals, which enables them to work as registered ASEAN professionals in another AMS in collaboration with recognized local professionals. As of June 2019, there were 3,733 engineers on the ASEAN Chartered professional Engineers Register, 545 architects registered as ASEAN Architects, and 3,205 accountants registered as ASEAN Chartered Professional Accountant.

Element A5 (Facilitating Movement of Skilled Labor and Business Visitors) of AEC blueprint 2025 provides guidance on ASEAN's work to facilitate the temporary cross-border movement of natural persons (MNP) and business visitors engaged in the conduct of trade in goods, trade in services, and investment. The ASEAN Agreement on MNP covers business visitors, contractual service suppliers, intra-corporate transferees, as well as other categories as specified in the Schedules of commitments of AMS. It does not, however, apply for the purpose of permanent employment, permanent residency, or citizenship. The MNP Agreement entered into force on 14th June 2016.

An essential part of facilitating the movement of skills is ensuring the comparability of educational qualifications. The ASEAN Qualifications Reference Framework (AQRF) is a common reference framework that enables comparisons of educational qualifications across participating AMS, which promotes and encourages education and learner mobility in all education and training sectors. The AQRF was developed in 2014 by the Task Force on the AQRF, which consisted of officials and experts from ASEAN ministries of trade, labor and manpower development, education, as well as other relevant qualification agencies. Since its first meeting in February 2017, the AQRF Committee has met six times, with two AMS successfully completing and having their AQRF referencing reports endorsed by the committee while other AMS are in various stages in preparing and completing their referencing reports.

The importance of FDI for a country's/region's economic growth and long-term competitiveness is widely acknowledged. As investment increases, the capacity of an economy to produce more and diversified goods and services also increases, driving economic growth. In ASEAN, investment has played a critical role in the formation of supply chains and production networks with AMS pursuing policies that allow FDI inflows as part of their industrialization strategies and drive the region to become a major production base in the global economy. Notwithstanding global economic uncertainties in recent years, the success of ASEAN's continuous efforts to establish a free and open investment regime is visible through steady investment inflows performance. With total foreign investment worth USD154.7 billion in 2018 from USD108.2 billion in 2010 (representing annual growth averaging of 4.6 percent), ASEAN's total FDI inflows exceeded those of other emerging economies, such as China (USD139.0 billion), ROK (USD14.5 billion), and India (USD42.3 billion). With the exception of the

EU and the US, each with total FDI inflows of USD277.6 billion and USD251.8 billion respectively, ASEAN's FDI inflows were also higher than some other developed economies, such as Canada (USD39.6 billion), Australia (USD60.4 billion), Japan (USD9.9 billion), and New Zealand (USD1.4 billion) as shown by UNCTAD, 2019. In 2018, Singapore remained the largest FDI recipient in the ASEAN region with a 50.2 percent share of total inflows to the region (USD77.6 billion), followed by Indonesia (14.2 percent), Vietnam (10.0 percent), and Thailand (8.6 percent).

Intra-ASEAN FDI inflows, which amounted to USD24.5 billion, took up the largest share at 15.9 percent, of total FDI inflows into the region in 2018. This figure was higher than the EU's USD22.0 billion (14.2 percent), Japan's USD21.2 billion (13.7 percent), and China's USD10.2 billion (6.6 percent). Intra-ASEAN FDI inflows have grown at an annual average of 5.2 percent from USD16.3 billion in 2010.

With USD154.7 billion worth of investment, the services sector received the highest FDI flows, or 60.7 percent, of total FDI inflows into ASEAN in 2018, and this was followed by the manufacturing sector with USD55.1 billion (35.6 percent). FDI inflows to the services sector has grown on average by 3.4 percent annually since 2011, with major contributions made by the sub-sectors, namely, financial intermediation (27.4 percent), trade and commerce (13.5 percent), and professional social and other services (9.9 percent) of total inflows in 2018.

ASEAN's present policy agenda on investment, as discussed earlier, is guided by Element A3 (Investment Environment) of the AEC Blueprint 2025. Under this characteristic, ASEAN aims to further enhance its attractiveness as a global investment destination through the establishment of an open, transparent, and predictable investment regime in the region. ASEAN's primary tool to achieve this objective is the ASEAN Comprehensive Investment Agreement (ACIA), which has been in force since 29 March 2012. The ACIA and its subsequent amended protocols are ASEAN's response to enhancing its competitiveness amid increased global competition. ASEAN's interest in sustainable investment has also been visible in its work in the area of responsible business conduct and/or corporate social responsibility (CSR).

Integration in the financial sector is envisaged under the first characteristic of the AEC Blueprint 2025 – a highly integrated and cohesive economy. Under Element A4 of the AEC Blueprint 2025, financial integration is required to be pursued through three strategic objectives, namely, financial integration, financial inclusion, and financial stability, and three cross-cutting areas – capital account liberalization, payment and settlement systems, and capacity building. To achieve these objectives, several areas of cooperation have been pursued in the areas of Financial Services Liberalization, Banking Integration, Capital Account Liberalization, Capital Market Development, Insurance cooperation, Payment and Settlement System, and Financial Inclusion. Work under these areas is guided by the SAPs for ASEAN Financial Integration 2016-2025, which were adopted at the 2nd ASEAN Finance Ministers' and Central Bank Governors' Meeting in April 2016. At the same time, another important area of financial cooperation – taxation – is guided by the Strategic Action Plan 2016-2025 for ASEAN Taxation Cooperation, adopted by ASEAN Finance Ministers in April 2017. The document outlines the broad strategies for enhancing tax cooperation on, among others, bilateral agreements on the avoidance of double taxation and withholding tax structures among AMS.

ASEAN's work on financial services liberalization (FSL) aims to gradually remove restrictions on the delivery of financial services within the region, covering banking, insurance, and capital markets, based on each AMS's state of readiness. The Working Committee on FSL was established in 2003 to carry out the process of FSL in the region. Progress has been made in the liberalization and integration of the insurance sector, starting with Marine, Aviation and Goods in International Transit (MAT) insurance as a non-sensitive sub-sector. In 2016, the ASEAN Insurance Forum was established to facilitate collaboration between the Working Committee on FSL and the ASEAN Insurance Regulators' Meeting, and work with the private sector to advance ASEAN insurance integration. The ASEAN Insurance Forum completed the Guiding Principles for the implementation of insurance liberalization in 2018 and is currently developing a Roadmap for the ASEAN Insurance Integration Framework. In 2019, the ASEAN Insurance Forum finalized the handbook for ASEAN insurers offering Cross-Border MAT Insurance, which provides greater clarity on MAT definition, its regulatory framework, and consumer protection mechanisms among AMS.

The ASEAN Central Bank Governors endorsed ASEAN Banking Integration Framework (ABIF) and its attendant guidelines in December 2014. The main objective of the ABIF is to establish a more integrated regional banking sector composed of a network of Qualified ASEAN banks, which will be provided with greater market access and operational flexibility comparable to that of domestic banks in the respective host countries. With the ABIF, any two or more AMS may enter into reciprocal bilateral agreements to provide Qualified ASEAN Banks with greater market access and operational flexibilities in host countries.

Financial integration in ASEAN also involves liberalizing the capital account to allow freer movement of investments and other flows. In 2015, the Working Committee on Capital Account Liberalization (WC-CAL) agreed to improve the CAL Heat Map, which is a tool for assessing the level of openness of the capital account regimes among the AMS, using a more objective scoring methodology. The revised CAL Heat Map methodology was finalized in 2016 and improved in 2017 and 2018. All AMS have begun its implementation in 2019. WC-CAL also continues to conduct policy dialogues on capital flows and safeguard mechanisms for capital account liberalization. The objective is to assist AMS in the formulation of relevant policies on safeguard measures during their respective CAL processes.

The integration of ASEAN capital markets involves the harmonization of standards and the development of infrastructure and connectivity among capital markets in the region. Two working committees are in charge of the work on capital market development, namely, the Working Committee on Capital Market Development (WC-CMD) and the ASEAN Capital Market Forum (ACMF). WC-CMD was established in 2003 to build the capacity and lay the infrastructure of the ASEAN capital market, with the long-term goal of achieving cross-border collaboration among the various capital markets in the region. The WC-CMD consists of representatives from finance ministries, securities exchange commissions and central banks. To monitor the development, openness and liquidity in ASEAN bond markets, the WC-CMD has developed the Bond Market Development Scorecard in consultation with members and private sector partners. The scorecard is continuously and progressively enhanced in order to improve the monitoring of developments in the bond markets and provide greater clarity and guidance. To enhance Stock Exchange Connectivity in the region, the ASEAN Trading Link was launched in 2012, connecting stock exchanges in Malaysia, Singapore, and Thailand. A study commissioned by the ADB at the ACMF's request identified key challenges facing the ASEAN Trading Link (Phase I in 2016), and recommended that the initiative be replaced with an entirely new connectivity solution (Phase 2 in 2017). In April 2017, the ASEAN Finance Ministers accepted the recommendation with a revamped ASEAN stock Exchange Connectivity strategy. Towards this, Malaysia and Singapore established a bilateral stock market trading link in 2018, with a view to expanding it to other ASEAN exchanges in the future.

With regard to ASEAN's efforts to enhance its participation in global value chains (GVCs), recent data shows that AMS' share of domestic value added (DVA) in gross exports, which measures the forward linkages of an economy's participation in the GVC that is common in a commodity-dominant economy, has been relatively high since 2010, and this has remained so until recently. Some AMS observed declining DVA shares in recent years, but this is more likely a result of these countries' declining reliance on unprocessed primary products exports, and transition to become exporters of more manufactured or processed products, which typically require more intermediate imports. Meanwhile, the share of foreign value added, which indicates the extent to which an economy uses imported intermediates to produce exports, tends to be higher in AMS that are involved more in manufacturing value chains and those with relatively high back-and-forth trading activities.

2. TOWARD COMPETITIVE, INNOVATIVE, AND DYNAMIC ASEAN

For ASEAN to be a competitive region with well-functioning markets, rules on competition need to be operational and effective. As of end-2019, nine out of ten AMS have competition laws in place, with Cambodia is expected to enact its competition law in the near term. All nine competition laws have been translated into English and compiled as the ASEAN Compendium of English Translations of National Competition Laws, which was annexed to the ASEAN Handbook on Competition Policy and Law for Business 2017.

As we understand that consumers are playing a key role in the market. Therefore, consumer protection is key to a modern, efficient, effective and fair market. ASEAN's cooperation in the area of consumer protection has deepened over the years. By end-2019, nine AMS have enacted their Consumer Protection Act, while Cambodia's consumer protection legislation is expected to be enacted by 2020. At the regional level, the ASEAN High Level Principles for Consumer Protection provide a common baseline for cooperation and exchange of experiences and best practices. Other recent milestones in ASEAN's cooperation in this area include the development of the ASEAN Self-Assessment Toolkit, the launch of the Handbook on Consumer protection Law in ASEAN, and the linking of the ASEAN Product Recalls Portal with the Product Recalls Portal of the Organization for Economic Co-operation and Development (OECD).

Intellectual Property (IP) promotion and protection supports innovation, creativity, and value creation in the market. Several noteworthy IP-related initiatives in the region since 2016 include the ASEAN Common Guidelines for the Substantive Examination of Trademarks and of Industrial Designs in 2017 and 2018 respectively; work under the ASEAN Patent Examination Cooperation, which allows patent applications to be processed faster and more efficiently; enhancements to the databases on registered trademarks and design registrations, namely the ASEAN TMView and DesignView platforms and the development of the ASEAN Geographical Indications Database; and the establishment of the ASEAN Network of Enforcement Experts. Continued efforts to strengthen IPR cooperation in ASEAN are critical for innovation and long-term competitiveness.

A competitive, dynamic, and innovative ASEAN requires regulations that are non-discriminatory, pro-competition, effective, coherent, and responsive. Good regulatory practices (GRP) are key to the successful delivery of AMS' development agenda as well as the overall implementation of regional commitments. GRP are newly embraced in the AEC agenda. Key achievements in this area are the adoption of the non-binding ASEAN GRP Core Principles in 2018 to assist AMS in improving their regulatory practices and to foster ASEAN-wide regulatory cooperation, and the conducting of a Baseline Study on Regulatory Management Systems in ASEAN, which is being finalized.

3. TOWARD ENHANCING CONNECTIVITY AND SECTORAL COOPERATION

Sectoral cooperation has been strengthened across different areas, while ASEAN connectivity has also been enhanced. In the transport sector, ASEAN's cooperation covers land transport, air transport, maritime transport, and sustainable transport. ASEAN's air transport cooperation achieved a significant milestone with the full ratification of the ASEAN open skies agreements in April 2016, establishing the ASEAN open sky. Continued progress has also been made in the upgrading of the ASEAN Highway Network road networks as well as efforts to complete the missing links of the Singapore-Kunming Rail Link, two key land transport initiatives in the region. In 2017, the region also saw the signing of the ASEAN Framework Agreement on the Facilitation of Cross-Border Transport of Passengers by Road Vehicles, along with the adoption of key documents on sustainable transport. Maritime transport cooperation also continued to advance with the launching of the ASEAN Roll-on-Roll-off Sea Linkage Route between Davao-General Santos, the Philippines, and Bitung, Indonesia, in 2017. The full implementation of the main transport facilitation agreements will significantly enhance connectivity in the region, and to this end, AMS should expedite the completion of ratification processes.

In today's world, digital connectivity is at least as important as physical connectivity. ASEAN's cooperation in the information and communications technology (ICT) sector is therefore of critical importance. The region has enjoyed rising internet access and a meteoric rise in mobile cellular subscriptions, but there has been a much slower increase in broadband subscription, access to which is fundamental to thrive in the digital age. Among the major milestones in ASEAN's ICT cooperation are the adoption of the ASEAN Framework on Personal Data Protection in 2016, the ASEAN International Mobile Roaming Framework in 2017, and the ASEAN Framework on Digital Data Governance in 2018.

Digitalization affects not only the way we connect, but also how we work, live, and trade. Underscoring the importance of electronic commerce (e-commerce), the ASEAN Coordinating Committee on Electronic Commerce was established in 2017, followed by the adoption of the ASEAN Work Program on Electronic Commerce in the same year. A key milestone in ASEAN's e-commerce work was the signing of the ASEAN Agreement on Electronic Commerce in 2018 to, among others, contribute to creating an environment of trust and confidence in the use of e-commerce in the region. A closely related, but broader, initiative was the ASEAN Digital Integration framework, which was adopted in 2018, and for which an Action Plan is also being finalized. In recent years, ASEAN's approach towards e-commerce has evolved to also cover cybersecurity as well as the empowerment of consumers and MSMEs.

In the energy sector, ASEAN continues to achieve milestones in clean energy and the reduction of energy intensity of consumption. The region achieved a 21.9 percent reduction in energy intensity in 2016, surpassing the 2020 target of 20 percent. Efforts are underway to further improve energy efficiency in cooling given the expected growth in demand, including through minimum energy performance standards for air conditioning. The vast richness of mineral resources in the region heightens the importance of ASEAN's cooperation in minerals. Aside from strengthening trade and investment in the mineral sector, ASEAN's current focus in mineral cooperation is on the promotion of sustainable mineral sector development through better monitoring, sharing of best practices, and promotion of sustainable standards adoption. Food, agriculture, and forestry (FAF) continues to play a strategic role in ASEAN's sectoral cooperation given its contribution to rural livelihood and links to food security and resource sustainability. Various initiatives have been put in place to further enhance the sustainability and competitiveness of the region's FAF sector. They include: in the case of agricultural sector, the ASEAN Public-Private Partnership Regional Framework for technology in FAF sectors and the ASEAN Roadmap for Enhancing the Role of Agricultural Cooperatives in Global Agricultural chains, launched in 2017 and 2018 respectively; and the Work Plan for Forest Law Enforcement and Governance, adopted in 2016, in the case of forestry sector. The tourism sector continues to demonstrate high potential in ASEAN, making a total contribution of 12.6 percent to the region's GDP in 2018 (WTTC, 2019). Beyond generating income, the sector also promotes local development and employment. Part of the efforts to enhance

ASEAN's competitiveness as a single tourist destination is the development and promotion of tourism standards, the later through avenues such as the annual ASEAN tourism Standard Awards. Mobility of tourism professionals is another area of cooperation that ASEAN is pursuing, with the signing of the ASEAN MRA on Tourism Professionals in 2012, and the launch of the ASEAN Tourism Professional System, a platform that facilitates the matching of tourism professionals and potential employers. ASEAN is also cultivating high-potential tourism market segments such as gastronomy tourism and cruise tourism. ASEAN's cooperation in the area of science and technology (S&T) is fundamental to the region's drive to become a globally competitive, innovative community. Moving the S&T agenda from the ASEAN Socio-Cultural Community to the AEC is an acknowledgement of the sector's significance to productivity and competitiveness. While early cooperation was focused on projects and activities supported by the ASEAN Science, Technology and innovation Fund, recently the sector has been taking a more holistic and programmatic approach. This started with the adoption of the ASEAN Declaration on innovation by ASEAN Leaders in 2018, followed by the development of the ASEAN Innovation Roadmap in 2019.

4. TOWARD A RESILIENT, INCLUSIVE, PEOPLE-ORIENTED, AND PEOPLE-CENTRED ASEAN

Efforts to make the AEC resilient, inclusive, people-oriented, and people-centred are key to ensuring that ASEAN economic integration leaves no one behind. ASEAN has recognized the role of inclusive business in fostering MSME development, including through the ASEAN Online Academy, ASEAN Business Incubator Network, the ASEAN Mentorship for Entrepreneurs, and also through the launch of the ASEAN Inclusive Business Framework in 2017. A more coherent and structured approach to private sector engagement is also being pursued in recognition of the private sector's contribution to the

AEC. The ASEAN Business Advisory Council was appointed as the apex private sector body in ASEAN, and is responsible for coordinating inputs from established business councils and entities in their interactions with various ASEAN sectoral bodies. The revised Rules of Procedures for Private Sector Engagement were endorsed in 2017 to ensure more effective public-private engagements. Contributing to the same objective, the ASEAN Secretariat has also initiated the AEC Dialogue as a regular interface with the private sector to discuss emerging issues facing the region's economy, and facilitate one-on-one consultations with individual business councils on specific subject of interest. Building on the improvements in narrowing the development gap among AMS over the past few years, ASEAN continues to intensify work in this area. The initiative for ASEAN Integration (IAI) Work Plan III (2016-2020), which consists of the five strategic areas of food and agriculture, trade facilitation, MSMEs, education, and health and well-being, was designed to assist Cambodia, Lao PDR, Myanmar, and Vietnam to meet ASEAN-wide targets and commitments towards realizing the goals of the ASEAN Community.

5. TOWARD ENHANCING EXTERNAL ECONOMIC RELATIONS

ASEAN, with its consistent commitment to open regionalism, continues to pursue active external economic relations with countries and regional groupings around the world in parallel to its internal integration efforts. Contributing towards its objective to become a global ASEAN, some of the key highlights in this area include the signing of the ASEAN -Hong Kong Free Trade Agreement and the ASEAN-Hong Kong Investment Agreement, as well as the conducting of upgrading or review of existing ASEAN Plus One agreements, such as the ongoing implementation of the ASEAN-China Free Trade Agreement upgrading protocol, the completion of the general review of the ASEAN-Australia-New Zealand Free Trade Agreement and the signing of the first protocol to amend the ASEAN-

Japan Comprehensive Economic Partnership by all AMS. The conclusion of the Regional Comprehensive Economic Partnership (RCEP) remains top of ASEAN'S external economic relations agenda. Negotiations are being intensified towards the target for conclusion to ensure the creditability of the RCEP process as well as in light of the urgency introduced by rising protectionism and global uncertainties. Once successfully concluded, RCEP will not only have immense economic potential through market and job opportunities, but also by providing a transparent, certain, rules-based framework for trade and investment among the 16 participating countries, hence safeguarding the stability of key production networks and value chains in the region and signifying ASEAN's central role in the region's economic architecture. The Fourth Industrial Revolution (4IR) has been high on ASEAN's agenda ever since the issue was given political recognition in 2017, when ASEAN leaders underscored the need for the region to be well prepared and able to maximize the opportunities from the 4IR, so as to foster the region's economic growth, and promote inclusive and equitable economic development. In 2018, the region saw the completion of the 'Assessment of ASEAN's Readiness for the 4IR', along with the signing of the ASEAN Agreement on Electronic Commerce, as well as the endorsement of the ASEAN Digital Integration Framework and the ASEAN Framework on Digital Data Governance. The 4IR had also been featured prominently in Thailand's 2019 ASEAN Chairmanship, where five out of 13 priority economic deliverables were focused on this emerging issue. As a next step, ASEAN will develop a consolidated strategy on the 4IR, which will articulate clearly and holistically ASEAN's 4IR agenda and directions.

Challenges

Despite progress and achievements to date, ASEAN should not be complacent. The bloc still faces number of challenges in promoting sustainable economic growth in the region. Internally, there should be urgency of ensuring the commitments are met and implemented effectively in a timely manner in each individual member country for the benefits to be realized. The absence of a strong enforcement mechanism or a functioning dispute settlement mechanism means that the implementation of ASEAN commitments depends on national efforts – including internal coordination and monitoring efforts, and peer-to- peer commitment to regional goals. Externally, ASEAN's economic integration agenda should be taken into consideration in working towards the implementation of those strategic measures in the Blueprint.

ASEAN states are located at a strategically important junction, bordering two of the world's most populous economic powers, China and India, which makes ASEAN a focal point for both regional and global powers. ASEAN member states are also entangled in territorial disputes with interested powers. However, closer coordination and common goals among ASEAN member states can help promote stability and lessen the prospect of conflicts.

ASEAN member countries need to translate regional commitments into national-level commitments, milestones, and targets that can be readily enforced, observed, and measured. This requires incorporating ASEAN's economic integration agenda into the realm of national policy making and implementation, such as in the formulation of national development plans and strategies. The same also requires regional coordination to be complemented with strong coordination at the national level to oversee the implementation of ASEAN commitments. While there is no uniform and universal mechanism, effective national mechanisms should facilitate inter-agency coordination, sharing of information, monitoring of implementation, and stakeholder consultation and feedback.

ASEAN is home to a wide variety of businesses, including a number of huge family-owned conglomerates and state-linked enterprises, like the Central Group in Thailand, Salim Group in Indonesia, state-linked Singtel in Singapore, and Vinamilk in Vietnam. But still, small and medium enterprises (SMEs) together with micro -entrepreneurs make up at least 89 percent of business activities in the region. There are conflicts of business interests among large conglomerates paired with widespread corruption and small and medium enterprises. To tackle this problem, ASEAN needs strong independent civic institutions to prevent corruption and to help the region compete globally (Ishtiaq Pasha Mahmood, 2018).

In terms of ASEAN's effort to create a highly integrated and cohesive economy, greater focus should be needed to initiatives beyond market opening, improving trade facilitation, transparency, and regulatory cooperation as well as providing efficient financial services. The ASEAN region offers a growing market of more than 600 million consumers. The intra-ASEAN market, in today's uncertain and everchanging world, has provided a meaningful buffer to external shocks. However, extra efforts are still needed for ASEAN to improve its intra-ASEAN trade and investment linkages, increasing the urgency for ASEAN to accelerate the full operation of its various trade facilitation initiatives. Given the fact that other competing markets are continuously and vigorously pursuing their own reform efforts, similar reform efforts must be maintained by ASEAN in the area of investment. Equally important is the deepening of financial integration, which is key to economic stability as well as economic connectivity. Although the level of financial integration in ASEAN is gradually rising, there is still ample scope for further progress. As rightly suggested in ASEAN Integration Report 2019, ASEAN needs to make long-term investments in financial infrastructure supported by sound institutional and legislative frameworks. Financial integration in ASEAN could accelerate in the coming years with the right balance of policy mix and the availability of digital infrastructure. Regional platforms should also be leveraged by member countries, amidst the advancement of new technologies brought about by the 4IR, to further strengthen and improve the relevance of the region's competition policy and laws, consumer protection regime, and IP cooperation in order to mainstreaming ASEAN's Good Regulatory core principles across its area of work.

Connectivity and sectoral cooperation are key to ensuring the success of regional economic integration. While cooperation in each particular sector should continuously be enhanced, closer attention should also be given to improving coordination and collaboration among the sectors on cross-sectoral issues. All these require AEC sectoral bodies to be more open in identifying strategic thematic intersections, and more proactive in pursuing appropriate cross-sectoral collaborations. This calls for more effective engagement and sharing of information at both the national and regional levels among the relevant sectors, beginning with the leveraging of existing platforms such as the coordinating committees or the Joint Consultative Meeting.

For ASEAN to become a resilient, inclusive, people-oriented, and people-centred, the AEC must deliver concrete benefits to the peoples of ASEAN. To do so, the further strengthening of ASEAN's engagement with the public is imperative. ASEAN is home to young, literate and increasingly urbanized and aspirational populations. Consumers in the region are increasingly demanding higher-quality products and services and presents an opportunity for businesses hoping to tap growing consumer markets. As more people migrate to cities, they create a pressure on existing infrastructure and job markets. Sustainable solutions of these problems will require innovative approaches. ASEAN governments will have to look at the issues ranging from affordable housing, quality health-care and education and will have to work closely with private sectors and non-government organizations. The consultation mechanism between ASEAN and the private sector—including through the institutionalization of feedback and consultation mechanism between sectoral bodies and the private sector, as well as efforts to track progress in addressing legitimate issues raised by the private sector – can be further strengthened. Cross-sectoral engagements with the broader ASEAN stakeholders should also be encouraged. Equally important is the effort to improve the socialization and utilization of ASEAN's initiatives. Also, in terms of inclusive growth and sustainable development, ASEAN member countries span a wide range of income levels. In Singapore, GDP per capita was USD58,829.60 in 2019. Whereas, in 2019, GDP per capita of Lao PDR was USD1,840.50, Cambodia's

USD1,643 and Myanmar's USD1,608.50. It is noteworthy that regional economic gains have fallen short of erasing significant differences among ASEAN member states. In terms of financial inclusion, it is generally measured in three dimensions: (i) access to financial services; (ii) usage of financial services; and (iii) the quality of the products and the service delivery. World Bank's Global Findex 2019 reported that despite considerable progress, large disparities in financial inclusion still persist in ASEAN region. For example. Japan and South Korea tend to be the global leaders with over 200 ATM machines per 100,000 adults compared to a global average of less than 50. Singapore was having 67 ATMs per 100,000 adults in 2019. On the other hand, countries such as Cambodia with 20 ATMs per 100,000 adults and Myanmar with only 2 ATMs per 100,000 adults are lagging behind. Comparative results hold, when using other indicators of financial inclusion such as bank accounts. These disparities show the need for broad, robust investment in infrastructure, financial institutions and strategic planning.

ASEAN should continue to work towards the attainment of a global ASEAN. With its continuously growing economic prowess, ASEAN has become significant global player in its own right. Given increased recent global uncertainties, ASEAN's enhanced role in the global economic community is more important today than ever. As multilateralism in general and multilateral trade in particular comes under pressure, there is a need for ASEAN to play a more active role in upholding the open and rules-based multilateral trading system. ASEAN also needs to be agile and flexible in addressing various emerging trends and issues that constantly arise in an increasingly uncertain global environment. Growing inequality, the emergence of disruptive technologies, climate change, unsustainable production and consumption, the shift in geo-strategic balance, and demographic shifts, to name a few, continue to pose challenges to the region's political and economic landscapes. ASEAN will need to address these issues taking into consideration various existing initiatives that are already in place, the diversity in it's membership, and its collective standing in the global economy.

CHAPTER-SEVEN
THE POTENTIALS AND CHALLENGES OF CAMBODIA AS A MEMBER OF ASEAN

The year 2019 marked the 20th anniversary of Cambodia being the 10th member of ASEAN. The roadmap of Cambodia's accession to this regional grouping has indeed come a long way and as a newer member, throughout these 20 years, Cambodia has been striving to catch up with other older members in different areas. During the last two decades after joining the ASEAN, Cambodia gradually gained more recognition internationally after decades of isolation due to civil war. On the other-hand, in the same time, Cambodia has become one of the fastest growing member states in ASEAN with an improved quality of life.

The year 2019 also marked the historical occasion when the Association of Southeast Asian Nations (ASEAN) turned 52 years old. Back in 1967, the five founding fathers of ASEAN namely, Indonesia, Malaysia, The Philippines, Singapore, and Thailand agreed to establish a regional organization and formed ASEAN. It was founded with the goal of promoting peace, stability, security, and economic growth in the region. Throughout, a basic assumption of its leaders has been that the achievements of the first three conditions are necessary for the fourth. The bloc of five countries then admitted Brunei in 1984, Vietnam in 1995, Laos PDR and Myanmar in 1997 and Cambodia in 1999 to become a ten member ASEAN region since 1999. These moves completed ASEAN's initial target of connecting all Southeast Asian countries, which are diverse in their political institution, economic structure, cultural identity, language and religion. ASEAN that we are having today, had undergone several stages – from Asian Relations Conference in 1947 to Southeast Asia Treaty Organization (SEATO) in 1954 to Association of Southeast Asia (ASA) in 1961 to MAPHILINDO in 1963. The Association of Southeast Asia (ASA), established in July 1961 by the Federation of Malaya (including Singapore), the Philippines, and Thailand folded within two years because of tensions between Kuala Lumpur and Manila over their Sabah territorial dispute. Maphilindo – formed of the Federation of Malaya (including Singapore), the Philippines, and Indonesia – lasted about one month in the summer of 1963. It was ended by the eruption of border clashes between Indonesia and Malay/ Malaysia from 1963-1966. Realizing one regional umbrella did not crystalize also because of the fragile political nature and social instability of some nation states as well as the undissolved problems between neighboring countries in the region. Moreover, countries in Southeast Asia except Thailand, had been under Western Colonization for long time. Therefore, some member countries of the region were not at ease until early 1960s even after the end of their colony status. The end of confrontation between Malaysia and Indonesia in 1966 created a new opportunity for regional cooperation in Southeast Asia. This was when Thailand's Foreign Minister Dr. Thanat Khoman put forth his initiative on establishing a Southeast Asian regional organization so that the member countries could get to know one another better, could start working together for common regional interest, and co-exist in peace. Following that initiative, on 8 August 1967, five leaders – the Foreign Ministers of Malaysia, Indonesia, the Philippines, Singapore and Thailand – sat down together in the main hall of the Department of Foreign Affairs building in Bangkok, Thailand and signed a document. By virtue of that document, the Association of Southeast Asian nations was born. The 1960s Cold War's dilemma and Vietnam war from 1965 till 1975 had a very disastrous effect on the region.

The outburst of Vietnam War had an unfortunate spillover effects on Cambodia's consecutive political regime changes in 1970s, included the genocidal regime of the Khmer Rouge and its aftermath for a few more decades until a complete package of peace and stability came to realize in 1998.

Pich Charadine quoted the argument of Martin Loffelholz and Danilo A. Arao as interesting that the Cold War between the US and the former USSR had encouraged the foundation of ASEAN, while decades later, the end of this global conflict opened the door for the expansion of the grouping in the late 1990s. The ASEAN Way was designed to reflect a trade mark benchmarking the non-binding partnership cooperation with minimal institutional bureaucracy, marginal supranational composition, and a strong proponent for consensus-building in relations to its decision-making process. ASEAN's fundamental principles, which was adopted in the 1976 Treaty of Amity and Cooperation (TAC) in Southeast Asia, stressed the 'mutual respect for independence, sovereignty, equality, territorial integrity, and national identity for all nations, and as well non-interference in the internal affairs of one another'.

ASEAN AND CAMBODIA (1967-1998)

Following the deferral in 1997 due to internal political crisis, Cambodia was eventually got admitted to be the 10th member of ASEAN in 1999 after years of being ASEAN's observer. Since the establishment of ASEAN in 1967 till becoming a member of this regional bloc in 1999, many incidents had occurred in Cambodia that led to several regime changes and ASEAN did not turn a blind eye on those Cambodia's affairs. At the time of the inception of ASEAN in 1967, despite the uncertainty and instability of Cambodia's political situation, Prince Sihanouk was approached for Cambodia to be part of ASEAN. However, Prince Sihanouk as the Head of State of Cambodia, stood firmly on the principle of neutrality and non-alliance in order to avoid being trap in the Vietnam War. But he clearly proclaimed to remain 'friend of ASEAN'. In March 1970, the situation in

Cambodia got worsened when General Lon Nol and Prince Sirik Matak staged a coup to overthrow Prince Sihanouk. Cambodia became a republic for the first time in history. However, ASEAN leaders did not accept the new Republican regime as the legitimate government of Cambodia, instead Prince Sihanouk gained support widely in the region. Cambodia gradually witnessed the major division in the country which led to a civil war under the pro-US military-led Khmer Republic regime. In April 1975, Lon Nol's government failed desperately and Cambodia fell into the atrocity regime of the Khmer Rouge with the withdrawal of US from the region. This genocidal regime isolated Cambodia from the rest of the world, including ASEAN, except China and several other communist countries. Cambodia and ASEAN's leaders were not in touch until the controversial intervention of the Vietnamese troops and the United Front for National Salvation of Kampuchea (UFNSK) in 1979. ASEAN condemned Vietnam for invading Cambodia's sovereignty after the collapse of the Khmer Rouge. ASEAN Foreign Ministers issued a joint statement against the presence of Vietnamese troops in Cambodia. ASEAN viewed, in that statement, the armed conflict between Vietnam and Cambodia as the 'armed intervention against the independence, sovereignty and territorial integrity of Kampuchea (Cambodia)'. ASEAN also called for the withdrawal of Vietnamese troops from Cambodia's territory. The People's Republic of Kampuchea (PRK) – a new political regime was established in Phnom Penh with the help of the Vietnamese. Simultaneously, there were also other movements along the Cambodia-Thai border, namely, FUNCINPEC of Prince Sihanouk, KPNLF of Son Sann, and the Khmer Rouge faction. These three movements, with the assistance of ASEAN for months, merged together officially and formed 'Coalition Government of Democratic Kampuchea (CGDK)' in 1982. This coalition 'faction' held the Cambodia's seat in the United Nations General Assembly. Until the late 1980s, there were occasional clashes between the PRK government and the CGDK coalition. In 1988, the negotiation (Jakarta Informal Meeting) took place between PRK government and

CGDK coalition under the benchmark of ASEAN and that was the initial attempt to restore peace and stability in Cambodia. The meeting continued to the third round, when Indonesian the then Foreign Minister suggested to form the Supreme National council (SNC) of Cambodia in order to initiate the power sharing mechanism and to brought about the peace process to a comparatively concrete level. In 1989, Vietnam began to withdraw its troops from Cambodia under the international pressure. Two years later, in 1991, the Comprehensive Cambodian Peace Agreement or Paris Peace Agreement was signed by 19 signatories and that led to the formation of the United Nations Transitional Authority (UNTAC) in Cambodia to operate the peacekeeping and peacebuilding mission. In 1993, the general election was conducted though Khmer Rouge boycotted that election. ASEAN recognized the UN-sponsored election. In order to avoid the political deadlock after the election, the new government was formed with two Prime Ministers, Prince Norodom Rannariddh of FUNCINPEC as the first Prime Minister, and Samdech Hun Sen as the second. In the subsequent couple of years, although the political environment in Cambodia was rather uncertain, ASEAN still used to invite Cambodia in various ASEAN Ministerial Meetings. In 1995, Cambodia signed the Treaty of Amity and Cooperation (TAC) and became ASEAN's observer in that year as well. ASEAN Foreign Ministers announced in Kuala Lumpur in May 1997 that Cambodia alongside Laos and Myanmar would become ASEAN member in July that year. However, the clash broke out between the loyalist forces of Prince Norodom Rannariddh and Samdech Hun Sen, and eventually led to the postponement of Cambodia's ASEAN membership. ASEAN even responded to the political violence of loyalist forces by establishing ASEAN Troika, which consisted of three ASEAN member states, namely, Thailand, Indonesia and the Philippines in an attempt to contribute to the peace process in Cambodia after July 1997 event. ASEAN proposed some conditions, such as requiring Cambodia to restore democracy, create a peaceful environment for the elections, and establish a Senate. Cambodia followed the recommendations and successfully fulfilled all conditions. After those political reforms in 1998, Cambodia was backed and proposed by Laos and Vietnam to be admitted as a member of ASEAN. In April 1999, in Hanoi, Cambodia was approved to be an ASEAN member state, making ASEAN to become ASEAN-10.

ASEAN AND CAMBODIA (1999 – 2019)

In the welcome statement to Cambodia, then ASEAN Secretary-General Rodolfo Severino said it was truly a historic moment that after 32 years of its inception, ASEAN had fulfilled the vision of the founding fathers to unite all nations of Southeast Asia under one roof. Mr. Severino also said 'the realization of ASEAN-10 has not only a symbolic significance, but also immense implications for the future of our region'. He added, 'With mutual respect and equality, we have turned our diversity to our advantage and pulled together to advance our common interest in strengthening peace and stability in our region'. He also emphasized, 'the Kingdom of Cambodia's membership will be a substantial contribution to this endeavor'.

During the last two decades, Cambodia has surely been able, beyond any doubt, to get the most benefit out of its membership in ASEAN. Cambodia has been benefitted from its ASEAN membership in many ways and in many aspects. However, there are both tangible and intangible benefits as well as challenges. Cambodia's benefits, interests and aspirations in ASEAN as well as challenges as an ASEAN Member State can be categorized as follows:

BENEFITS

1. Political, Territorial, and Security Interests

Cambodia, as an ASEAN member, can view ASEAN as an important safeguard protecting its sovereignty and independence against foreign invasion and interference.

The Potentials and Challenges of Cambodia as a Member of ASEAN   169

ASEAN contributed to political change and helped bring peace and stability in Cambodia. Cambodia regards ASEAN as an important shield to ward off the adverse impacts deriving from power shifts and power contestation. ASEAN, so far, helped Cambodia to diversify its strategic and economic partners as well as enhance Cambodia's capacity to offset security risks and uncertainties. ASEAN's Treaty of Amity and Cooperation (TAC) which Cambodia signed in 1995, sets clear basic principles of international relations within the region – with emphasis on mutual respect for independence, sovereignty, equality, territorial integrity and national identity, and the right of every member state to be free from external interference, subversion or coercion. In other words, from its inception, ASEAN has always emphasized the spirit of equality and partnership towards peace and non-interference. This effectively means that Cambodia's ASEAN membership bolsters overall security, especially along the borders of individual countries. However, it was disappointed with ASEAN when this regional organization failed to address the border clash between Cambodia and Thailand in 2008 and 2011 due to the lack of consensus. In that time, Cambodia had invited ASEAN to mediate in the dispute, but Thailand preferred using the bilateral negotiation mechanism. ASEAN has become even more relevant in Southeast Asia in the context of rising tensions and uncertainty resulting from geopolitical competition between major powers, particularly between the US and China. Due to the concern that internal conflict in some ASEAN member countries might lead to regional instability, the Cambodian Defense Minister in 2012 proposed to his ASEAN counterparts the establishment of Free of Conflicts ASEAN. He suggested ASEAN to consider creating 'ASEAN Security Connectivity' to better link security issues and security actors, both state and non-state actors, in order to better and timely address complex regional security issues. However, these two proposals have not been realized due to lack of consensus. Against all odds, it is evident that Cambodia has been continuing to consider ASEAN as a reliable security shield as well as the catalyst for dynamism during the last few decades. Institutionally and diplomatically, ASEAN has capacity to encourage major powers to behave peacefully and responsibly.

For furthering security and safety for the peoples of ASEAN, law enforcement agencies of Member States have been playing a key role in engaging themselves in dialogue through meetings, trainings, workshops and conferences with the intention of exchanging experiences and to establish channels of communications to assist their daily operations. Such cooperation also includes the combat against terrorism. Another is on humanitarian assistance and disaster relief. ASEAN Member States, so far, had shown their effective cooperation and support to each other at the time of natural disasters.

Cambodia's ASEAN membership is also a platform to promote its defense and security capacity. The ASEAN Defense Ministers' Meeting (ADMM), established in 2005, and ADMM Plus, created in 2010, have significantly promoted practical security cooperation among Member States and the Plus eight countries, namely, Australia, China, India, South Korea, Japan, New Zealand, Russia, and the United States. Within the framework of ADMM Plus, the following are the five areas of security cooperation: (1) maritime security; (2) humanitarian assistance and disaster relief; (3) counter- terrorism; (4) peacekeeping operations; and (5) military relief. Under the umbrella of such a cooperation framework, Cambodia has sent its security officers to participate in training workshops, skill and expertise building programs and joint exercises. In the process, Cambodia is strengthening its security personnel as well as the system to meet the new challenges including the non-traditional security threats. The ASEAN Chiefs of Police (ASEANAPOL) Conference is another platform of which Cambodia's national police has been a part. The forum has provided law enforcement agencies of ASEAN Member States the opportunity to review their strategic cooperation and discuss the whole range of transnational crime issues such as terrorism, drugs, arms smuggling, human trafficking, piracy, cybercrime, money laundering, and economic crimes that impact the region and beyond. These exercises make law enforcement agencies of all the Member States of ASEAN a well-informed body with expanded network to fight transnational crimes in the region and beyond. The Senior Officials Meeting on Transnational Crime (SOMTC) was established to annually discuss and share intelligence information on these crimes in the region. Cambodian law enforcement bodies, through these meetings, have gathered a lot of knowledge and experiences to prepare them in a better way to combat transnational crimes.

ASEAN membership contributed to promoting Cambodia's image and prestige in the regional as well as in the international arena. Although Cambodia is the youngest member of ASEAN, yet it has been given an equal footing with its rights and obligations in this regional grouping. Cambodia has been active in all areas of cooperation – from international politics to security, and from economic to functional cooperation. The country has also been strongly committed in participating in regional and global platforms to serve common interests and to shape common values. Cambodia has contributed, for instance, more than 1000 peacekeepers to different parts of the world with ASEAN identity under the United Nations (UN). This gesture has promoted Cambodia's image in international relations and diplomacy. The country has also been able, through ASEAN multilateral diplomacy, to engage and participate actively in other important forums, dialogues and meetings, namely, the WTO, Asia Cooperation dialogue, the Asia-Europe Meeting, and the Forum for East Asia-Latin America Cooperation. Given the growth of regionalism in other parts of the world as well as full blown globalization, without ASEAN platform, small and medium-sized states of Southeast Asia would have little influence or role in international affairs. Moreover, the small states in Southeast Asia are also vulnerable to the external influences of the major powers. Therefore, in order to maintain central role of ASEAN, these small states in the region have been participating in realizing the ASEAN community.

2. Economic, Trade and Investment Interests

Cambodia has witnessed considerable economic and social achievements during the last two decades. In end-2019, Cambodia has one of the fastest economic growth rates in the world. Moreover, with a low inflation rate of 2.37 percent in 2019 and a stable local currency (riel), Cambodia portraits a stable macro-economic prospect in the medium and long term. Cambodia's gross domestic product (GDP) increased from USD7.27 billion in 2006 to USD18.5 billion in 2015 and to USD26.73 billion in 2019. The GDP in Cambodia expanded7.1 percent year-on-year in December 2019, following a growth of 7.5 percent in the previous year. The GDP growth rate reached all time high of 13.2 percent in 2015. GDP per capita also increased from USD666.5 in 2006 to USD1,020.9 in 2015 and USD1,693.80 in December 2019. According to the World Bank, Cambodia became a lower middle-income country in 2015 when its GNI (gross national income) per capita reached USD1,070. Cambodia's gross savings rate was measured at 24.4 percent in December 2019. Garment and apparel industries, construction, tourism, and agriculture sectors accounted for the bulk of the country's growth. As of end- 2019, around 700,000 people, the majority of whom are women, are employed in the garment and footwear sector. An additional 500,000 Cambodians are employed in the tourism sector, and a further 200,000 people in construction. Mining also is attracting some investor interest and the government has touted opportunities for mining bauxite, gold, iron, and gems. All the above statistics show the beneficial outcomes for Cambodia of being part of ASEAN for the last twenty years despite being the last one to join the regional grouping.

ASEAN is also Cambodia's one of the main platforms to promote trade-oriented development. Cambodia has been working through the ASEAN regional framework since its joining in 1999 to promote its trade in goods and services, while also pursuing its own bilateral approach. Cambodia is having the access to a market of about 600 million people in the whole of Southeast Asia under the umbrella of the ASEAN Free Trade Agreement. Given the latest development of ASEAN economic integration through the deepening and growing cooperation among Member States, ASEAN as well as the PLUS Three countries (China, Japan, and South Korea) and India have become even more important for overall economic development of Cambodia. Cambodia's trade volume remarkably increased during the last two decades, from USD7.2 billion in 2005 to USD26.36 billion in 2015, and to USD36.7 billion in 2019 (figures from the National Bank of Cambodia). Cambodia's exports increased from USD3.09 billion in 2005 to USD11.96 billion in 2015. Cambodia shipped an estimated USD25.2 billion worth of goods around the globe in 2019. That dollar amount reflects a 111 percent increase since 2015. During the period, Cambodia's imports were amounted to USD3.93 billion in 2005 and USD14.4 billion in 2015, and USD22.19 billion in 2019, a year-on-year increase of 18.6 percent. The latest available data shows, in 2018, Cambodia exported 24 percent of its global total to United States, 8.6 percent to Germany, 8.5 percent to Japan, 8 percent to United Kingdom, 6.8 percent to China, 6.1 percent to Canada, 4 percent to Spain, 3.9 percent to Belgium, 3.4 percent to Netherlands, 3.4 percent to France, 2.8 percent to Vietnam, and 2.5 percent to Thailand. From a continental perspective, in 2018, Cambodia exported 38.7 percent of its global total to European countries while 30.7 percent was sold to North America. Cambodia exported another 28.4 percent worth of goods of its global total to Asia. Cambodia also shipped 0.8 percent of its global total export to Latin America excluding Mexico but including the Caribbean, Africa (0.5 percent), and Oceania led by Australia (0.9 percent). When it comes to Cambodia's exports to ASEAN countries, these increased from a mere 4.3 percent of total exports in 2000 to 22.1 percent in 2017. This figure signifies the increasing market share of ASEAN for Cambodia's exports. From the trend over the years, it is obvious that the ASEAN market holds great potential for Cambodian exporters. Cambodia's exports, in 2019, were dominated by textile goods, which accounted for around 70 percent of its total exports. Other export products included timber, rice, tobacco, footwear, natural rubber and fish. Cambodia imported, in 2019, petroleum products, cigarettes, gold, construction materials, machinery, motor vehicles, and pharmaceutical products from its main import partners. Cambodia's main import partners include Thailand, China, Vietnam, Hong Kong, and Singapore. Cambodia's total exported goods represent 32.7 percent of its overall Gross Domestic Product in 2019.

Cambodia reformed its tariff structure by reducing the number of tariff bands from 12 to only 4, in order to be in line with ASEAN and the WTO. Cambodia also abolished the high tariff rates of 40 percent, 50 percent, 90 percent, and 120 percent. At present, there are only four tiers in Cambodia's tariff structure: 0 percent, 7 percent, 15 percent, and 35 percent. Over 53.4 percent of tariff lines are duty free or subject to the minimum 7 percent tariff rate, compared with 44 percent in 2001. 35 percent tariff rate is used to protect several semi-processed goods and consumer goods, such as processed meat and dairy products, processed vegetables and fruits, beverages and tobacco, footwear, and motor vehicles. Overall tariff lines were reduced from 10,700 to 8,314 from 2007 to 2011, based on the Harmonization System of 2007 nomenclature. Under preferential treatment, Cambodia implemented the ASEAN Trade in Goods Agreement (ATIGA) by 2015. In this context, Cambodia implemented tariff reduction since 2009 and eliminated import duties on all products by 2018 with the following schedule: (i) import duties of at least 80 percent of tariff lines, are equal to or less than 5 percent since 1st January 2009; (ii) import duties on ICT products were eliminated since 1st January, 2010; (iii) import duties on unprocessed agricultural products in High Sensitive List are having their respective applied MFN (most favored nation) rate; (iv) import duties on Priority Integration Sector Negative List (PIS-NL) were reduced to 0 percent in 2015; (v) import duties on unprocessed agricultural products in Sensitive List were reduced 0 percent to 5 percent (0-5%) by 2017.

Cambodia, as member of ASEAN since 1999, has also been able to expand its economic and trade relations with the countries in the region and beyond. The Regional Comprehensive Economic Partnership (RCEP) is currently the most important multilateral trading system for Cambodia. Hence, Cambodia is strongly supportive of and looking forward to the early conclusion of RCEP negotiations.

Cambodia's ASEAN membership in 1999 has also opened its door for foreign direct investment (FDI). Business interest in ASEAN has recently been increased due to the (a) relatively low wage in most of the ASEAN member states compared to China, (b) formation of the ASEAN Economic Community (AEC), (c) large scale consumer market covered by ASEAN, (d) economic partnership network with a core of ASEAN countries. Despite a 3 percent drop, intra-ASEAN investment (USD25 billion in 2018) was still the largest source of FDI. Governments of ASEAN are also encouraging the adoption of fourth industrial revolution technologies in industry, and promoting investment by start-ups and producers of relevant technologies. Combined FDI flows to the CLMV (Cambodia, Laos, Myanmar, and Vietnam) countries rose by 4 percent in 2018, to a record level of USD23 billion, representing 15 percent of flows into ASEAN. To compete with ASEAN member states, Cambodia has been implementing many reforms, since its admission to ASEAN, in the policy and legal framework to attract foreign direct investment (FDI). As of 2019, Cambodia has an open and liberal foreign investment regime with a pro-investor and pro-business legal and policy framework. Investment incentives available to foreign investors include 100 percent foreign ownership of companies, corporate tax holidays of up to 8 years, a 20 percent corporate tax rate after the incentive period, duty-free import of capital goods, and no restriction on capital repatriation. To facilitate foreign investment, Cambodia has created special economic zones (SEZs), which provide companies with ready access to land, infrastructure and other services to facilitate the set-up and operation of businesses. By 2019, there are 13 SEZs, and according to the US Department of State, in recent years, the Phnom Penh Special Economic Zone alone has attracted American companies such as Coca-Cola (which alone invested USD100 million), American Licorice and Tiffany & Co.

Cambodia's Foreign Direct Investment (FDI) registered a growth equal to 13.5 percent of the country's Nominal GDP in December 2019, compared with a growth equal to 13.1 percent in 2018. Cambodia's FDI as percentage of Nominal GDP data between December 2010 to December 2019 shows that the data reached an all-time high of 14.1 percent in December 2012 and a record low of 10.1 percent in December 2015 (CEIC 2020). According to the latest figures by the Bank of Cambodia, in dollar terms, in 2019 FDI inflows reached record high at USD3.5 billion, of which USD2.3 billion were directed to the financial sector. It is evident that FDI inflows to Cambodia have grown exponentially in the last two decades due to its gradual adoption of sound macro-economic policies, political stability, regional economic growth, and open investment market.

3. Promotion of Tourism Interest

Cambodia's ASEAN membership has been playing a crucial factor to promote tourism in Cambodia during the last two decades. The open Skies Policy, also known as the ASEAN single aviation market, designed to increase regional and domestic connectivity, integrate production networks of all member states, and enhance regional trade by allowing airlines from ASEAN member states to fly freely throughout the region through liberalization of air services under a single, unified aviation market. As a result, as a member of ASEAN, Cambodia's tourist market has become integrated with other ASEAN tourist destinations. It is to be noteworthy that Cambodia has also increased connectivity, tourist marketing, and air transport in a big way with a strong commitment to implement the ASEAN Open Skies Policy and the allied frameworks. Tourism is one of many key areas where Cambodia has comparatively successfully been able to work with ASEAN over the last ten years in particular. ASEAN's regional cooperation and integration process has contributed to the growth of the tourism industry of the region because the ASEAN connectivity plan designed a favorable condition for air, maritime, and land transport connections and for the movements of tourists across the region. Simultaneously, the tourism products of all member states of ASEAN have also been marketed in a better and fruitful manner. Cambodia, like other regional partners, has teamed up and worked closely with all the Member States to promote tourism to the benefit of all dialogue partners. Cambodia was, so far, benefited much in pro-poor tourism, and that has reduced the development gap noticeably in the country as well as in the region. In 2018, Cambodia experienced the third largest increase in international tourists in ASEAN, behind only Vietnam and Indonesia, according to data released by the Ministry of Tourism. The total number of international tourist arrivals in Cambodia increased from only 367,743 in 1999 (the year Cambodia joined the ASEAN) to 5.01 million in 2016, and to 6.60 million in 2019, up 6.5 percent over 2018 (Tourism Ministry of Cambodia). According to the latest data from the Ministry of tourism, in 2019, China remains Cambodia's largest tourism market, accounting for nearly 38.7 percent of all tourists. It is followed by Vietnam, Laos, and Thailand, ranking second, third and fourth, respectively.

4. Social and Cultural Interests

ASEAN is also a platform which has been helping Cambodia to promote and strengthen its national identity throughout the region and beyond. Cultural identity has been one of the key national interests of Cambodia's foreign relationships. As Chheang Vannarith of Asian Vision Institute rightly mentioned that Cambodia is having comparative advantage in projecting its soft power within ASEAN through cultural diplomacy as the country is rich in historical and cultural assets. As per ASEAN Secretariat report, the ASEAN Socio-Cultural Community (ASCC) is the commitment to lift the quality of life of its peoples through cooperative activities that are people-oriented, people-centered, environment friendly, and geared towards the promotion of sustainable development. The ASCC Blueprint was substantially implemented from 2009 to 2015 and was found effective in developing and strengthening the coherence of policy frameworks and institutions to advance human development, social justice and rights, social protection and welfare, environmental sustainability, ASEAN awareness, and narrowing development gaps. The ASCC, more precisely, has been helping heighten commitment in the form of policy and legal frameworks, such as the Declaration on the Elimination of Violence Against Women and elimination of Violence against Children in the region. ASEAN has also depicted collective will in offering quick and tangible action in humanitarian assistance through the ASEAN Coordinating Centre for Humanitarian Assistance. Cambodia's gain from its ASCC participation is huge, although it can't be measured. Cambodia witnessed the following social changes and important developmental outcomes in the country from its participation in the ASCC initiatives: (i) the rate of poverty (people living on less than USD1.25 per day) fell from 53 percent in 2004 to 20 percent in 2011, and to 12.9 percent in 2018 (Asian Development Bank); (ii) life expectancy rose from 54.9 years in 1999 to 69.66 years in 2019, a 0.32 percent increase from 2018; (iii) the net enrolment rate for children of primary school age rose from 78 percent in 1999 to 85 percent in 2012, and to 91 percent in 2018 (World Bank); (iv) the proportion of seats held by women in parliament increased from 10.6 percent in 1998 to 20 percent in 2019; and (v) maternal mortality per 100,000 live births fell from 830 in 1990 to 160 in 2017 (World health organization).

The Asian Cultural Council (ACC) has been launched in January,2019 and Cambodia is hosting ACC's Secretariat. Cambodia is having a plan, as reported, to institutionally connect the ACC with the ASEAN Socio-Cultural Community. Since 1998, when Cambodia first introduced its five-year development plan called the Triangular Strategy, Cambodia has always identified regional integration as one of the key pillars of national economic development strategy. Triangular Strategy's second pillar stresses the importance of regional integration in the country's socio-economic and cultural development. Similarly, through the country's latest five-year development strategy 2018-2023, also known as Rectangular Strategy Phase IV, Cambodia also commits, among other things, to actively participate and involve in realizing the ASEAN goal of rules- based, people-oriented, and people-centered ASEAN through socio-economic and cultural integration in the region and beyond.

5. Other Benefits

ASEAN is committed to maintain sustainable and inclusive economic development together with regional socio-economic integration. Towards that commitment, a certain set of institutional and legal frameworks for economic management, public administration, and the judicial system have already been evolved and practiced in ASEAN member countries. Besides, new laws, fresh amendments, and new frameworks are also getting added on a regular basis to accelerate as well as to strengthen the process to achieve the goal. Cambodia, even as a preparatory work for getting admission to ASEAN, had to introduce many reform programs to be consistent with ASEAN. Cambodia's ASEAN membership has also been the pushing factor for many useful and effective reforms for sustainable and inclusive economic development through regional economic integration. Cambodia has no choice but to adhere to the changes through reform process to narrow the gap with other member states and to compete at the regional level in order to realize maximum benefit from such a dynamic regional integration process by providing better and favorable conditions for production, trade, investment for the country's economic survival.

Cambodia has been consistently benefited in the area of its human resource development from ASEAN integration framework. Training and human resource development are important for Cambodia since the country are in desperate need to train and develop its human resources in many fields for overall socio-economic development of the country. Cambodia sends, every year, many of its officials, bureaucrats, technocrats, and students to various training programs and workshops in Member states as well as in dialogue partner countries of ASEAN.

Cambodia, as member of ASEAN, is also having the opportunity to be benefitted from bilateral as well as multilateral projects, funded by ASEAN dialogue partners, such as Plus Three countries. The recent creation of the ASEAN Infrastructure fund is another important milestone linking ASEAN infrastructure, particularly in the least developed countries of ASEAN. As a member of ASEAN, Cambodia is also having the opportunities to even participate in other related regional and sub-regional cooperation such as in the Greater Mekong Subregion (GMS), ASEAN Mekong Basin Development Cooperation, the development triangles, CLMV (Cambodia, Lao PDR, Myanmar, and Vietnam) cooperation, the Ayeyawady – Chao Phraya – Mekong Economic Cooperation Strategy, and Lower Mekong Initiative.

CHALLENGES

In Cambodia, the internal development gap is very wide between its capital city, Phnom Penh, provincial capitals, and rural areas. There are noticeable big disparities in public utilities, wealth, and infrastructure amongst the national capital, provincial capitals, other urban areas, and rural places. The development projects till now are mostly concentrated in Phnom Penh, attracting migration, traffic, and pollution problems, and causing speedy urbanization. Attention is needed on a regular and urgent basis to take the necessary steps to reduce this internal developmental gap.

Cambodia, as a country of lower income compared to other ASEAN members, requires to implement further reforms in many areas, especially in the economic sector to catch up with the older members as well as to narrow down its development gap gradually and consistently with the rest of the ASEAN. In order to ensure that the least developed members of ASEAN can fully integrate their economies into the regional and the global economic system, Cambodia requires to put extra effort toward ASEAN integration, the sub-regional development projects, and the CLMV cooperation. ASEAN dialogue partner countries, and the other interested countries and institutions will presumably be helpful to further ASEAN's integration and in reducing the development gap within the region.

Although Cambodia has implemented many reforms, however, some problems still exist due to many reasons. One of those reasons is poor law enforcement. Non-tariff barriers (NTBs) and non-tariff measures (NTMs) still create trouble for trade in Cambodia as well as in some other ASEAN Member countries.

Cambodia's weak position in regional competition is one of its biggest challenges and that brings negative impact to Cambodia as ASEAN member. Cambodia still suffers with its low production base, poor skilled labor, weak infrastructure, high cost of electricity, in-adequate transport avenues, and comparatively poor logistics and marketing mechanism. As a result, Cambodia has been facing difficulties to compete with imported products sold locally and also for getting export market of local indigenous products. Practically speaking, so far the regional free trade in goods and services has seriously affected Cambodia's local small and medium-sized enterprises (SMEs). Cambodia needs to recover from its existing problems to give its SMEs a level playing field to compete with the SMEs of other Member States.

To extract maximum benefit from regional integration and also to reduce regional development gap, Cambodia is needed to focus on the creation of resources in the country's public sector enterprises as well as in the private sector enterprises. The public sector in Cambodia still needs leadership, legal regulations, and expertise in strategic planning besides technological upgradation and investment capital. Similarly, the private sector in Cambodia still lacs skilled labor, trained professionals, innovation, and research and development (R&D). Moreover, according to surveys, both the public and the private sectors in Cambodia still have limited awareness of ASEAN. However, awareness is required to join regional integration and to meet changes in the business environment.

It is observed that Cambodia's economy is driven by few sectors. Therefore, the country strongly requires to find out some other viable and feasible sectors in order to avoid the vulnerability of its economy.

Having a proper and strong logistics system, among other thigs, is a pre-requisite to become a successful player in cross-border state. Logistics connectivity can be measured both in terms of cost and time. Cambodia's most bulk cargo and containers use the road transport system, resulting in quick deterioration of road networks, which is comparatively costly for the government to repair and maintain. Since container shipping has become prevalent, Railway normally offer an efficient interface between land and maritime transport systems. However, Cambodia's rail transport is considered the weakest link in the regional logistics infrastructure. At present, the operation of Cambodia Railways is privatized, but it is not ready to fulfil the need. On the other hand, waterway transport is also limited despite the country's good waterway system in the Mekong River. There is lack of effective, time saving and cost saving links in logistics between ports, airports, railways, and waterway and maritime transport. Cambodia needs to take care to improve its logistics system undoubtedly to be more competitive in the regional and global trade.

Conclusion

Overall, Cambodia worked hard and reaped remarkable benefits over the last two decades. From being frequently engaged in war, destruction, isolation, and political strife, Cambodia has been transformed into a stable and peaceful country. Cambodia has also been advanced from a low-income or least developed country to a lower middle-income economy. ASEAN, since 1999, has influenced Cambodia's political, security, economic, and socio-cultural aspects. ASEAN has also acted as a shield to protect its sovereignty and independence; and also as a platform to promote its national identity. Cambodia also has been fully supportive of an evolving ASEAN-driven regional integration. However, there are challenges as discussed earlier in this chapter. Cambodia should address all those challenges, exert intensified effort to accelerate its reforms, and focus more in implementing all ASEAN agreements, frameworks, and protocols to maximize its benefits from regional integration.

CHAPTER-EIGHT
ACHIEVEMENTS ON POVERTY REDUCTION, PUBLIC HEALTH & HEALTH SERVICES AND PUBLIC EDUCATION DURING 1999-2019

Cambodia became an observer of ASEAN in 1995. In 1999, the country became the full member of this regional organization. During the last two and half decades, Cambodia worked hard and achieved remarkable results in many areas. After emerging from destruction of war, political strife, and isolation, Cambodia changed itself from a centrally planned economy to a market economy and has become a lower middle-income economy by 2015. In light of its turbulent history, Cambodia made substantial progress on poverty reduction and other development indicators over the last two decades. Inequality has also been improved during this period. With significant gradual improvements in some health indicators over the past one and half decades, the major challenges in health care going forward are now becoming clearer. Also, Cambodia's Ministry of Education, Youth and Sport (MoEYS) made considerable progress in improving opportunities for all Cambodian children to access education services. It enhanced the quality of learning, and improved the delivery of efficient and effective education services.

ACHIEVEMENTS IN POVERTY REDUCTION

Despite three decades of devastating civil conflict, Cambodia has achieved remarkable progress in poverty alleviation and reducing inequality. Economic growth averaged nearly 7.1 percent over the period 1994-2019. Cambodia's open borders to international trade and investment during the last two decades, have helped attract foreign direct investment to support manufacturing, construction, and tourism. As a result of Cambodia's sustained high growth, the percentage of Cambodians living below the national poverty line fell from 53 percent in 2004 to around 17 percent in 2012, and to 12.9 percent in 2018 (Asian Development Bank). Gross national income per capita in Cambodia also rose from USD290 in 1998 to USD1,060 in 2015, when the country has been classified as a lower middle-income country by World Bank, and reached to USD,1,480 in 2019. Growth has also been inclusive. That is the reason, Cambodia's income inequality is also low among the Association of Southeast Asian Nations (ASEAN).

Normally, poverty lines are based on the monetary value of a person's consumption in relation to his or her minimum nutritional needs, clothing requirements, and shelter needs. The world bank, as of October 2015, set the international poverty line at USD1.90 per person per day and reported a reduction of global poverty from 37.1 percent in 1990 to 12.8 percent in 2012 (Cruz et al. 2015). However, critics of the World Bank's global poverty benchmarks and calculations pointed out that such calculations could be driven by political agenda and ignore the impoverished conditions of those who live as just above the official poverty lines (Hickel 2015). National governments used to set their own poverty thresholds based on the local costs of essential food and non-food items. In contrast to income-based or consumption-based poverty calculations, critics suggest the concept of multi-dimensional poverty which use to identify the broad range of deprivations people experience in the areas such as health, nutrition, education and standard of living (including access to sanitation, clean drinking water and modern cooking fuels). It shows how poor people recognizes their own poverty and identifies the various barriers that prevent them from achieving a decent quality of life (UNDP, 2016; Oxford Poverty and Human Development Initiative, 2015).

In terms of methods of identifying poor people, targeting method requires a measurable definition of poverty. In developed countries, eligibility for social benefits is usually determined through a means test which measures the amount of income and savings a person has, or can involve a detailed consumption survey. Proxy means tests correlate easily quantifiable or observable 'proxies' – such as assets (ownership of a radio, type of roof material on the house) or behaviors (children attending which school)-with consumption, allowing interviewers to calculate a score and then apply an established eligibility cut-off line. Proxy means tests can also fail to account for the multidimensional character of poverty and ignore communities' perceptions of poverty (Savadogo et al, 2015). Other targeting methods include (i) categorical targeting based on one or more criteria such as age, gender, disability status; (ii) geographical targeting focusing on people living in an identified high-poverty area; and (iii) self- targeting i.e. participants self-select for benefits that are designed to deter the non-poor (Lavallee et al, 2010). Dissatisfaction with the prevailing methods used by many poverty alleviation programs led to greater emphasis on community-led targeting methods in the 1990s. This method involves community members themselves gathering to identify those households that they consider as poor on the basis of the pre-discussed and determined criteria or definition of poverty by the said community. Community targeting can be more accurate where monitoring and transparency are strong. Community targeting method, as community is involved, can provide greater satisfaction with fewer disagreements in the identification of really poor people. Another option is to combine the proxy means test with community-based targeting. Such an approach involves transparency and acceptance by the community with some consistent criteria and reducing the chance of biasness.

Cambodia's growing population (16.5 million in 2019) is steadily becoming more urbanized, stood at 19.5 percent in 2008 to 21.4 percent in 2013, and to 23.39 percent in 2018, whilst still remaining overwhelmingly rural. However, as levels of poverty reduce, so does inequality. Yet a noticeable percentage of Cambodia's population are still classified as poor or nearly poor or slightly above the poverty line. Inequality started to rise between 2004 and 2007, but has steadily declined since 2007. A very big percentage of population is concentrated toward the bottom of the income distribution, and the poverty rate is highly sensitive to where the line is drawn. According to the latest Cambodia Socio Economic Survey (2019), disposable income per capita in Phnom Penh is much higher as those in rural areas and higher than in other urban areas. There is a considerable distributional gap in household disposable income. Rural households' monthly disposable income equals 71 percent of that of households in other urban areas, and 57 percent of that of households in Phnom Penh. The 20 percent of households in the highest quintile have a monthly disposable income per capita that is about ten times that of the 20 percent of households with lowest income (Henny Anderson, Multidimensional Poverty Analysis, December 2019). The multidimensional poverty analysis (MDPA) is one input to the process of preparing a Swedish country strategy for development cooperation with Cambodia from 2020, by identifying the deprivations in terms of resources; opportunities and choices; power and voice; and human security to finally say who are the poor. In terms of resources, being poor means, one is not having access to or power over resources that can be used to sustain a decent living standard and improve one's life. Such resources can be material and/or non-material nature, for example, reasonable income, reasonable capital, educated or professionally trained, understandably healthy. In terms of opportunities and choice, being poor means what possibility one is having to develop and/or use one's resources in order to move out of poverty. Opportunities and choice can be like access to land, capital, infrastructure, social services, and/or natural resources. In terms of power and voice, being poor means the lack of ability of one to articulate one's concerns, needs and rights in an informed way, and to take part in decision making relating to those concerns. In terms of human security, being poor means that violence and insecurity are the obstacles for any individual or a group to come out of poverty. As World Bank reported in May 2019 that poverty reduction has been continuing in Cambodia. However, the bottom 40 percent are doing less well than before. Though impressive gains continued to be made, the reduction in poverty during 2013-2018 was less than during 2009-2013, mainly because economic growth benefited the non-poor more, while urban poverty stagnated compared with the earlier period. Consumption per capita for the bottom 40 percent grew at 13 percent during 2013-2018, while it expanded at 22 percent for the top 60 percent. World Bank also suggested that there are many households that are only just above the poverty line and have limited ability to absorb shocks, even small ones. Any negative shock reducing consumption per capita by less than USD1.00 would double the poverty rate. The decline in income poverty has been driven mostly by successful creation of labor-intensive jobs for the people including women in industries as well as in services. This allowed a large number of rural households to diversify their livelihoods to rural non-farm economy and in other industries. The non-agricultural wage also played a major role in reducing poverty during 2013-2018. The proportion of Cambodians living in multidimensional poverty also declined over the years. It is noteworthy that the main source of Cambodian household income in 2018-2019 is wage and salary. In 2014, self-employment was the main source of income. Female-owned businesses are more than 50 percent of all business establishments in Cambodia, although they are generally smaller and less profitable. Also, women are more dependent on agricultural income, and that is why they are immediately exposed from negative external shocks, climate change, and natural resource degradation. Studies suggest that a quarter of Cambodia's population have migrated internally and/or cross border and their remittances contribute significantly to household income in migrant households (WFP 2019; UNICEF 2016; NIS/MoP 2013). About 35 percent of rural households are having at least one member migrated during 2010-2016, except for a lower 17 percent in the Plateau area. Four out of five (79 percent) migrants are aged between 17 years to 35 years old. More than 50 percent of the total migrants are men (WFP 2019). Rural-urban migration accounted for 57 percent of all migration, cross border (mostly Thailand) for 31 percent, and from one rural area to another rural area a low 13 percent (WFP 2019). However, recent survey suggested that besides poverty, there are also some other facilitating factors for the above migration. Such factors are the prospect of higher income generation opportunities, mobility, and the aspiration of the young generation to live a life outside their villages. In terms of natural resources and agricultural land ownership, nearly 59 percent of all households in Cambodia own less than one hectare (10,000 square meters) of agricultural land with variations across the zones. Only 6 percent of all total households own more than 3 hectares of agricultural land. Small household landholdings are generally to prevent a sustainable transfer to increasing commercialization of agricultural production. It is also noteworthy that employment opportunities created during the last two decades also played a pivotal role to reduce poverty remarkably. Cambodia experienced an extraordinary increase in working age population, aged 15 years to 64 years, an increase from 4 million in 1980 to about 10.5 million in 2018. Cambodia's working age population is growing faster than its total population, 2.4 percent compared to 1.9 percent over the last decade. Cambodia added an average 164,000 people to its labor force each year during the last decade. Unemployment in Cambodia, in 2019, was less than 1 percent and youth unemployment was less than 1.6 percent (ILO 2019). Both of these figures are the lowest in the Asia Pacific region. It helped to reduce household poverty. Since 2012, non-agricultural sectors such as services and industry have been the main sources of job growth. The percentage of salaried or wage workers (employees) grew from 29.8 percent in 2010 to 49.64 percent in 2019. By contrast, contributing family workers fell from 19.4 percent to 3.6 percent over the same period (ILO). All these statistics are the reflection of steady economic growth-related activities in Cambodia during the last two decades and such economic growth-related activities created the opportunities to reduce the poverty in Cambodia remarkably.

As mentioned earlier in this chapter that Cambodia's inequality started to decline steadily from 2007. Effective poverty alleviation requires the targeted orientation of development activities towards the poor. The Cambodian Ministry of Planning has developed the IDPoor Program (identification of Poor Households mechanism) with support from Deutsche Gesellschaft fur Internationale Zusammenarbeit (GIZ) GmbH, to regularly update and guide governmental agencies and NGOs through providing target services and assistance to the poorest and most vulnerable households. Before the project began its work, there was no standardized, universally recognized and nationally applied procedure for recognizing poor households in Cambodia. Through ID Poor Program, the Cambodian Government implemented a standardized procedure for identifying poor households nationwide. In 2011, the Cambodian government confirmed IDPoor by law as the country's official poverty targeting mechanism to be used nationwide by the public and private social sectors. Millions of poor and vulnerable Cambodians have been given access to social services, such as free health care, reduced government fees, assistance with shelter, school feeding programs, running water, and more through ID Poor mechanism during the last decades. As per government data, between 2015-2017, ID Poor reached more than 550,000 poor households in rural areas only. By 2019, the poor living in Cambodia's towns and cities were also included for the first time. Since the Royal government of Cambodia is progressively taking over the responsibility for funding ID Poor's operational costs, the program's sustainability is understandably assured.

ACIEVEMENTS IN PUBLIC HEALTH AND HEALTH SERVICES

The health of the Cambodian population has improved significantly during the last two decades. Cambodia has made remarkable progress towards some of its health-related Millennium Development Goals. In the decade to 2010, Cambodia's maternal mortality rate (MMR) dropped from 437 to 288, and to 160 in 2017 (per 100,000 live births). The infant mortality rate dropped from 43.5 in 2008 to 30.5 in 2013, and to 24 in 2018 (per 1,000 live births) (Statista 2020). In 1990, the average life expectancy from birth was just 53.6 years. But between 1997 and 2019, the average life expectancy rose from 56.2 years to 69.3 years as revealed by United Nations Development Program's data. During this period, the percentage of the population using improved sanitation facilities rose from 12.3 percent to 48.8 percent. As per Government data, government allocations to the health ministry as a percentage of the overall state budget was 6.6 percent in 2019. Child mortality rate for 12-60 months old decreased from 37 to 22 (per 1,000 live births). In the decade to 2010, measles immunization coverage in Cambodia improved from 79 to 93 percent, and in 2015, Cambodia received its measles elimination status following years of hard work by the Cambodian government and health partners like WHO. However, it has not been immune to the global measles resurgence. From 1st January to 4th May 2020, Cambodia recorded 341 measles cases, a significant increase from the 44 cases recorded during the same period in 2019. Of the recorded cases, 65 percent had not been vaccinated. DTP immunization coverage improved from 82 to 92 percent during 2000-2010, and improved to 98 percent in 2018. Births attended by skilled health staff rose from 44 in 2000 to 71 percent in 2010, and to 89 percent in 2015 (UNICEF Health Survey).

In terms of access to health care, even though Cambodia has a well-established network of public health systems, access to good quality health care is far from universal including those at the provincial and community levels, and in operational districts. Despite the expansion of the Health Equity Fund and service delivery grant systems, health expenditures are largely financed through out of pocket spending (58 percent) (WHO 2017). Since more women than men work as own account workers, more women than men are thus not entitled to health insurance of any sort. Therefore, more women likely bear more out-of-pocket health spending burden than men do (OECD 2017). In 2017, among patients seeking treatment for illness, injury or other health problems, 75 percent went to private health care providers, whereas 21 percent only accessed public facility. The share of traditional healers, self-care, and others is higher in rural areas than urban areas, but has decreased remarkably over the years (down from 13 percent in 2014 to less than 2 percent in 2018).

The two most common household sources of financing treatment for health care are the household income and household savings. In 2017, about 38 percent of money spent on health care came from household savings, around 1 percent from borrowing, and more than 58 percent from household income. In Cambodia, even relatively modest out-of-pocket health expenditure frequently causes indebtedness and can lead to poverty (CSES 2017). Despite significant improvements in coverage of essential maternal and child health services, only around two-thirds of children receive all basic vaccinations by age 12 months, over one-quarter of children age 12-23 months are not fully vaccinated, and most of them are remotely-settled urban and rural population and children of migrant families (World Bank 2019). As of December 2019, it can be summarized that health services in Cambodia have become more pro-poor through the Health Equity Fund, which pays for health-related costs when citizens use public health facilities, and covers more than 3 million people. The risk of poor households being unable to pay for their medical expenses declined from 8.8 percent in 2009 to 3.7 percent in 2016, and the risk of households falling into poverty due to medical expenses declined from 5.7 percent in 2009 to 1.6 percent in 2018 (RGC 2018). Nevertheless, a new UNSW study, in 2019, found that unless healthcare is better funded for low socio-economic households in Cambodia, efforts to achieve universal health coverage (UHC) will be futile. The Health Equity Fund is currently a joint contribution between government and development partners, with the government expected to take over the fund with state revenues by 2025. This would obviously require significant reallocation of state revenues (Eng 2019).

Cambodia Government's major Health reforms have, so far, been guided by a long-term process of national health planning. This process culminated in the adoption of three consecutive Health Strategic Plan (HSP) for 2003-2007, 2008-2015, and 2016-2020. As the government emphasized that the goals of the HSP1 for quality improvement and institutional development were largely achieved. HSP2 pursued targets on six priority areas: service delivery, quality improvement, human resource development, behavioral change, health financing, and institutional development. HSP3 (2016-2020) outlined a clear development framework for the health sector, which included, but was not limited to, strategic direction and strategic objectives supported by potential priority areas for action at both supply and demand side in pursuit of achieving Health Development Goals, ultimately moving to Universal Health Coverage in line with the Cambodia Sustainable Development goals.

Despite some significant improvements in health indicators over the last two decades, there are following major issues and challenges in health care in the country:

1. Child mortality in Cambodia, like many developing Countries, is closely related with wealth, especially for children of 1-12 months old. Children in the poorest quintile are 3.3 times more likely to die before age five than children in the wealthiest quintile – a ratio that has remained unchanged since 2005. Child mortality for rural children is 3.0 times than for urban children. Children born to mothers with no education are twice as likely to die compared with those born to mothers with secondary education or higher. Poor mothers are less likely to be educated. Neonatal (from birth to one month) mortality is the predominant source of child mortality for both child and poor. Neonatal mortality (death under 28 days) is strongly influenced by the quality of maternal and child care, including prenatal, delivery, and post-delivery care. U5 mortality (death from 1 to 5 years) is mainly because of complications at birth, from diseases that can be prevented by timely vaccines, and from lack of access to clean drinking water and good sanitation. Also child deaths increase, as data analysis suggests, when births are attended by unskilled birth attendants (World Bank Report, 2018).

2. According to World Health Organization, non-communicable diseases in Cambodia are now-a-days the major source of mortality. Growing burden of non-communicable diseases (NCDs) is affecting the poor adversely. Initiatives on primary prevention and treatment will be necessary to reduce the disease burden and costs both for the individuals and the health system.

3. Coverage of health services remain highly inequitable for some preventative interventions, especially those that require multiple visits. As a result, poor mothers fail to obtain essential nutritional support, which affects the quality of the subsequent delivery. The poorest still suffer from lower immunization rates. Another problem is while over 75 percent of the rich people seeks medical care in private pharmacies, clinics, or hospitals, over 90 percent of the poor goes to unlicensed drug shops and markets when they are sick. Those un-licensed drug shop owners are not having any medical training, and the medications are prone to counterfeiting since they are not monitored or regulated.

4. Health spending remains a significant burden on the poor and is a major source of debt and impoverishment for the poor and near-poor, and the chronically ill. Medical expenses are a major burden for at least 10 percent of households in Cambodia where at least one family member is chronically ill or injured. In addition, coverage and use of Health equity funds (HEFs) remain low. While the Cambodian government was committed to achieving national coverage of HEFs by 2015,

latest Cambodia Socio-Economic Survey (CSES) found that a major percentage of the poor still did not make use of free or subsidized treatment when seeking health care. World Bank public expenditure analysis in health found that Cambodia's (a) primary care and preventive spending is pro-poor, while spending on hospitals is not mostly pro-poor; (b) resource allocation among provinces lacks transparency, and could use poverty as a better criterion for allocation; (c) at least 70 percent of the total resources are managed centrally and that should be more decentralized; and (d) the MoH spends more than 50 percent of its budget on pharmaceuticals, and pays more for drugs than is necessary. Such amount could be channelized to scale up and broaden coverage of priority equity enhancing, namely, HEFs.

5. Maternal support through nutrition and education is crucial for both mothers and their children. While improvements have been seen in levels of anemia, high levels of anemia are still found in mothers with many children, uneducated mothers, women in poor households and in rural areas. Twenty percent of the prenatal mortality and ten percent of maternal mortality are thought to be attributable to iron deficiency worldwide, while anemia is a common cause of premature delivery and low birth weight. In Cambodia, there is significant scope for reducing maternal and prenatal mortality by improving the coverage of micronutrient supplements, possibly through cash transfers to poor pregnant women in order to encourage them for antenatal and postnatal care. Also, despite progress, more attention is needed to promote breast feeding, further reduce open defecation, and more access to drinking water.

6. In 2011, the Cambodian government approved the first Nationwide Social Protection System (NSPS) to protect households vulnerable to financial shocks. But since then, the implementation of the strategy has been slow for different reasons. But now, with the decaying traditional family-based safety-net systems due to growing urbanization, there is an urgent need to adequately implement the NSPS.

Finally, Universal Health Coverage (UHC) is an agreed target of Cambodia within the newly accepted sustainable development goals. Moving towards UHC by 2030 is thus an obligation for the Royal Cambodian Government (RCG). The health sector certainly require to be upgraded to achieve this UHC aspiration. Cambodia's health system needs sufficient public funding to tackle many pressing issues along the path toward UHC. The health system also falls short of professional services that its citizens require. The shortage of qualified and trained medical personnel also has adverse effects on the government's efforts to move toward UHC. Therefore, achieving UHC requires overall actions across the health system including health financing reforms. In the short-run, Cambodia's Ministry of Health should improve efficiency, equity in the distribution of resources, transparency, and accountability, which are the immediate objectives for UHC. Over the medium to long-term, the Cambodian government should be able to ensure access to quality health-care services as well as to reduce out of pocket spending (OOP) for the population at large, especially the poor and near poor, by (i) initiating a social health insurance law to determine individuals who will benefit from such insurances; (ii) establishing an appropriate national institution in order to govern the three main social health protection schemes to reduce administrative cost and for easy reporting system; (iii) aligning the provider payment methods, benefit packages, claiming process, and criteria for quality of care of the three main schemes keeping in mind to merge them into one administrative authority at a future stage; (iv) considering to provide subsidies to the informal sector through general tax as the informal sector population is quite large in Cambodia; (v) strengthening the regulations regarding medical licenses; and (vi) giving special allowances with specialized training opportunities to doctors and nurses as an incentives to work at the remote health centers.

ACHIEVEMENTS IN PUBLIC EDUCATION SECTOR

Cambodia has a long history of education development and also witnessed many changes in its education policy since 1860s (French colonization of Cambodia started at 1863). Those changes in the education policies also affected development prospects of Cambodia time to time. However, the discussion of the country's contemporary education sector usually begins with the Post-French colonization period (1954 – 1969). French officially granted independence to Cambodia on July 3, 1953. Cambodia of King Sihanouk's regime introduced new ideology of Buddhist Socialism and the Sangkum Reastr Niyum (the People's Socialists Community). The change of politics from the French protectorate to the monarchy also marked the significant changes in education policy during Sangkum Reastr Niyum (Sokunrith POV and Norimune KAWAI, 2019). Cambodia, after independence, adopted education as the main development policy to accelerate economic growth and modernization. King Sihanouk's central nation-building perspective was to embrace formal education as the policy to transform the country to be an industrial and technologically advanced modern nation. The public education system was divided into primary, secondary, higher, and specialized education under the management of the Ministry of Education (MoE). Sihanouk government used the schooling model developed by the French administration. However, Sihanouk government, during the period of its 15 years tenure (National election of 1955 to 1970) increased the education budget substantially and also rapidly increased the number of primary schools, secondary schools, and universities in the capital and provincial regions. Cambodia enjoyed a massive expansion of education from 1953-1970 (Fergusson & Masson, 1997), but such expansion started to decline during the civil war of the 1970s and then totally dismantled during 1975-1979 by the policy of Khmer rouge. The Khmer Rouge's regime, during 1975-1979, tore apart the social fabric of Cambodian society at the cost of over two million lives and incalculable disruption and destruction to the economic and social functioning of the country. Following the fall of the Khmer Rouge in January 1979, the Vietnamese supported government established social systems from scratch (Ayres 2000). Education and other social sectors were reborn with financial and technical support from the socialist blocks (Sitha Chhinh & Sideth S. Dy). The new government was known until 1989 as People's Republic of Kampuchea (PRK) and later the State of Cambodia (SOC). Although the PRK seemed to put much effort to develop the education sector in Cambodia after the severe social destruction of Pol Pot's regime, the literacy rate was still restricted below 30 percent. In the capital city, there was a high primary enrolment rate, but it was very low in the rural areas. Also, the high dropout rates were a major concern, especially for girls. Public education sector was chosen as the most important sector to restore after the 1991 Paris Peace settlement and return of the monarchy in 1993. The ravages of previous two decades of scattered violence, frequent conflicts and civil war involving several factions left a significant legacy of damaged infrastructure and a generation with minimal education. The newly elected government adopted education as the primary focus for the national development in order to boost human resource development as the key to socio-economic development. The international development aids also started to flow into Cambodia since the early 1990s. The right to quality education was guaranteed in the Cambodian constitution adopted on September 21, 1993. Cambodia experienced mostly stable political and educational development since 1993.

The 4+3+3 education system established in 1979 soon after the fall of the Khmer Rouge was expanded to a system of 5+3+3 during 1987-1994 and then to 6+3+3 (six years of primary education, three years of lower secondary, and three years of upper secondary) from 1994 until now. Since 1994, education in Cambodia has made significant progress. But schools in remote areas are still lacking in different ways. The education system does not yet capable to provide quality and relevant learning for children and youths of the country as a whole. Because, many schools lack teachers, when there are too many students per class. There are insufficient materials, core textbooks and library resources. Some schools are located far from the villages. The school drop-out rate is high. Furthermore, some teachers require to be absent during the harvest season. Some children are often needed to join the workforce at a young age leaving the school classes. The lack of literacy among the labor force is another issue in Cambodia. The recent Cambodia Economic Survey revealed that about 15 percent of the labor force (aged 15-64) were either illiterate or had only basic literacy skills, while more that 30 percent had not completed primary education. Another challenge to the education system is that teachers' pay has traditionally been low, compelling teachers to take a second job to increase their income in order to support their families. In 2005, teachers in Cambodia earned only USD35-40 per month in primary schools and USD60 in upper secondary schools, while it was estimated that a teacher needed a minimum salary of USD150 to support a typical Cambodian family of five members. In 2012, such salary was USD60 for primary school teachers, and USD80 for junior high school teachers. However, in 2015, Cambodia's Ministry of Education, Youth and Sport (MoEYS) increased the teachers' salary to USD124.46 per month for primary school teachers and USD186.62 for lower secondary teachers. This salary was subsequently raised to USD250 per month in accordance with MoEYS' promise of a further 20 percent rise.

Cambodia's Ministry of Education, Youth and Sport (MoEYS) already set and executed four education strategy plans from 2000 until 2018 to address the problems of the education sector. The fifth education strategy plan (2019-2023) is currently in operation. The first Education Strategy Plan (2000-2005) emphasized on enrolment in primary school by: (a) starting to cancel the enrolment payments; (b) giving school funding to rural schools in poor areas; and (c) establishing primary schools across the whole country in order to create maximum opportunities for at least primary education for the young population of the country. The second Education

Strategy Plan (2006-2010) focused to improving education in secondary schools by: (a) establishing lower secondary schools in all communes and secondary schools in all districts across the country; and (b) providing scholarships to poor students in order to encourage as well as enable them to complete at least up to Grade 9. The third Education Strategy Plan (2009-2013) shifted the focus on improving internal efficiency within the education system by: (a) reducing repetition and drop-out rates among the students; and (b) strengthening institutions for decentralization. The fourth Education Strategy Plan (2014-2018) emphasized on (a) equality and the quality of education; (b) the response and the contribution of education to the needs of the economy; and (c) effective management of MoEYS staff. The fifth and ongoing Education Strategy Plan (2019-2023) has been designed for: (a) implementing education, youth and sports reforms in order to establish a robust base for education by 2030 and beyond; and (b) responding to the vision of Cambodia's socio-economic development and the reform programs of the Royal Government of Cambodia. The Education Strategy Plan (ESP) (2019-2023) applies sub-sector structural management approaches to address logical relationships between sub-sector objectives, strategic frameworks, main activities and resource requirements, monitoring and evaluation, and mechanisms for continuous quality improvements.

In 2016, Cambodia's MoEYS reviewed the implementation of the ESP 2014-2018 at mid-term and revised its policies from three down to two, to be consistent with Cambodia's National Strategic Development Goal, and to respond the various policies in order to contribute to the implementation of the Royal Government of Cambodia's (RGC) policies for employment growth, equity and efficiency towards achieving the goals of poverty reduction and promoting citizens' livelihoods. The Year 2016's two medium-term education policies were: (i) ensuring inclusive and equitable quality education and promote life-long learning opportunities for all; and (ii) ensuring effective leadership and management of education officials at all levels.

The past three decades witnessed systematic improvements in Cambodia's education system, which particularly accelerated since 2000. The following four areas are indicative of progress achieved: (1) the abolition of start-of-year school fees in 2000 across the country, coupled with extensive outreach and enrolment campaigns, led to a massive surge of new students with the number of primary school pupils rising from 2.2 million to 2.7 million between 1999-2000 and 2001-2002. The greatest increases occurred in remote areas, where the number of pupils almost tripled (Chansopheak, 2009). Achievements were equally dramatic at the lower secondary level with an average annual increase of 24.2 percent between 1999-2000 and 2003-2004 (Bray and Seng, 2005). In 2018, there were a total 3.2 million children enrolled in public schools from pre-primary to upper secondary levels (50.9 percent girls). In terms of Early Childhood Education (ECE), access to ECE improved year on year as a result of interventions and the provision of education services. The percentage of five-year old children accessing all aspects of ECE services, was increased gradually from 59.9 percent in 2013-2014 to 68.5 percent in 2017-2018, achieving the ESP target of 68 percent. The enrolment of four-year old children increased from 24.5 percent in 2013-2014 to 39.9 percent in 2017-2018, achieving the target of 38 percent by 2017-2018.

Cambodia's MoEYS expanded pre-schools over the period of 4th Education Strategy Plan from 5,625 in 2013-2014 to 7,587 in 2017-2018, an increase of nearly 34 percent over the five years period; 31.2 percent in terms of the number of public pre-schools, 33.1 percent in terms of community pre-schools, and slightly higher for private pre-schools (Education Sector Performance by MoEYS, 2019). During this period, MoEYS implemented many plans and programs, such as school operational budgets and school improvement plans, an inclusive education program, a multilingual education program, parents' education linked to community pre-schools, and a floating pre-school program in flooded areas. The number of Public pre-schools implementing the inclusive education program increased from 27 in 2013-2014 to 183 in 2017-2018. The number of Community pre-schools implementing the inclusive education program increased from 10 in 2013-2014 to 64 in 2017-2018. Towards teacher capacity development, MoEYS deployed 200 new pre-school teachers annually and recruited 200 pre-school teacher trainees during the 4th ESP period. However, the Cambodian government acknowledges that still the challenges to enrolment in early child education (ECE) include a lack of pre-school teachers and infrastructure for expanding ECE services. In terms of Primary Education Sub-sector, net enrolment rates at primary education level achieved 98 percent, while completion rates reached 80 percent during 4th ESP period. In 2019, primary schools are largely available in all geographic locations in Cambodia. The number of students enrolled at the right age increased reasonably by 2019, which indicates that the Cambodian people realize the value of education. The efficacy of primary education, as evident from drop out and repetition rates, also improved during the 4th ESP period. Nevertheless, as of 2019, there were still high student drop-out rates at Grade 6 of primary school. The pupils to teacher ratio in primary education in Cambodia in 2018 was 41.7 pupils for every teacher available. However, as MoEYS acknowledged, the main challenges in Cambodia's primary education sub-sector, included a lack of teaching and learning materials for teachers and students, and teachers not using enquiry-based learning activities. MoEYS requires to strengthen classroom management and teaching and learning processes in primary education level.

In terms of Secondary and Technical Education Sub-sector, enrolment in lower secondary education improved to 56.8 percent in SY 2017-2018, with the average gross enrolment increasing at 3.5 percent during the 4th ESP. The gross enrolment rate increased to 28.5 percent in SY 2017-2018 for upper secondary education. 4th ESP targets were 54.6 percent and 27.7 percent for lower secondary and upper secondary enrolment respectively. During the 4th ESP period, the drop-out rate for lower secondary school declined significantly, from 21.2 percent in SY 2013-2014 to 15.4 percent in SY 2017-2018. Nevertheless, the drop-out rate from lower secondary school is still high because of few factors such as schools being far from houses, lack of core textbooks, teaching methods and scholarships. In the upper secondary school level, drop-out rate is high, at 18.3 percent in SY 2017-2018. More specifically, the drop-out rate from the upper secondary school level is higher in rural areas, as students of the rural areas need to work to earn money and support their families. Transition rates from primary to lower secondary school were quite low during the 4th ESP period due to the vast geographic spread of lower secondary schools. The pre-school education and primary education are 1,050 hours per school year and 30 hours per week. Lower secondary education and upper secondary education are 1,400 hours per year and 40 hours per week. Although, significant improvements occurred in the secondary school level education in Cambodia during the last two decades, there is still room for MoEYS to pay more attention to reduce student drop-out by addressing geographical issues and other reasons that students do not pursue their learning. Enhancing the scholarship program, new curricula and classroom management, and encouraging students to participate the classes more actively could be the few strategies of MoEYS to assist students to stay in school. In the area of technical education, the number of technical high school students gradually increased during the five years of 4th ESP through the provision of scholarship program, dormitories for students, and increased advertising that explained the importance and value of technical education. The rate of technical students didn't reach the target of the 4th ESP in SY 2017-2018 as some technical education students moved to general education. Although there are distinct signs of improvements in technical education in Cambodia in the past five years, MoEYS still needs to focus on providing career counselling, orientation, learning workshops, internship programs and collaboration with enterprises to foster technical education further.

In terms of Higher Education Sub-sector, enrolment rate at higher education level did not change significantly during the period of 4th ESP. The gross enrolment rate for higher education was 11.6 percent in SY 2017-2018, which was lower than the target of 23 percent. Increased student accesses to education in science, technology, engineering, and mathematics (STEM) at higher education level were promoted by MoEYS through the creation of a new training program and new higher educational institutions specializing on STEM. During the ESP period, nine new Higher Education Institutions were established of which four are public institutions. MoEYS also promoted the culture of research at higher education level and developed the research and innovation capacity of higher educational institutes through research funds and capacity building. MoEYS also organized an education researchers' forum in 2015-2019 to further support research at the higher education level. As a result, Cambodia's higher educational institutes now have the capacity to accept research projects through partnerships with the Erasmus+ framework of the European Union as well as with the other international universities.

Although the implementation of the Education Strategy Plan (ESP) 2014-2018 made noteworthy progress towards achieving its policy objectives, there are still some challenges, as mentioned in the Education Congress Report 2018, that require further strengthening, further improvements, and appropriate strategies to achieve the desired goals. Accordingly, in ESP 2019-2023, MoEYS identified sub-sector wise priorities for action towards achieving the goal. Under Early Childhood Education Sub-sector (ECE) of ESP 2019-2023, MoEYS identified priorities for strengthening ECE services, such as increasing the access to quality, equitable and inclusive education, improving the quality of pre-schools in accordance with standards, and strengthening the capacity of ECE sub-sector management. Under Primary Education Sub-sector of ESP 2019-2023, MoEYS identified priorities on improving access to education, completion of primary education for all children, especially children from disadvantaged groups, and strengthening the quality of education through a comprehensive early grade learning program. This comprises Khmer literacy, mathematics, subject-based mentoring, and teacher qualifications. Under

Secondary and Technical Education Sub-sector of ESP 2019-2023, MoEYS identified priorities to focus on: (a) STEM, school administration; (b) new generation schools; (c) work skills at the secondary school level, and (d) English and other foreign languages as required by the school, along with ICT. Under Higher Education Sub-sector of ESP 2019-2023, MoEYS identified priorities to strengthen and promote quality in higher education towards regional and international standards, and to respond to the Rectangular Strategy Phase IV of the Royal Government of Cambodia in this new mandate. MoEYS is also committed to define policies, strategies and key activities to ensure inclusive and equitable quality education and also to develop a governance and management system to support Higher Educational Institutions to become fully autonomous. Under the Non-Formal Education (NFE) Sub-sector of ESP 2019-2023, MoEYS identified priorities to increase the number of literate students and to increase access to NFE programs for out-of-school children and youth, as well as access to full NFE services within a framework of life-long learning, knowledge, skills and attitudes. MoEYS also require to strengthen the implementation of a fully functioning results-oriented management system of NFE programs and to enhance capacity of NFE staff at each level. Under the Physical Education and Sport Sub-sector of ESP 2019-2023, Cambodia government's priority is to develop human resources and infrastructure, and promote the physical education and sport sector. In 2023, for the 32nd South East Asian Games in Cambodia, the country has an ambitious goal to rank fifth among the 11 countries, and accordingly MoEYS identified priorities to increase access to physical education and sport in schools and communities to improve people's well-being and livelihoods. MoEYS also expressed its determination to promote the performance of national sports teams to win more gold medals by 2023; and to develop the institutional, managerial, and technical capacities of the physical education and sport sub-sector for improved effectiveness and quality.

CHAPTER-NINE
ECONOMIC PERSPECTIVES OF INDUSTRIALISATION: 1989-2019

During 1989 to 2019, Cambodia underwent a significant transition, reached lower middle-income status in 2015 and aspiring to attain upper middle-income status by 2030. Cambodia's economy sustained an average growth rate of 8 (eight) percent between 1998 and 2018, making it one of the fastest growing economies in the world. While eased slightly, growth remained strong at 7.1 percent in 2019, after the better than expected growth rate of 7.5 percent in 2018. In 2019, the share of industrial economic sector in Cambodia's gross domestic product was 34.23 percent, whereas in 2009, industry contributed only 21.66 percent of Cambodia's GDP. In 1988, the total value of Cambodia's industrial production including handicraft was only USD20 million and it was dominated by state-owned enterprises (Slocomb 2010); whereas in 2019, Cambodia exported industrial products, including garment products, worth USD11.18 billion, a year-on-year increase of 14 percent (Agence Kampuchea Presse, 17th February 2020).

Cambodia faced many challenges since its independence in 1953. During this period, Cambodia also experienced a number of very different political ideologies which strongly influenced its industrial policy of the time. During 1970-1989, Cambodia largely underwent through much hardship, including a protracted civil war, political genocide, and international isolation. After 1989, Cambodia slowly stated transforming its economy. Subsequently, with Paris Peace Settlement in 1991 and the establishment of the new coalition government in 1993, the Royal Government of Cambodia started implementing macroeconomic and structural reforms to reconstruct and develop the country. Cambodia has managed to achieve relative political stability over the last nearly three decades, under governments formed by the Cambodian People's Party, led by Prime Minister Samdech Hun Sen, initially in coalition with Royalist Party. In line with peace, social order, political stability, national reconciliation and with international assistance, the country has already transformed from a war zone into a dynamic and emerging country with fast development. Cambodia also transformed itself, in the process, from a centrally planned economy into a free market economy. It is evident that free trade in Cambodia significantly contributed so far to reduce poverty and improved people's living standard. Thus, the Royal Government has been continuing to liberalize trade and ensure the free flow of goods and services both within the country and between Cambodia and the key regional and global partners. Such policies have been providing Cambodia with the desired economies of scale and opportunities that attract investment, increase incomes, accelerate economic growth, create more employment, and thus continuously reducing poverty. In this context, Cambodia's membership in ASEAN in 1999, and in the World Trade Organization (WTO) in 2004 should be considered as historical and strategic steps towards its miracle of national rehabilitation and development. The Royal Cambodian Government acknowledges and recognizes that to reap the maximum benefit from those memberships, especially ASEAN, the country requires adequate efforts in the formulation, adoption, and implementation of necessary laws, regulations, procedures in order to increase the country's capability in production and competitiveness.

Cambodia has been in transition to a full market economy since 1993 election overseen by the United Nations (UN). While the dream of industrialized Cambodia has been in mind since its independence in 1953, for different political and ideological reasons, the expansion of industry, as a major policy in true sense, has been observed since 1993. Following is a snap-shot of the growth and development of Cambodia's industrial sector focusing on the structure of industry in terms of output, employment, and the characteristics of enterprises, and addressing industrial policies as well as the various macroeconomic, trade, regulatory and labor market policies of relevance:

State of Cambodia and the UN period (1989-1993)

In 1989, Vietnam completed its promised military withdrawal from Cambodia following ten years of occupation. The decision to withdraw the last one of Vietnam's military forces in Cambodia by the end of September 1989, a year earlier than the planned 1990 deadline, was a difficult one. Once Vietnamese troops left, Hun Sen declared Cambodia 'permanently neutral' and claimed that the country's neutrality would take precedence over Cambodia's mutual defense pact of 1979 with Vietnam. With the fall of the Soviet Union and the Eastern Bloc and Vietnam's launching of 'Doi Moi' economic reform policy in 1989, Cambodia also started to adopt radical reforms of its economic management system and transition from a centrally planned economy to a market-oriented one. In 1989, Cambodia launched a broad reform program. The foreign investment law was brought into force in 1989, enabling private companies to engage in foreign trade. In the early 1990s, trade policies were further liberalized, largely removing restrictions on firms and individuals engaged in international trade. Most quantitative restrictions and the licensing of imports were eliminated. In 1989, the two-tier price system for rice, introduced in 1984, under which farmers were taxed indirectly by being compelled to sell a portion of their output to the state at below market prices, was abolished. The process of becoming market-oriented economy was compounded by the signing of the Paris Peace Accord in October 1991. As part of the Paris Peace Agreement, the Cambodian government had to relinquish the role of rehabilitation and reconstruction to the United Nations Transitional Authority (UNTAC) during the transition period. The Peace Agreement also defined the transitional period beginning with the entry into force of the Paris Agreements, i.e. 23rd October 1991, and ending when a Constituent Assembly, elected in conformity with the Agreements, approved the new Cambodian constitution and transformed itself into a legislative assembly, creating a new Cambodian Government. Social development and the provision of basic needs such as food security, health, housing, training, education, public utilities, and basic transport infrastructure were the priorities for the rehabilitation phase. Entrepreneurship and private sector development were promoted during the reconstruction phase in order to get prepared for entry into a free market economy. UNTAC became operational on 15th March 1992. Towards Reconstruction of Cambodia, UNTAC monitored the process of transition. This body, which subsequently evolved into the consultative group, met annually to provide loans and grants for development, on the condition of reforms being implemented by the government. Cambodia's political and economic developments moved, through these reforms, from a command to a laissez faire economy, and from a domestic oriented to export-oriented production (Slocomb 2010).

The industrial sector accounted for only 5 percent of Cambodia's GDP in 1985, down from 19 percent in 1969. Industrial activity continued to be concentrated in the processing of agricultural commodities, mostly rice, fish, wood, and rubber. Manufacturing plants were small, and they employed an average of fewer than 200 workers. These plants aimed to produce enough consumer goods to satisfy local demands. By late 1985, there were reportedly 60 factories in the state sector producing household goods, textiles, soft drinks, pharmaceutical products, and other light consumer goods (Nations Encyclopedia). Most plants used to operate below capacity because of poor management and shortages of electricity, raw materials, and spare parts. Recovery efforts continued in the early 1990s, but were hampered by dilapidated equipment and shortages that continued to affect industrial production, mainly textiles and rubber production. For instance, following the cutback of assistance from the former Soviet Union in 1990, Cambodia's primitive industrial sector suffered from raw material shortages; three of six government-owned textile mills shut down because of shortages of cotton. Major industries, during this period, included rice milling, fishing, wood and timber products, cement and gem mining. Construction in urban areas boomed with the signing of the Paris Peace Accord in 1991. After Cambodia opened oil fields to foreign investors in February 1991, sixteen companies expressed interest in oil exploration. By end-1993, it was reported that five oil companies were conducting offshore oil and gas exploration (Nations Encyclopedia).

Table: 9.1 illustrates some of the successes achieved during this period with GDP experienced strong growth in 1988 at 9.8 percent, a slowdown in 1989 and 1990, and then a recovery largely driven by the buildup of UNTAC operations. Industry contributed around 15 percent of GDP during this period while agriculture accounted slightly over half of GDP, and service sector around 33 percent. However, these successes and market reforms were undermined by macroeconomic imbalances caused by declining state revenues due to the humanitarian aid, increased unit cost of goods and services procured for operations and investments, and high inflation caused by monetary financing of the budget deficit (Royal Government of Cambodia 2009). The inflation rate accelerated, as a consequence, from 70 percent in 1989 to 200 percent in 1992 (Table: 9.2). Inflation was, however, stabilized in 1993 through reduction in the government deficit, but the high inflation rate of the previous years led to a permanent dollarization of the economy because of the decline in public confidence in national currency.

TABLE 9.1: GDP growth and different sector's share of GDP, 1988-1992

	1988	1989	1990	1991	1992
GDP growth	9.8	3.5	1.2	7.6	6.9
Agriculture	5.9	7.1	1.2	6.7	4.8
Industry	15	1.8	-2.1	8.9	8.4
Services	13.6	-1.1	2.7	8.4	9.5
GDP by sector					
Agriculture	50.5	52.2	52.3	51.8	50.8
Industry	15.7	15.4	14.9	15.1	15.3
Services	33.8	32.4	32.8	33.1	33.9

Source: based on Irvin,1993

TABLE 9.2: Inflation Rate, 1989-1992

YEAR	1989	1990	1991	1992
Rate (%)	70	157	121	200

Source: Nations Encyclopedia.

KINGDOM OF CAMBODIA (1993 – present)

Polling for the election of Cambodia's first Constituent Assembly took place from 23rd to 25th May,1993. Subsequently, the Constituent Assembly had its first sitting on 14th June,1993. Cambodia started to enjoy national reconciliation and political stability, overcoming protracted civil war and political strife, after the formation of the new government in 1993. In line with peace, stability, and social order, the Royal Government of Kingdom of Cambodia has been implementing macroeconomic and structural reforms, and thus achieved remarkable success in stabilizing the macroeconomic foundation. In the late 1990s, there were more deliberate phases of positive steps towards a highly liberal trade regime. To promote industrial development, the government also provided generous incentives to attract foreign direct investments (FDIs) and equally strived to find export markets for FDI-manufactured products. In addition, tax exemptions were provided on imported intermediate goods and on the exporting of finished goods. Cambodia has become increasingly integrated into the region after joining ASEAN in 1999 and other regional and subregional mechanisms. Another important milestone in global economic integration was finally reached when Cambodia was admitted as the 148th member of the World Trade Organization (WTO) on 13th October 2004. Cambodia's WTO membership, with limited human resources and expertise in international trade, has imposed greater responsibility on the country to adhere to strict protocols and standards, while it has opened up tremendous opportunities for trade with the world as a whole on a competitive basis. Membership of these organizations placed further requirements on Cambodia to liberalize trade in goods and services and foreign capital ownership.

Cambodia's economy, with an average growth of 8.4 percent per year during 1994-2008, was considered as one of the fastest growing in the world. Economic growth during 2004-2008 averaged 10.3 percent. Cambodia's growth performance ranked 7th across all countries in the world and had higher exports per capita than other countries of Cambodia's level of economic development (World Bank 2009). However, Cambodian economy, after a double-digit growth during 2004-2008, registered a growth of only 0.1 percent in 2009 as it was severely affected by the global financial crisis. But the Royal government led the Cambodian economy out of the crisis in a 'V' shaped recovery path and successfully addressed all the negative impacts of the crisis. The growth rate, after declining in 2009 due to the crisis, increased to 5.5 percent in 2010. Inflation was around 3.5 percent in December 2010 over December 2009. Manufacturing and agro-industry sectors also continued to grow in 2010. The garment sector, in 2009, severely affected by the world economic crisis, grew nearly 30 percent in 2010, generating total revenue of more than USD3 billion. FDI played a significant role in creating a production base, especially to exploit trade opportunities in advanced economies. The inflow of FDI increased from just USD124 million in 1993 to nearly USD520 million in 2009 (Ministry of Economy and Finance).

The Royal government of Cambodia, starting from 1994, began privatizing small and medium-sized state-owned enterprises, especially those that did not make a profit such as public transports, engineering firms, rice mills, soft drinks, textiles, and wine breweries. The Cambodia Royal Railways was transferred to an Australian company named TOLL in 2009. By end of 2010, only a few strategic enterprises remained as 100 percent state-owned enterprises, including international ports, electricity, and water supply. Some enterprises, for example national airlines and air traffic control, remained as partly state-owned. As per Economic Census Reports 2011, conducted by the National Institute of Statistics and the Ministry of Planning, by end 2010, private establishments accounted for 96 percent of the total number of establishments, while state-owned establishments accounted for only 3 percent of the total establishments. Also, during that time, private establishments and state-owned establishments absorbed 90 percent and 8 percent respectively of the total number of persons engaged in establishments.

Driven by a robust manufacturing sub-sector, during 1995-2008, Cambodia's industry's value added had been growing by more than double the annual rate of agriculture's value added. Manufacturing became the largest contributor to industry output, accounted for at least 70 percent since 1998, with construction added another 24 percent. Mining and utilities accounted 4 percent. Manufacturing also contributed most to industry growth – averaging 9.4 percent during 2000-2012 (excluded 2009 data, when growth declined abruptly because of world economic crisis, to avoid distortion of average). Construction and mining and utilities contributed 2.3 percentage points each per year during 2000-2012. The production of garments, textiles, and footwear dominated manufacturing, and their share of sector output rose from 15 percent in 1995 to 75 percent in 2010. During this period, Cambodia became an attractive production site due to its low wages, preferential tariffs, and quota-free access to major markets. The food, beverage, and tobacco sub-sector continued to grow, but its relative importance diminished with the rise of garments, textiles, and footwear. Food, beverages, and tobacco accounted for 36 percent of manufacturing output during 1995 – 1999, but reduced to only about 10 percent during 2006-2010. The share of other sub-sectors, including rubber, wood, paper, and publishing experienced a similar decline during that period. The output of garments, textiles, and footwear grew 60 percent annually during 1995-2000, but slowed to 8 percent in 2006-2010. Exports increased four-fold between 2001-2013, from USD1.2 billion to USD4.9 billion, including a contraction of almost 20 percent in 2009 due to the global financial crisis. Over reliance on global clothing retailers in Europe and the United States left this sector susceptible to adverse demand shocks. Footwear exports were less affected by the crisis and recorded positive growth since 2006. Cambodia experienced the lack of export diversification, with garments dominated exports for more than a decade (2001-2012) (ADB, 2014).

The Royal Government of Cambodia has set directions to become a middle-income economy by 2030 and a high-income country by 2050, as projected in the National Strategic Development Plan for 2014-2018. The role of industry and small and medium enterprises are being emphasized as the key driver of future growth (Ministry of Planning, 'National Strategic Development Plan 2014-2018'). In March, 2015, the government prepared and adopted an Industrial Development Policy (IDP), 2015-2025 as a guide towards systematic solutions to developing a more competitive industrial sector in Cambodia. The Royal Government considers the industrial sector as a growth strategy priority to promote economic diversification by introducing profound structural change and thereby improving competitiveness. The structural transformation is designed to ensure the sustainability and robustness of national economy with strengthened role of financial intermediaries, modernized and up-to-date logistic system and distribution channel, gradual advancement and introduction of new techniques and technologies, and improvement in governance and capacity of public institutions in managing economic development.

Since 1993, the industrial sector of Cambodia has been playing important role in the country's economy. It's share of GDP increased from a mere 12.6 percent to 26.2 percent in 2006. The sector suffered a short decline and remained steady at 22 percent at 2012 due to the change in international trade regime and the global economic crisis. Cambodia's industrial sector's share of GDP rebounded to around 24 percent in 2013 and to 34.23 percent in 2019. In that light, the industrial sector in Cambodia is a key performer towards achieving the country's desired growth.

Cambodia's industrial sector is also the main provider of jobs. In 1993, about 72 percent of the total labor force was in the agriculture sector as compared to only 5 percent in the industrial sector. Jobs in the industrial sector accounted to nearly 600,000 or an equivalent to 8.6 percent of the total jobs in Cambodia as envisaged in 2008 Population Census. As per 2012 Socio-Economic Survey, nearly 1.4 million people were engaged in the industry or an equivalent of 18.6 percent of the total jobs. However, it is noteworthy that these jobs are seasonally adjusted. The dry season of the year 2012, there were nearly 1.8 million workers in the industries in Cambodia or an equivalent of 25.2 percent of the total jobs. By end-2019, jobs in the industrial sector accounted to more than 2.7 million or an equivalent to 29 percent of the total jobs (World Bank 2020).

One of the most remarkable developments from the economic reforms was the growth of Cambodia's manufacturing sector. According to a report by the Asian Development Bank, Cambodia's manufacturing sector accounted for 31 percent of the country's economy in 2018. The manufacturing sector continued to account for more than one-third of Cambodia's economy in 2019. The country's growth rate for value added in industry is the highest in South-east Asia. The Asian Development Bank forecasted in 2018 that the country's manufacturing sector to continue to grow by around 9.6 percent, with a slowdown in garments and footwear off set by stronger growth in emerging industries, such as electrical parts, automobile components, bicycles, milled rice, and rubber. In 2017, Cambodia became the European Union's number one supplier of bicycles. During the first half of 2019, Cambodia strengthened its leading position with an export to the European member states of 835,000 regular bicycles. After garments and footwear, bicycles export is the third largest export category of Cambodia. Cambodia's light manufacturing assembly sector, located primarily but not exclusively in special economic zones, are mainly labor-intensive operations. The productions of construction materials, machinery, electronics, engines, and chemical products are still comparatively small by end-2019. Electrical and vehicle parts exports together reached USD430 million in 2017.

In the beginning of 2019, as per figures from the Ministry of Industry and Handicraft, there were 1,528 factories in Cambodia, with almost two-thirds i.e. 922 factories were being operated by weaving, bag, garments, and footwear manufacturers. 178 new factories opened in 2018, compared to 150 in 2017. Production of both domestic and export products generated total income of USD13.17 billion in 2018, an increase of 23 percent over 2017. Cambodia's garment sector continues to be the front-runner in the country's growth process. Garment sector provided, on average, 635,000 jobs in 2017 at 643 factories. Almost 90 percent of the workforce are female. Exports totaled USD8.02 billion in 2017, up 9.5 percent from 2016, and made up 72 percent of Cambodia's total merchandise exports. Garments and textiles continued to be the largest export industry in Cambodia in 2018 as well as in 2019. In 2018, the industry shipped USD13.1 billion worth of goods, accounted for 63 percent of the country's total exports. The primary markets for these exports, which also included accessories such as buttons, Velcro and zippers, were the European Union (40 percent), United States (30 percent), and Canada (9 percent). Footwear exports grew by 14.4 percent year-on-year, to USD873 million in 2017. However, in 2018, the industry shipped products valued at USD2.3 billion, or 11 percent of Cambodia's total exports. Footwear and headwear were collectively Cambodia's second largest export in 2019. The primary destinations of these exports were the European Union (46 percent), the United States (17 percent) and Japan (12 percent). The ILO reported that footwear and headgear's share of exports grew by 4.4 percent between 2013 and 2018. Food and beverage is the third largest export industry in Cambodia. Cereals, vegetables, roots and fruits and nuts made up the bulk of the sector's USD1.5 billion (7.2 percent of the country's total exports) in exports in 2018. There is reasonable confidence within the industry that the sector will prosper in the coming years and it's contribution towards country's export growth will increase.

Cambodia's current economic growth does not rely much on investment, as an analysis suggests that the contribution of expenditure to GDP indicates that the source of growth of GDP still largely depends on private consumption. By the standard of developing countries, the contribution rate of investment to GDP should be between 40 percent or above in order to boost the economy to jump to the next level of development. It means, there is still room for more investment in Cambodia. Cambodia's economic growth, so far, relied heavily on the garment, construction, tourism, and rice sectors, implying there is need to invest more to invigorate new economic growth.

BFC (Better Factories Cambodia) – a partnership between the ILO (international Labor Organization) and the International Finance Corporation, a member of the World bank Group, was established in 2001 in Cambodia to improve mainly the working conditions and competitiveness of the factories of Cambodia. A tripartite memorandum of understanding (BFC, Cambodia Government, and Garment Manufacturers' Association) has been renewed six times since then, the current renewal is effective from 21st December 2019.

In 2015, Cambodian economy was at a crucial transformation stage after sustaining high growth over the decade since 2004. The country required comprehensive structural reforms aimed at strengthening economic diversification and competitiveness to ensure sustainable economic growth with equitable redistribution of wealth. The Royal Government felt to consider for a new development approach vis-à-vis expanding development opportunities and investment in new growth sectors by way of improving the necessary socio-economic infrastructure, supply of energy, expansion of transport infrastructure and development of logistics, promotion of technical and science education, and institutional strengthening. In this regard, the Cambodian government adopted its Industrial Development Policy (2015-2025) in March 2015 in order to provide a policy framework and a specific mechanism for driving the country's economic growth and creating jobs with focus on the manufacturing sector, agro-industrial sector and SMEs. In pursuance of this policy, Cambodia has been aiming to succeed in its economic structural transformation by moving from an agriculture based economy toward a manufacturing and agro-industry based economy, and subsequently in the final phase toward diversification in other sectors especially those that use technology and innovation.

In terms of vision of the Industrial Development Policy (IDP), the Royal Government envisages a transformation and modernization of Cambodia's industrial structure from a labor-intensive industry to a skill-based industry by 2025, linking with global value chain, integrating into regional production networks and developing clusters, while strengthening competitiveness and improving productivity of domestic industries, and marching toward developing a technology and knowledge based industry. In line with the vision, the Royal Government is committed to pay close attention to driving structural change in three important phases by continuing to promote its industrial potentials and diversifying its labor intensive industries, such as manufacturing and agro-industry; and by initiating a comprehensive industrial restructuring through diversification of production; and finally by undertaking further change by way of specialization based on sciences and technology development and innovation. The core objectives of the country's Industrial Development Policy have been to address structural challenges and to invest in key industrial infrastructure, both hard and soft, to be in line with the potentials, competitive advantage and development of the Cambodian industry. In order to realize the vision and to fulfil the desired objectives, the Royal Government has set three targets, namely, transforming and strengthening the industrial structure in the national economy; increasing and diversifying export products; and strengthening and promoting of SMEs.

In terms of policy measures and action plans to implement the IDP, the Royal Government has put forth the following key policy measures:

(1) **Investment Promotion through**, among other things, (a) Offering Favorable Investment Climate by reviewing and amending the law on investment and other relevant regulations to respond to the concrete needs for developing the industrial sector by way of making the business climate conducive to attracting investment, enabling technology transfer, creating jobs and enhance skills training and increasing value-addition; (b) Development of Special Economic Zones (SEZs) and Industrial Zones by reviewing the incentives framework for foreign and domestic firms and SMEs located in SEZs, as well as by promoting the establishment of large industrial parks and clusters by enacting the law on Special Economic Zone aimed at supporting, in a comprehensive way, the development of these zones to meet international standards including infrastructure management system, adequate supply of electricity and clear water, provisions of raw materials and other inputs, trade and transport facilitation, provisions

of incentives and other supporting measures to promote investments in SEZs.

(2) **Expansion and Modernization of SMEs** through, among other things, (a) Institutional Arrangements and Incentives by strengthening the SME development framework and mechanism, focusing on the preparation of registration, monitoring and tracking the progress of this sector with an intention to encourage Cambodian enterprises to register in the formal tax regime, thus allowing the Royal government to have accurate information about the sector so that it can initiate proper supporting policies to enable better access to credit information and other business advises to grow their businesses and investments; (b) Registration and Accounting Practices by amending the law on corporate accounts, audit and accounting profession to introduce a simplified accounting standards for SMEs, and by strengthening the single-window mechanism for registering SMEs by way of using their registration and account ledgers as the basis for evaluating and determining criteria for providing incentives and receiving support from the Royal Government; (c) Promotion of Agro-Industrial Development by exploring possibilities of establishing agro-processing zones such as furniture manufacturing, rubber processing, seafood processing, food processing for domestic use and export through public-private partnership.

(3) **Improvement of Regulatory Environment** through, among other things, (a) Trade Facilitation and Export Promotion Measures by accelerating the finalization of the implementation of trade facilitation reform plan and the utilization of the National Single Window Service at all international border checkpoints and ensuring its integration with the ASEAN Single Window Service in order to support the international logistic network, and by establishing trade information center that consists of internet based information on trade measures, tariff and formal fees imposed by the Royal Government; (b)

Industrial Standards and Property Rights by continuous strengthening institutional framework and the capacity in managing metrology and standards, which are the foundation of industrial activities. Additional efforts are dedicated to develop the appropriate regulatory framework and to get international recognition of key national institutions such as the National Metrology Center and the Institute of Standards of Cambodia; as well as by improving the effectiveness of the process of registering industrial property rights by way of implementing collaborative procedures to recognize registration agents of partner countries and to facilitate to the registration of IP agents through automation; (c) Facilitation for Payment of Tax and Excise by reviewing the tax and customs system by transforming it into a tool not only for revenue collection but also for promoting industrial development; and by rationalizing revenue collection mechanism and improve taxpayer services to promote tax culture among enterprises and taxpayers; (d) Labor Market Development and Industrial Relations by continuous strengthening the tripartite labor relation mechanism among the government, employers and employees through the Labor Advisory Committee in order to promote mutual understanding, while developing an effective mechanism for setting minimum wages consistent with labor productivity, socio-economic conditions and status of industrial development in Cambodia; and also by preparing Law on Union and Law on Labor Court.

(4) **Coordination of Supporting Policies** through, among other things, (a) Skills and Human Resource Development by offering a second opportunity for students to finish secondary education by establishing a testing based equivalent education system, which allows students to receive general education certificate, albeit from the non-formal education sector; and by strengthening the quality of education at primary and secondary levels by focusing on strengthening basic knowledge for children and youth

in mathematics, sciences, literature and technology; (b) Sciences, Technology and Innovation promotion by expediting the preparation of regulatory framework and measures for the development of sciences, technology and innovation; as well as by promoting and encouraging the transfer of new technology in manufacturing, including for handicraft; (c) Establishment and development of industrial infrastructure by creating a coordinating mechanism for investing in transport infrastructure (road, rail, air and port) by linking to targeted industrial areas; and by direct energy supply to major production zones by ensuring the most sufficient and stable electricity supply, which allow factories to plan their production effectively; (d) Financing measures by continuous implementing the Financial Sector Development Strategy 2011-2020 as the framework for financial sector development in Cambodia; as well as by preparing appropriate finance mechanism for industrial development by way of providing financing to SMEs in priority industries.

In addition to the above mentioned policy measures and action plans, the Royal Government implemented four key concrete measures by end 2019 to ensure that the vision, objectives and goals of the IDP are realized:

(1) Prepared and implemented a plan of reduced electricity tariffs for industrial and commercial purposes including strengthened reliability and expanded coverage of electricity supply. The Royal Government introduced the electricity tariffs reduction and price differentiation schedule for the industrial and commercial purposes toward 2020.

(2) Developed and implemented a master plan for transport and logistic system development with the aim of creating an integrated and highly effective multimodal transport and logistics system, focusing on connecting the major economic poles and the three economic corridors, Phnom Penh – Sihanouk Ville, Phnom Penh – Bavet, and Phnom Penh – Poipet, to become key national economic corridors

through the construction of internationally standards highways and the setup of an effective logistics system.

(3) Further strengthened labor market mechanisms and skills training development in order to ensure stability of the labor supply, increase productivity, and improve living standards of workers by promoting skills training programs, strengthening the mechanism for setting minimum wage, and enhancing harmony in industrial relations based on the principles of positive union and the kindness of employers towards their employees. In this regard, Labor Advisory Committee and the Cambodia Productivity Committee are the existing mechanisms.

(4) Developed and transformed Sihanouk Province into a model multi-purposed Special Economic Zone, following the concept of Special Administrative Region. Accordingly, a master plan, legal and regulatory framework and other administrative arrangements are being developed and designed to provide full authority and jurisdiction for mobilization of resources, talents, investments, and businesses. The province is now an industrial, trade and tourist hub of Cambodia in line with sustainable and environmentally sound development concepts, and is now being considered as the ASEAN Green Industry and Metropolitan City.

The targets of Industrial Development Policy 2015-2025 in certain key areas through structural transformation and the respective achievements by 2019 are being reflected through the following performance indicators:

(1) **TARGETS:** Transforming and strengthening the industrial structure in the national economy by increasing the GDP share of industrial sector to 30 percent in 2025 from 24.1 percent of GDP in 2013 with the manufacturing sector growing from 15.5 percent in 2013 to 20 percent in 2025.

ACHIEVEMENTS: In 2019, the share of Industry in Cambodia's GDP was 34.23 percent, thereby already surpassed the 2025 target. As per Asian Development Bank's Asian Development Outlook 2018 report, Cambodia's manufacturing sector accounted for 31 percent of Cambodia's economy in 2016, and thereby surpassed the 2025 target.

(2) **TARGETS:** Increasing and diversifying export products by increasing the export of manufacturing products (non-textile products) to 10 percent of all exports by 2020 and 15 percent of all exports by 2025, Garment and Footwear to 55 percent of all exports by 2020 and 50 percent of all exports by 2025, increasing exports of processed agricultural products to 10 percent of all exports by 2020 and 12 percent of all exports by 2025 as well as exporting new products.

ACHIEVEMENTS: The following export product groups represented the highest dollar value as well as percentage share of overall exports in Cambodian global shipments during 2019: (i) Knit and crochet clothing, accessories – USD8.8 billion (35 percent of total exports); (ii) Clothing, accessories (non-knit or crochet) – USD4.1 billion (16.3 percent); (iii) Gems, precious metals – USD3.8 billion (15percent); (iv) Footwear – USD2.5 billion (10 percent); (v) Leather / animal gut articles – USD1.5 billion (6.1 percent); (vi) Electrical machinery, equipment – USD579.5 million (2.3 percent); (vii) Furniture, bedding, lighting, signs, prefabricated buildings – USD526.8 million (2.1 percent); (viii) Vehicles – USD516 million (2 percent); (ix) Cereals – USD440.8 million (1.7 percent); (x) Plastics, plastic articles – USD312.4 million (1.2 percent). The above statistics reflected that the Cambodia's exports of 2019 surpassed the IDP targets.

(3) **TARGETS:** Strengthening of the management mechanism and development of SMEs by promoting their official registration including large enterprises and promoting good corporate governance with proper accounts and balance sheets. By 2020 target, to officially register 80 percent and by 2025 target, to officially register 95 percent of SMEs, out of which 50 to 70 percent of them to have accurate accounts and balance sheets.

ACHIEVEMENTS: Statistically, the 2018 Annual Report of Cambodia's Ministry of Industry and Handicraft, newly named Ministry of Industry, Science, Technology, and Innovation indicated that SMEs play a significant role in contributing to Cambodia's economy as they accounted for 70 percent of employment, 99.8 percent of companies and 58 percent of GDP. The development of SMEs is significant for the robust and resilient economic growth of Cambodia. However, in terms of the above target of official registration and having proper accounts and balance sheets, it is yet to be achieved by end of 2019.

In conclusion, it requires to be mentioned that the rapid transformation of global and regional architecture combined with the geopolitical landscape have visibly highlighted the opportunity for Cambodia's industrial development. In the framework of regional economic liberalization and integration, especially with the establishment of the ASEAN Economic Community (AEC) and the Regional Comprehensive Economic Partnership (RCEP), Cambodia will secure its physical and institutional connectivity, along with its full economic integration, which will contribute toward opening new market opportunities, attracting investment, and securing technology transfer to Cambodia.

As a whole, the rate of structural industrial transformation in Cambodia is expected to be defined by three important pre-requisite factors, namely, Change in Regional Cost Structure along with labor costs; Trend in Regional Industrial Connectivity whereby Cambodia is favorably situated; and the Trend to ensure reliability of the Supply Chain to mitigate risks arising mainly from geo-political factors and other unexpected events.

CHAPTER-TEN
CAMBODIA'S FOREIGN RELATIONS—POLITICO AND SOCIO-ECONOMIC CONTEXTS

Cambodia, in its glory days of the Khmer Empire from the 9th to the 15th century, was a major power in Southeast Asia in terms of military might, diplomacy and trade. But the collapse of the empire combined with internal conflict signaled the beginning of the dark ages of Cambodia including colonization, and conflict. Nevertheless, during the last three decades, the country has proved its potential by starting a promising new chapter, one in which it pursues its core national interests, most notably stability, sovereignty, economic development, diplomatic ties, and image building. After successful regional integration, Cambodia is very much on its way to becoming a lower middle-income country with annual GDP growth of around 7 percent.

However, with the changes of the international landscape, for example with the rise of China and the U.S. rebalancing to Asia, new regional challenges are emerging. In order to deal successfully with these challenges and to become a relevant player within the region, Cambodia requires to have a grand strategy for its foreign policy with an integrated set of principles and priorities to navigate a complex and dangerous international environment toward achieving its national interests.

While looking at what the Cambodian government has done with its foreign policy to date, it appears that Cambodia's grand strategy rests on three pillars:

(1) The first of those pillars could be termed as the 'Asian Century'. It is getting gradually clear that the gravity of global power has shifted to the Asia-Pacific and the 21st century is shaping up to the Asian century, with most countries in the region, such as China, India, and the ASEAN countries, among them Cambodia, enjoying strong economic growth in recent years. China, the world's second largest economy after the United States, is also ASEAN's largest trading partner. While Cambodia has focused most of its diplomatic efforts on ASEAN and other ASEAN-led regional forums, such as the East Asia Summit, it has also strengthened its existing diplomatic ties with major powers in the region, such as China and Japan by upgrading its diplomatic relations to the level of strategic partnership in 2010 and 2013, respectively.

Cambodia has also extended its diplomatic relations with countries like Belarus and Azerbaijan, with a hope to promote economic and trade relations. This signals another major shift in its foreign policy, from political diplomacy to economic diplomacy. In a regional context, ASEAN and its Dialogue Partner countries have been negotiating comprehensive free trade deals, such as the Regional Comprehensive Economic Partnership (RCEP). All these efforts are designed to reap the benefit of regional integration, and represent a golden opportunity for Cambodia to focus on the Asia-Pacific to sustain its economic growth. In the context of the Asian century, ASEAN should remain the cornerstone of Cambodia's foreign policy. But Cambodia also require to balance its economic, military and political interests among its immediate neighbors as well as China, the U.S. and ASEAN. Cambodia is reasonably well aware that this balancing is needed to be done with skill if it wishes its gradual, increasing prosperity over the long term.

(2) The second pillar is post-conflict Cambodia, which has been favorable for its own development effort. The post-cold War period offered Cambodia both challenges and opportunities for development and proactive engagement with the regional and international communities. Today, one of the major priorities

of Cambodia's foreign policy is to put all round diplomatic efforts to rebuild its prestige in the region. Cambodia, today, is asserting active foreign policy in order to mobilize resources and international assistance for its development, especially in physical infrastructure and poverty eradication. After decades of civil war and chaos, Cambodia has been slowly improving its status in regional and international forums. During the last three decades, Cambodia's government has been exhibiting its vision which entails democracy, rule of law, good governance, a free market economy, and peace and stability in order to reap opportunities and address challenges in the long run.

(3) The third pillar is Cambodia's observance of a set of six foreign policy principles, described in Article 53 of its Constitution. First, it follows a strict policy of permanent neutrality and non-alignment. Second, Cambodia maintains a policy of peaceful co-existence with its neighbors and with all other countries. Third, it will not invade any country, nor interfere in any other country's internal affairs, and shall solve problems peacefully. Fourth, Cambodia is prohibited from having any military alliance or military pact with any other country that is incompatible with its policy of neutrality. Fifth, it shall not permit any foreign military base on its territory and shall not maintain its own military bases abroad, except within the framework of United Nations Peacekeeping missions. Sixth, it reserves the right to receive foreign military assistance and training of its armed forces for self-defense purposes.

The annual conference of Cambodia's Ministry of Foreign Affairs and International Cooperation wrapped up in the last week of January 2020 with several key observations and messages on international politics and Cambodia's foreign policy priorities. In that conference, Cambodian leaders expressed their view that the world order is in transition towards multi-polarization or even a multiplex world where old and new global actors, state and non-state actors are dynamically interacting and are evolving along a complex, uncertain and dangerous trend. Cambodia re-iterated their beliefs that multilateralism and rules-based international order are the keys in maintaining world peace, promoting shared prosperity and addressing emerging global issues. No country can singly address such interconnected and complex global issues. Therefore, international collaboration and partnership is needed. Addressing the closing ceremony of the annual conference, Cambodian Prime Minister Hun Sen stressed that rules-based international order and multilateralism are under assault in the recent years because of protectionism and unilateralism. He also mentioned that small and weaker countries are becoming more vulnerable to fast-evolving global geopolitics at varying degrees. Simultaneously, he raised questions concerning who creates the rules, who enforces the rules and who are affected by the rules. Heightening power competition and rivalries between major powers, foreign intervention and international sanctions are posing significant threats to international peace and stability. Striking a balance between national interests and international responsibility is a real challenge nowadays. For Cambodia, maintaining a balance and permanent neutrality in its external relations is not easy, but it is a must. PM Hun Sen maintained that Cambodia could achieve peace, stability, and prosperity only if the country could protect independence, sovereignty, and neutrality. Prime Minister Hun Sen set out five main tasks in foreign policy: (i) protecting independence, sovereignty, territorial integrity and neutrality, and maintaining peace, security, social order and social unity; (ii) effectively implementing the slogan, 'expanding international friends based on the spirit of independence'; (iii) promoting economic diplomacy to attract more foreign direct investments and expand export markets for Cambodian products; (iv) supporting and strengthening multilateralism to address emerging global issues and challenges, enhance rule-based international order and work towards the realization of sustainable development goals; and (v) increasing the capability and professionalism of diplomats.

Compared to its fellow ASEAN members, Cambodia enjoys a unique position. First, it has maintained closer relations with China. Second, Cambodia is not a claimant state in the South

China Sea. Third, Cambodia has balanced foreign policy interests and objectives with regards to its neighbors and ASEAN. Cambodia's government has established diplomatic relations with most countries, including the United States, the United Kingdom, France, all of its Asian neighbors, to include the People's Republic of China, India, Japan, Vietnam, Laos, South Korea, North Korea, and Thailand. Cambodia is also a member of most major international organizations, including the United Nations and its specialized agencies such as the World Bank and International Monetary Fund. Cambodia is also a member of Asian Development Bank (ADB), a member of ASEAN, also a member of WTO. In 2005, Cambodia attended the inaugural East Asia Summit.

MAJOR BILATERAL RELATIONS

1. Cambodia – Vietnam relations

Cambodia and Vietnam share a land border and share historical links as being part of the French colonial empire. During the period of the Vietnamese emperor Minh Mang (1820-1841), Cambodia was brought under Vietnamese control with the occupation of Phnom Penh. State-encouraged Vietnamese settlement in Phnom Penh accelerated, and in order to weaken Khmer resistance, Vietnamese occupying forces spirited away native Cambodian leaders like Ang Mey to inland Vietnam. However, the policy of direct rule became inconvenient and expensive for the Vietnamese Court because of Khmer uprisings in southern Vietnam during 1840-1845. They finally opted to keep Cambodia as a tributary state after the death of Minh Mang. Cambodia became a vassal state under Vietnam and Siam after the Siamese-Vietnamese wars in the 1830s and in 1840s. The Thai-raised King Norodom of Cambodia (1860-1904) signed a treaty with the French Empire in 1863, granting them mineral exploration rights in exchange of security from Thai and Vietnamese attacks. However, during the French colonial rule, French authorities imported Vietnamese laborers to Cambodia who subsequently started to dominate businesses and water resources in the country. Cambodia and Vietnam established diplomatic relations in 1967. During the Vietnam War, the Viet Cong used Cambodia as a base to fight. The United States Army also bombed Cambodian territory in pursuit of Vietnamese communists, resulting in deaths of nearly 150,000 Cambodians. In 1975, Khmer Rouge opposition came to power in Cambodia, shortly before the fall of Saigon to Northern forces. In 1979, Vietnam overthrew the Khmer Rouge through Cambodian-Vietnamese War, and established the People's Republic of Kampuchea. By late 1989, Vietnam officially withdrew its troops from Cambodia. Subsequent chronology of Cambodia's political history vis-à-vis Vietnam's role have already been mentioned in the earlier chapters of this book. It is evident that Cambodians have had long cultural ties with Vietnamese people. In terms of recent political events, in 2005, Cambodia and Vietnam signed a supplementary treaty to the original 1985 Treaty on Delimitation of National Boundaries. Accordingly, Cambodia would have to give up two of its villages to Vietnam in return for keeping two villages that was deemed Cambodian territory according to the 1985 treaty, Thlok Trach and Anlung Chrey. It was not known which two villages Cambodia would have to give up. To resolve the dispute, the Cambodian government announced in 2011 that it would speed up the demarcation process with Vietnam. The year 2017 marked 50 years of diplomatic relations between Cambodia and Vietnam. During this period, the relationship ebbed and flowed with changing geopolitics and domestic politics in both the countries. Despite all constraints, linkages between the two countries seem to expand to all the areas beyond political and defense aspects. Although Cambodia has tilted towards China economically in recent years, the strong relationship between Vietnam and Cambodia has seemingly endured with frequent official visits on a wide range of topics highlighting the push for cooperation. However, still some complexities are visible in the ties between these two neighboring countries. Cambodia is the only country with which Vietnam has not yet finalized border demarcation. In December, 2018, when both the Prime Ministers Nguyen Xuan Phuc of Vietnam and Hun Sen of Cambodia met, both sides agreed to speed up the border demarcation process which has already completed 84 percent of the 700 miles border line. In January 2019, Vietnamese National Assembly Chairwoman Nguyen Thi Kim Ngan met with Cambodian leaders on the sidelines of the 27th Annual Meeting of the Asia Pacific Parliamentary Forum (APPF-27) to enhance further border collaboration. In February 2019, the 10th meeting on cooperation and development of border provinces between the two nations was convened to promote border security ties and the upgrading of border checkpoints as well as infrastructure projects and further cooperation. In March 2019, Vietnamese President Nguyen Phu Trong visited Cambodia in his second overseas trip in office. His visit was being seen as a reiteration of Vietnam's policy to view Cambodia as an important strategic neighbor, with which Vietnam shares many common interests and regional concerns.

Defense ties between the two countries have also been strengthened over the past few years, with Vietnam providing the Royal Cambodian Armed Forces with military equipment, infrastructure, and training. In this regard, the defense ministers of the two countries signed the Protocol and Plan for cooperation in Ho Chi Minh City in March 2015. Prior to the above meeting of the Defense ministers of the two countries, in February 2015, the Cambodian army inaugurated a military maintenance, repair and overhaul (MRO) facility funded by the Vietnamese defense ministry. In early February 2015, the military headquarters of Vietnam's southern province of Tay Ninh and the Cambodian province of Tbong-Khmum signed a MOU on military cooperation focusing on seven areas of cooperation, including combating trans-border crime, mutual support on border delineation, land marker planting, and maintaining public order. In December 2018, Vietnam's Defense Minister Ngo Xuan Lich paid an official visit to Cambodia for discussions on defense cooperation, ranging from military information dissemination to the repatriation of Vietnamese soldiers' remains from Cambodia.

Since the 1990s, the economic relations between the two nations have begun to improve. Both Cambodia and Vietnam are members of multilateral regional organizations, namely, ASEAN and the Mekong-Ganga Cooperation. These days Cambodia and Vietnam find themselves more closely attached through economic relations. Bilateral economic ties between Cambodia and Vietnam have been expanding dramatically in the last few years. In 2019, Vietnam was Cambodia's fourth largest trading partner. The volume of bi-lateral trade reached USD3.8 billion in 2017, an increase of about 25 percent over the previous year, while it was around USD2.3 billion in 2010. In 2018, the figure rose to nearly USD4.7 billion, up a further 24 percent (United Nations COMTRADE database on international trade). It was projected that the bi-lateral trade to reach USD5 billion in 2020. However, because of coronavirus pandemic, such target surely could not be met. While Cambodia's imports from Vietnam was USD3.79 billion in 2018, it was only USD1.2 billion in 2007. During the first eight months of 2019, Cambodia's imports from Vietnam hit USD2.866 billion, a year-on-year increase of 18.3 percent. Significant growth was seen in aquatic products by 54 percent, steel and iron products (62 percent), chemicals (34 percent), and garments and textiles (28 percent). Similarly, Cambodia's exports to Vietnam reached USD683 million during the first eight months of 2019, an year-on-year increase of 3.2 percent. Six out of nine export products of Cambodia enjoyed robust growth, including fruit and vegetables, cashew nut, soybean, rubber, machinery, and spare parts.

The two nations also have a blueprint for promoting border trade with the planned construction of 116 warehouses along the border crossings of Vietnam, Cambodia, and Laos, highlighting the scope for growth in this trading relationship. As of 2018, Vietnam was among the top five investors in Cambodia, with cumulative registered investments of approximately USD3 billion. Metfone, a telecommunications company backed by Vietnam's Viettel group, was assessed to be the most valuable brand in Cambodia. In 2019, Vietnamese tourists made up the second largest proportion of inbound arrivals in Cambodia, only behind China. Vietnam exported USD1.2 billion worth of goods to Cambodia in 2007. While Cambodia is only the 16th largest importer of Vietnamese goods.

Vietnam, in addition, extended aids in various forms to Cambodia in order to strengthen their bi-lateral ties. In 2017, Vietnam agreed to fund the construction of an administrative building inside the Cambodian National Assembly as a USD25million gift. In 2018, Vietnam offered 930 scholarships to Cambodian nationals for both degree and non-degree programs in different training areas. Vietnam also opened high quality Vietnamese hospitals and schools in the capital city of Phnom Penh.

2. Cambodia – Thailand Relations

A major part of Cambodia's history has been shaped by its relations with Thailand and Vietnam. To prevent the two neighbors, Siam, as Thailand was called, and Vietnam, from swallowing Cambodia, King Norodom invited France on 11 August 1863 to make Cambodia its protectorate. Cambodia remained under France's rule until 9 November 1953. Relations between the newly elected Cambodian Government after the UN-sponsored election in 1993 and Thailand were rather complicated given the Thai Military and business groups' continuing trade relations with the outlawed Khmer Rouge. Article 10 of the Paris Peace Agreement stipulated that 'upon entry into force of this Agreement, there shall be an immediate cessation of all outside military assistance to all Cambodian Parties'. Thailand, however, as reported, indirectly continued to finance the Khmer Rouge's survival through gemstone and timber business deals in the Khmer Rouge territories. Following the outlawing of the Khmer Rouge in July 1994, First Prime Minister of Cambodia Prince Ranaridh appealed to all nations (though primarily aiming at Thailand) to bar Khmer Rouge members from their territory and 'arrest those outlaws'. However, successive Thai governments until 1996 constantly faced pressure from the Thai military and business interest groups to authorize them to engage in logging and the buying of gemstones from the Khmer Rouge. In spite of Thailand's business relations with the outlawed Khmer Rouge, the new Cambodian coalition government had little choice but to accept this reality. Cambodia's relations with Thailand (under Hun Sen and Thaksin, respectively) during the early 2000s were very cooperative. Along with Thai investments and exports to Cambodia, Thai movies and serials dominated TV screens in Cambodia. Even before coming to power, Thaksin had already made a personal investment in the telecommunications industry in Cambodia through his company known as CAMSHIN (i.e. 'Cambodia Shinawatra'), which saw the revenues from sales and services rise from 3.7 billion baht in 2002 to 4.3 billion baht in 2003. In addition, 'sister cities programs' along the border were also encouraged to promote regular contacts among the peoples of both countries. In June 2001, Cambodia and Thailand also signed the MOU regarding the Area of their Overlapping Maritime Claims and 'vowed to make use of the Joint Commission (JC) for Bilateral Cooperation, first established in 1995, to promote all areas of cooperation including the issues of border demarcation and maritime delimitation through the Joint Border Commission (JBC)'. However, Cambodia's close relations with Thailand came to a halt in January 2003. The problem stemmed from the appearance of an article on January 18, 2003 in a small Cambodian newspaper, Rasmei Angkor (light of Angkor), which alleged that a Thai actress had stated Angkor Wat properly belonged to Thailand and she looked down (on Cambodians) by saying that she was reincarnated, she would rather be a dog than be a Khmer national. The alleged interview could not be verified, even if many Cambodians believed that it was true. The immediate impact of the story was infuriation among Cambodians, who had always held a view that Thai people always looked down upon them. The problem got out of hand on 29th January 2003, when riots led to the burning of Thai embassy and destruction of several other well-known Thai business establishments. Hundreds of Thai immigrants fled Cambodia to avoid the violence. In Bangkok, hundreds of Thais responded to the violence by protesting outside the Cambodian embassy on the same day. The country's emblem and sign were ripped off the compound wall and burned along with shredded Cambodian flags. This eventually led to the Thai government to down grade diplomatic relations with Cambodia. Thailand also demanded an apology, an investigation, and compensation for the damages incurred. Cambodia was apologetic and agreed to pay compensation worth about USD50 million. After Cambodia made the initial instalment of the compensation sum, compromise was reached and relations were normalized.

Once diplomatic relations were restored, investments and cross-border trades resumed. While bilateral trade in 2002 reached USD445 million, the figure rose to USD1 billion in 2006. Even after Thaksin ousted by the coup in late 2006, relations between Cambodia and Thailand were not severely affected. Following the signing of MOU on labor cooperation between Cambodia and Thailand on May 31, 2003 (which spelled out how to send new migrant workers legally) and registration rounds conducted by the Thai government (which offered opportunities for undocumented workers to register) in 2004, some 110,000 Cambodian migrant workers were able to receive their legal work permits. The Thailand Migration Report 2019 suggested that there are nearly 1.7 million to 2 million Cambodian migrant workers in Thailand, with 20 percent being undocumented.

In December 2007, the two countries agreed in principle to introduce the 'single visa' scheme to facilitate tourists' entry, i.e. tourists need to apply for their visa at a single place only in order to visit Cambodia and Thailand. However, such plan was finally actually implemented in December 2012.

Between 2008 and 2011, the border around the ancient Khmer temple of Preah Vihear (Phra Viham in Thai), UNESCO World Heritage Site, was the site of repeated clashes between Thai and Cambodian troops. Open conflict was put on hold when Cambodia submitted the dispute to the International Court of Justice in 2011. More than two years later, the Court confirmed Cambodia's ownership over part of the disputed territory, leaving the adjacent area subject to bilateral negotiations.

Relations between the two countries also plunged to a record low when Thaksin, who was in exile, was appointed as an economic advisor of the Cambodian government in November 2009, in defiance of Thailand's request to extradite Thaksin to Thailand. In protest, Thailand, on November 5, 2009, recalled her ambassador from Cambodia. Cambodia followed suit on November 6, 2009. Thailand's foreign ministry revoked the 2001 MOU on overlapping maritime boundaries between the two countries on November 10, 2009. However, in late August 2010, when Thaksin decided to quit his post as an economic advisor to the Cambodian government citing his personal difficulties in fulfilling his role effectively, relations between the two countries started to improve again. Ambassadors to both countries were reappointed immediately after that. In early September, 2010, both sides agreed to waive visa requirements for each other's citizens to mark the 60th anniversary of their relationships. In July 2011, Thaksin's sister's party, Pheu Thai Party won a landslide victory in Thailand's national election. Yingluck, Thaksin's sister, became the Prime Minister of Thailand. Cambodian-Thai relations have been relatively amicable since then. They preferred to leave aside the contentious issue of border disagreement. In the aftermath of the 2014 coup, Thailand shifted its diplomatic stance by adopting an amicable attitude. Thai Prime Minister of the Junta Government Prayuth Chan-ocha has, so far, been keen to amend its ties with Cambodia. Cambodian Prime Minister also responded positively towards improvement in bilateral relations.

In terms of economic and trade relationship between the two countries, it is noteworthy that the relationship has improved significantly in recent years. The volume of trade between Cambodia and Thailand was USD6.18 billion in 2017, up almost 10 percent over 2016. Cambodia – Thailand trade volume was USD8.38 billion in 2018 as indicated by the Thai government source. Trade between the two countries grew by 12 percent to USD9.4 billion in 2019, increasing from USD5 billion in 2015. Trade is very heavily one-sided. Exports from Thailand to Cambodia were valued at USD5.2 billion in 2017, a rise of almost 13 percent from the previous year. Thailand exports to Cambodia was USD6.95 billion during 2019, according to the United Nations COMTRADE database on international trade. Latest data from Cambodia's Ministry of Commerce showed that Cambodia exported some USD2.27 billion worth of products to Thailand in 2019, up 195 percent compared to a year earlier. Spokesperson at the Cambodia's Ministry of Commerce, said that the Government has been working hard to minimize the trade deficit with Thailand.

3. Cambodia – Philippines Relations

Cambodia and Philippines formally established their diplomatic relationship in August 1957. Between 1958 and 1965, Philippine interests in Cambodia were overseen and managed by the Philippine Embassy in Saigon, Vietnam and at some point by the Philippine Embassy in Bangkok. The first resident diplomatic mission in Cambodia was established in 1965. On March 1975, the Philippine government closed the Embassy in Phnom Penh when the defeat of the Lon Nol government by the Khmer Rouge became imminent. In January 1995, after a 20-year hiatus in diplomatic relations, both the countries formally re-established their diplomatic relationship. Both Cambodia and Philippines have been maintaining cordial ties since then.

If we go to the history, it reveals that prior to European colonization, the people of Cambodia and the southern Philippines had traded with each other through the barter system for hundreds of years. The trade was negated after Spain subjugated and took control of the Philippines in the 16th century. There is historic record of commercial contact between Cambodia and Spanish Manila in the seventeenth century. Cambodia was a source of boat building for Philippines because of the excellent timber that used to come from the country's forests. When Cambodia became a French Protectorate, some of the Filipino troops were transferred to Cambodia and assigned as palace guards and cannoneers for King Norodom 1. King Norodom 1 visited Manila in 1872 as part of a goodwill tour of several countries. Before ending his Philippine visit, he made arrangements to bring a group of Filipino musicians to Phnom Penh to form the Royal Brass and Reed Band. The Filipino militia and musicians settled in Phnom Penh and outlying areas and married into Khmer and Vietnamese families. General Sosthene Fernandez, the son of one of the Filipino musicians, became a police chief and, later, a prominent politician in Cambodia. President Lon Nol, after Prince Norodom Sihanouk was deposed in 1970, appointed Gen. Fernandez as the Commander-in-Chief of the Khmer National Armed Forces. In more contemporary times, during 1992-1993, Filipinos were commissioned as peacekeepers for the United Nations Transitional Authority in Cambodia (UNTAC).

Both Cambodia and Philippines are now the members of the Association of Southeast Asian Nations (ASEAN). Political and economic relations between the two countries remain strong despite a rift in early 2012 over the ASEAN's failure to issue a joint declaration on territorial disputes in the South China sea. Cambodia also stopped an ASEAN unified stance in 2016 using the case ruling that the Philippines won against China. However, political observers believe that Cambodia's such stance on the issue may impact in future its own longstanding territorial disputes with Thailand since the significance of the Philippines' case against China is identical to the dispute of Cambodia with Thailand. In December 13-14, 2016, Philippine President Rodrigo Duterte visited Cambodia as a part of his regional tour of Southeast Asian states ahead of Philippines' ASEAN chairmanship in 2017. As reported that the Cambodian side had rolled out the red carpet for Duterte, upgrading the visit from a working visit to a state visit, with King Norodom Sihamoni taking the time to meet him and hosted a royal banquet at the Royal Palace.

During the above visit of President Duterte, substantively, four agreements were signed: (i) a Memorandum of Understanding on transnational crime involving the police forces; (ii) two memoranda of agreements on labor and sports cooperation; (iii) an implementation program of tourism cooperation out to 2020 that included establishing more direct flights between the two countries; and (iv) exchange program for students. The authorities of both the countries expressed their opinion that these agreements were important to deepen bilateral cooperation between the two countries. In this context, it would be meaningful to mention some of the major (already in place) agreements between the two countries are: (i) Agricultural and Agribusiness cooperation (September 2015); (ii) Cultural Agreement (June 2015); (iii) Rice trade (April 2013); (iv) Air Services (Aril 2012); (v) recognition of Training and Certification for Seafarers (October 2002). Coming back to Duterte's December 2016 visit, apart from the agreements, Duterte also stressed to spur Cambodian investment into the Philippines. Cambodian Prime Minister Hun Sen also congratulated Duterte on the Philippines' assumption of the ASEAN's chairmanship for 2017, the 60th anniversary year of the bilateral relationship of the two countries, while Duterte emphasized that both the countries had a common stake in keeping ASEAN strong, relevant and responsive.

In a bid to boost defense cooperation, Philippines-Cambodia Joint Defense Cooperation Committee (JDCC) inaugural meeting was held in March 2019 in Phnom Penh. Both sides, as reported, discussed a string of regional defense and security issues and ways on how the two countries can further boost cooperation to face these challenges.

In terms of trade and business relationships, Cambodia's exports to Philippines during 2019 was USD84.72 million, as per United Nations COMTRADE database on international trade. On the other-hand, Cambodia's imports from Philippines was USD32.85 million during 2018 (UN COMTRADE database). As of 2019, the footprint of Philippine businesses in Cambodia is still quite small. However, their operations are growing rapidly. By end-2019, there are more than 50 Filipino businesses. These companies are engaged in everything from brewing and food production to aviation and telecommunications. Cambodia is home to more than 6000 Filipino nationals.

4. Cambodia – Indonesia Relations

Cambodia and Indonesia have shared a close historical, cultural and political relationship. However, the closeness between the two countries in terms of economic cooperation still needs to be strengthened in order to bring greater benefits to the people of both the nations. The relationship between ancient Indonesia and Cambodia dated back from the Kingdom of Chenla, Javan Sailendra and also Srivijaya. As it was mentioned in the history that King Jayavarman 11 had resided for some times in Java during the reign of Sailendras, and in 802 declared sovereignty of Cambodia from Java and proclaimed himself as universal monarch, thus started the Angkor period.

Bandung Conference, also known as the Asia-Africa Conference, was held in April 1955. The landmark conference which was attended by Cambodia also, led to the establishment of the Non-Aligned Movement. Indonesia and Cambodia, in 2019, celebrated the 60th anniversary of their diplomatic relations that were initiated on February 1959. During Sukarno administration in the 1960s, the president of Indonesia visited Cambodia. Similarly, as an exchange goodwill visit, Prince Norodom Sihanouk also visited Indonesia. Indonesia was one of those countries that provided troops in 1992 for United Nations Transitional Authority in Cambodia to assist the country in its security and peace effort. In 1999, Indonesia also welcomed and supported Cambodia's membership in ASEAN.

In the area of culture, we have observed striking similarities between 9th century Bakong and Borobudur temple. It suggests that Borobudur was served as the prototype of Bakong. There must had been exchanges of technical as well as architectural details, besides travelers, between Khmer Kingdom and the Sailendras in Java. Both nations have similar archaeological heritages that are held as UNESCO World Heritage Sites. During ASEAN Tourism Forum in Manado, North Sulawesi, in January 2012, both the temple of Borobudur and Angkor Wat were proclaimed as sister sites. During this event, the sister cities agreement between Yogyakarta and Siem Reap was also proposed. Indonesia with its experience on Borobudur restoration projects, lent its architectural expertise on Angkor preservation efforts. Not only that, Indonesia also provided financial aid to Angkor restoration project, especially for the three main gates of Angkor Royal Palace archaeological site.

In the area of security, both Cambodia and Indonesia historically shared a close military relations. Back in 1972, Indonesian Kopassus trained and assisted the formation of Cambodian Para-Commando Battalion. Cambodia and Thailand agreed to allow Indonesian monitors to go to the border between the two countries to help prevent further military clashes as both Cambodia and Thailand trusted Indonesia as a fair and impartial observer to solve intra ASEAN disputes. Accordingly, Indonesia was appointed as observer in Cambodia -Thai border dispute in 2012.

In terms of economic relations, Cambodia and Indonesia signed a free visa agreement in June 2010. The governments of Indonesia and Cambodia had agreed at a meeting between the two countries' foreign ministers in February 2018 to strengthen relations through the enhancement of bilateral mechanisms, particularly aimed at improving economic cooperation, especially in the area of investment, trade, and tourism. Before that, Indonesian Ambassador to Cambodia Sudirman Haseng observed that investment cooperation between Indonesia and Cambodia, considering six decades of bilateral relations, has not developed rapidly. As of end 2019, Indonesian investment in Cambodia was about USD350 million. As of end 2019, no Indonesian state-owned enterprises (SOEs) or companies had invested directly in Cambodia. However, there is an increase in interest from Indonesian entrepreneurs to invest in Cambodia. Indonesian businessmen and SOEs were encouraged to start doing business by utilizing natural resources in Cambodia that were relatively unexplored and had yet to be optimally managed.

Trade cooperation between Cambodia and Indonesia, unlike investment, has been relatively good. The trend of trade balance between the two countries during the five-year period from 2013 to 2017 had continued to increase by an average of 10.86 percent. The total bi-lateral trade value between Indonesia and Cambodia jumped to a record high of USD661.11 million in 2019. It was USD542.23 million in 2017, an increase of 19.9 percent from the 2016 bi-lateral trade value of USD452.19 million, while their bi-lateral trade volume was only USD220 million in 2012. Cambodian exports to Indonesia surged to USD42.59 million in 2019, a significant increase from USD25.37 million in 2016. Thanks to the then Cambodia's Ambassador to Indonesia – Hor Nambora. Commodities imported by Indonesia from Cambodia included apparel, rice, rubber, and footwear. Meanwhile, Cambodia is also a potential alternative market for Indonesian products. Indonesian products that have, so far, penetrated the Cambodian market comprise packaged food and beverage products, home care and automotive products, personal care, pharmacy, batik, and motor vehicles. Indonesian pharmaceutical products are currently well-known among the Cambodian public, according to Indonesian government sources. The Indonesian Embassy in Phnom Penh holds annual business meetings, and trade promotions, such as the Indonesian Trade and Tourism Promotion (ITTP) event in order to help more Indonesian potential products penetrate the Cambodian market. Similarly, Cambodia also has been arranging its export-import exhibition.

Cambodia is more fortunate, unlike in trade, in the tourism sector as more Indonesian tourists visit Cambodia than Cambodians visiting Indonesia. This is partly because Indonesia has a much larger population than Cambodia. In 2018, the number of Indonesian tourists visited Cambodia had reached 55,753 people, while 8,819 Cambodian tourists had visited Indonesia in the same year. The number of Cambodian tourists visiting Indonesia has been increasing by about 15 percent per year. But the Indonesian government's target to increase it at an average of 20 percent in the coming years following a rise in the number of middle-class people in Cambodia. Nevertheless, it is rightly assumed that the absence of direct flight service between the two countries posed major obstacles towards increase in tourist arrivals in both the countries. Both the governments have already taken initiative to open direct flight in the Jakarta and Phnom Penh flight route.

Finally, both Indonesian and Cambodian governments stressed that sound economic cooperation and relations between the two nations are not only about efforts to seek benefits from each other but also to help each other to improve the welfare of people in both the countries.

5. Cambodia – Malaysia Relations

Diplomatic relations between Cambodia and Malaysia was formally established on 31st August 1957. However, the Malaysian embassy in Phnom Penh was closed in 1975 after the Khmer Rouge regime reached the capital and took power of the country. Following the signing of the Paris Peace Accord on 23rd October 1991 and establishment of the United Nations Transitional Authority in Cambodia, Malaysia re-opened its embassy in Phnom Penh on 26th November 1991. Since then, both the countries expressed their repeated commitments time to time to strengthen their bilateral relationship in trade, investment, tourism, and security. The bilateral relations between the two nations have always been supported by the Kings of both the countries.

Cambodia and Malaysia acknowledged that the area of defense cooperation needed to be strengthened through more training and information sharing. In September, 2019, after a bilateral meeting between the then Prime Minister of Malaysia Dr. Mahathir Mohamad and Prime Minister Hun Sen of Cambodia, the two leaders reiterated the growing threats of terrorism and radicalism globally, hence better coordination in terms of security needs to be established between the two countries. They also underscored the importance of security cooperation, especially in maintaining peace and stability in light of the security challenges and threats in the region. Both the leaders also encouraged the relevant agencies to continue strengthening the framework agreed upon in terms of employment and to further promote close cooperation and coordination to promote the rights and to address the welfare of Cambodian migrant workers in Malaysia. The leaders took the opportunity of their meeting in Phnom Penh in September 2019, to exchange views on regional and global issues of common interest and concern, including cooperation amongst ASEAN member states, issues related to the South China Sea, developments in Rakhine State, counter-terrorism and other current global issues.

In terms of trade, in 2019, Cambodia was the 8th largest trading partner of Malaysia among the other Southeast Asian nations. In 2018, the value of Cambodia-Malaysia trade was USD558 million. In the first seven months of 2019, the value reached USD484.9 million, an increase of 42.1 percent compared to the corresponding period of last year. Goods exported from Malaysia in 2019 included petroleum products, textiles, footwear, processed food, chemical products and transport equipment. During the first six months period of 2019, petroleum products exported from Malaysia amounted to USD167.9 million, while textiles, apparel and footwear were valued at USD44.5 million. Processed food exports recorded USD30.7 million and Chemical products exports were valued at USD18.3 million. Exports of transport equipment from Malaysia to Cambodia during the period amounted to USD13.5 million. Meanwhile, in 2019, Malaysia became the largest Cambodian rice importer among ASEAN members. Top products imported from Cambodia to Malaysia during the same period of 2019 included textiles, apparel and footwear (USD33.1 million), natural rubber (USD9.4 million), palm oil and palm-oil based products (USD2.5 million), electronics products as well as optical and scientific equipment (USD1.5 million). In 2019, Malaysia's the then Prime Minister Dr Mahathir Mohamad visited Cambodia with his main agenda to witness the signing of the Double Taxation Avoidance Agreement (DTA) between the two countries. The agreement was also hoped to boost investment and trade between the two countries. Cambodia was the last country in the region to sign the agreement with

Malaysia, which would supposedly bring long-term benefits for the business community in both the countries.

In terms of investment, Malaysia is the fifth largest foreign investor in Cambodia during 2014-2019, according to a report from the Council for the Development of Cambodia. The country attracted a total investment of USD481 million from Malaysia during 2014-2018. However, between 1994 to 2006, Malaysia was on the top of Cambodia's foreign investors ranking and then gradually fell to fifth place. Speaking at the seminar in October 2019, Malaysia's Ambassador to Cambodia said that Malaysia would soon be able to get to second place. Early August 2019, IG Tech Group, a Cambodian Enterprise, signed a MOU with four Malaysian tech companies aiming to bring new solutions to the Cambodian market in key areas, such as, cyber security, systems to combat money laundering, school support systems and insurance solutions. Malaysia's banking sector has also established a presence in Cambodia. Besides Maybank, other financial institutions include CIMB, RHB, and Public Bank. To increase the investment volumes between Cambodia and Malaysia, the top leaders of both the countries agreed to allow the institutions concerned in the two countries to explore ways to further expand their cooperation in this field. Both the countries shared their views that the Regional Comprehensive Economic Partnership (RCEP) will contribute to regional economic integration and growth as well as in safeguarding multilateral trading system.

Towards cooperation in the tourism sector, in September 2019, the Prime Ministers of Malaysia and Cambodia signed the latest MOU. The Cambodian Prime Minister Hun Sen said that the two countries were considering the use of one visa for two countries, meaning that foreign tourists getting visas to enter Malaysia can also visit Cambodia and vice versa. Cambodia's Ministry of Tourism reported on 14th August 2019 that during January to June 2019, tourists arrivals from Malaysia were 91,905, a 7 percent increase in numbers compared to the corresponding period of 2018.

6. Cambodia – Singapore Relations

Cambodia and Singapore established their diplomatic relationship on 10th August 1965, immediately after Singapore became an independent country. Cambodia was one of the first countries to recognize Singapore's independence. The year 2020 marked the 55th anniversary of the diplomatic relations between Cambodia and Singapore. The diplomatic ties between the two countries were suspended in 1975, but the trade relations continued. Cambodia's diplomatic ties with Singapore resumed in 1992 after the signing of the Paris Peace Agreement in 1991. During the Khmer Rouge regime, in 1980s, Singapore provided timely humanitarian assistance to Cambodia in order to rehabilitate and reconstruct the economic sectors essential to its needed economic growth. Singapore had been a key supporter of Cambodia during the oppressive period of Khmer Rouge. Singapore had also played a major role in the post-war economic recovery as well as reconstruction of Cambodia. It resulted in a strong bilateral relations between the two nations and its people. In fact, both the countries maintained excellent overall relations that continue to grow and work in building a united and cohesive Association of Southeast Asian Nations or ASEAN. This relationship was strengthened through continuous exchange of visits by the countries' government leaders. All these high-level visits have resulted in the promotion of Singapore's foreign direct investment in Cambodia, enhancement of human resource development in Cambodia, and tourism development plan for Cambodia. Both the countries have been working closely on technical cooperation through the Singapore Cooperation Program (SCP). In 2002, Singapore established the Cambodia-Singapore Training Centre in Phnom Penh under the Initiative for ASEAN Integration to train Cambodian officials The Cambodia-Singapore Training Centre was upgraded to a Singapore Cooperation Centre in 2018 in order to boost economic integration and the adoption of technology in the region.

In terms of trade, it is noteworthy that in 2019, Singapore

was one of Cambodia's top five trading partners. In 2017, bilateral trade was valued at USD3 billion. In the same year, Singapore was Cambodia's second largest investor with more than USD250 million in approved fixed-asset investments. During 2019, Singapore's exports to Cambodia was USD2.27 billion, and Singapore's imports from Cambodia was USD2.1 billion according to the United Nations COMTRADE database on international trade. The Cambodian Commerce Minister during his official visit to Singapore in July 2019, met with Singapore's Minister of Trade and Industry and discussed boosting bilateral trade, particularly by increasing the number of agricultural goods that Singapore buys from Cambodia. Both the Ministers mentioned that enhancing trade cooperation between the two countries is in line with the ASEAN policy of boosting regional trade.

7. Cambodia – Laos – Myanmar- Vietnam (CLMV) Relations

The CLMV is a sub-region within ASEAN. The CLMV sub-region consists of four countries, namely, Cambodia, Lao PDR, Myanmar, and Vietnam. All the four countries are also members of global and regional organizations, such as the United Nations, World Bank, Asian Development Bank, and ASEAN. The countries of the CLMV sub-region are relatively new members of Association of Southeast Asian Nations (ASEAN). Cambodia joined ASEAN in April 1999, while Laos and Myanmar in July 1997, and Vietnam in July 1995. The admission of these four countries into ASEAN widened its political, economic and cultural diversity. CLMV nations share a number of similarities, while they differ, among other things, in terms of their economic priorities as well as the size of their markets. While talking about the similarities, CLMV economies are primarily agro-based – transitional economies – insufficient infrastructure – lack of strong institutions for a shift to a market economy. Although CLMV have been experiencing a high rate of growth and certain degree of macroeconomic stability in recent years, they are still facing major challenges especially towards narrowing gaps in wealth among the population, and in addressing development gaps within the region. While Vietnam, even within CLMV, has attained comparatively high levels of economic development, per capita income, and industrialization, the other members of the sub-region still have comparatively low per capita income and limited skilled human resources. Each country in CLMV is having different development constraints. But CLMV, as a group, has a great potential for sustainable development depending on individual country efforts and supports from development partners within and outside the region.

We noticed that the CLMV countries started getting admission into ASEAN from the mid-1990s onwards, just when economic integration of ASEAN -6 was accelerating. Before the admission of the CLMV countries, economic disparities had already been existing within and between the six older members of ASEAN. Such economic disparities grew larger in ASEAN-10, with the admission of CLMV countries. Since economic disparities perceived to be a hindrance to economic integration, there were fears that ASEAN-10 may become irrelevant in the global economy if effective integration cannot take place because of the economic divide within the region. Therefore, integrating the transitional economies of the CLMV countries with those of the older ASEAN members has always been one of regional grouping's greatest challenges. ASEAN leaders agreed in November 2000 to launch the Initiative for ASEAN Integration (IAI) program to narrow the development gap between it's older and newer members, as well as to strengthen the latter's capacity, capability, and resolve to meet the challenges towards enhancing the grouping's competitiveness in the world market. Accordingly, a six year IAI Work Plan (July 2002-June 2008) was formulated and launched in August 2002. In this context, it is to be noted that economic integration has been a trend during the last two decades. Broader regional integration in East Asia have also been started. During the first East Asia Summit in December 2005, leaders from ASEAN countries, China, Japan, South

Korea, India, Australia, and New Zealand vowed to focus on, among other things, promoting cooperation in development, economic integration and growth, eradicating poverty and narrowing the development gap in East Asia through technology transfer and infrastructure development, capacity building, good governance and humanitarian assistance. The Fourteenth East Asia Summit was held in Bangkok, Thailand on November 4, 2019. American delegation to the summit was headed by the country's National Security Advisor. United States Secretary of Commerce was also in the delegation. It is more likely that economic disparities may increasingly become even more pronounced and therefore more of a concern in the context of East Asian regional integration. ASEAN including CLMV must be aware of that and should be ready to address the situation.

The Eleventh CLMV Economic Ministers' meeting was held on 5th September 2019 in Bangkok, Thailand. In that meeting, the ministers noted the favorable growth of CLMV's trade and investment. CLMV's merchandise trade continued on an upward trend, not only in terms of value, but also as percentage of ASEAN's total trade. In 2018, CLMV's total merchandise trade amounted to USD541.5 billion, which was 19.3 percent of ASEAN's total merchandise trade. In 2018, foreign direct investment (FDI) into CLMV grew by 4.2 percent, amounting to USD23.5 billion, while it was USD22.5 billion in 2017. The percentage of CLMV's contribution to ASEAN's total FDI slightly decreased to 15.2 percent in 2018, while it was 15.3 percent in 2017.

CLMV Economic Ministers commended the progress in the implementation of the CLMV action Plan 2019-2020. In the first six months of implementation period, the 29th Vietnam Expo held on 10-13 April 2019 in Hanoi, and the Viet-Laos Trade Fair 2019 held on 27June-1July 2019 in Vientiane, Laos. An 'Assessment of Legal and Regulatory Frameworks on Electronic Commerce in CLMV' was being undertaken to identify the gaps in regulatory framework and capacity building needs of CLMV countries to facilitate e-commerce, particularly in the MSMEs in order to access the wider market place. Also workshops on 'Consumer protection in Online Transaction' – an activity related to the project of 'E-tourism: An Innovative Approach to Tourism MSMEs in CLMVs', was held in April 2019 in Hanoi, Vietnam. The project delivered a guiding manual to serve as a reference for government authorities in designing their respective domestic policies and regulations. The Ministers jointly endorsed the Framework for CLMV Development, which aims to provide a unified strategy for CLMV countries to become a sustainable middle-income economy by 2030. The framework comprises three main aspects, namely connectivity, enablers and sectors with comparative advantage. The focused areas of connectivity are transportation and facilitation, logistics hub, internet backbones, digital readiness, and financial services, which will be supported by strong legal institutions, competent workforce, and access to sufficient electricity to create a conducive business environment. Cooperation in agriculture and food, and tourism will be enhanced in order to increase the competitiveness of these sectors that have comparative advantages in all CLMV countries. The CLMV countries, as an advanced global business hub, will be physically connected to facilitate trade, investment, tourism, and other economic activities.

8. Cambodia – Japan Relations

The modern relations between Cambodia and Japan started when the two countries first established their diplomatic relations in 1953. The relationship subsequently improved when King Norodom Sihanouk made an official visit to Japan in 1955 to sign a friendship treaty between the two countries and Japan's adoption of a resolution of gratitude regarding Cambodia's act of abandoning the rights to claim reparation from Japan after World War 11. The bilateral relations were disrupted from mid 1970s to early 1990s after Khmer Rouge cut diplomatic ties with Japan in 1975. After 1979, although new government in Cambodia was established, but Japan did not have official relations with that government. Japan reopened its embassy in

Phnom Penh in 1992, after the Paris Peace agreement and conflict resolution in 1991. Cambodia reopened its embassy in Tokyo in 1994. At the end of the Cold War, Japan actively returned to Cambodia through its official development assistance (ODA), peace building and national reconstruction efforts.

Japan has been Cambodia's biggest donor since 1992. Japanese aid placed emphasis mainly on rebuilding Cambodia's infrastructure, which had been destroyed by years of war and negligence. Japan has been helping directly to construct roads, bridges, and irrigation systems, connecting rural areas to major cities across the country and improving the lives of many Cambodians. Japan provided millions of dollars in Grant Aid in strengthening the healthcare system in Cambodia. In early 2014, Japan gave USD11.5 million to expand Cambodia's National Maternal and Child Health Center. In 2016, Japan's Sunrise Healthcare Service Co. opened the first Japanese hospital in Cambodia by spending more than USD35 millions, which is equipped with state-of-the-art healthcare equipment and highly trained medical staff. There are many more healthcare initiatives in Cambodia which were funded by Japan.

Japan has also been working closely with the Cambodian Government to strengthen the country's education system, which remains weak and underfunded. Many schools have been built with Japanese aid. In addition, hundreds of Cambodian students receive scholarships each year either from private funding or from the Japanese government to pursue their studies in Japan and other countries. Japan has been consistently providing aid in monetary terms to address the problem of skills shortages, particularly in the area of science, technology, and engineering. Since early !990s, Japan's financial assistance to Cambodia went beyond economic development and poverty reduction to include country's governance issues. The Japan International Cooperation Agency (JICA) which is tasked with coordinating Japan's official development assistance to developing countries, has been providing Cambodia since 1993 with technical assistance and financial resources to reform its legal and judicial system, promote gender equality, and improve public finance management.

Japan and Cambodia also signed a memorandum to strengthen their defense cooperation. It is true that the rise of China has shaped the relations between Cambodia and Japan in many important ways. However, expecting Cambodia into choosing Japan abandoning China is unrealistic. Because, as a small developing country, Cambodia requires to engage with all countries and seldom can afford to isolate itself from a major economic power, whether that be Japan or China. To become an upper middle- income country by 2030, as Cambodia has targeted, the country needs to embrace economic restructuring and revamping its manufacturing sector. Japan can play a major role in Cambodia in that direction.

From 2010, Japan's participation in Cambodia's economic development has been remarkable. Japanese investment increased from USD35 million in 2010 to USD328 million in 2012, nearly tenfold. According to Japan External Trade Organization (JETRO) in Cambodia, the number of registered Japanese businesses also surged from 19 in 2010 to 195 in 2013. Japan started to operate its direct commercial flight to Cambodia since September 2014, encouraging more Japanese tourists and investors to come to the country. JETRO also reported that in 2015, Cambodia ranked among the top countries as an investment destination for Japanese firms. More specifically, from 1994 to the first quarter of 2019, the Council for the Development of Cambodia approved 137 projects being carried out by Japanese companies with a total capital investment of about USD2.5 billion. As per sources from Cambodia Chamber of Commerce, more Japanese investors are also turning to the Kingdom, especially within the Phnom Penh Special Economic Zone and in Koh Kong province. As per report from the National Bank of Cambodia, during January to September 2019, Japanese-owned companies accounted for eight percent of Cambodia's total exports to the international market.

Bilateral trade between Cambodia and Japan increased by nearly 13 percent in 2019, compared with 2018, as the Japan

External Trade Organization (Jetro) reported. It said that during January to November 2019, Cambodia and Japan's bilateral trade totaled USD2.1 billion, a 12.95 percent increase compared to same period in 2018 when trade reached USD1.86 billion. Cambodia's export to Japan were worth nearly USD1.60 billion in 2019, up by 7.7 percent from USD1.48 billion in 2018. Cambodia's imports from Japan were worth USD502.88 million in 2019, up by 33.9 percent from USD375.70 million in 2018. It would be relevant to note that Cambodia maintained a positive trade balance with Japan during the period. Cambodia mostly exported garments, footwear, electronics, and bicycles to Japan.

9. Cambodia – Russia Relations

Diplomatic relations between Cambodia and USSR were established on May 13, 1956. King Norodom Sihanouk of Cambodia, in December 1991, announced the recognition of the Russian Federation as the successor state to the USSR. The Soviet Union, and subsequently Russia, played an active part in unblocking the Cambodian conflict, initiating and concluding the Paris Peace Agreement in 1991, and implementing the United Nations peacekeeping mission during 1991-1993. Meanwhile, in 1990, the USSR promoted the recognition of Cambodia by the United Nations as an independent state. Subsequently, the signing of a Joint declaration on the Basics of Friendly Relations in 1995 was of great importance towards developing bilateral legal framework between the two countries. The bilateral relationship between the two nations has noticeably strengthened since early 2000. The beginning of highest level dialogue was started by the meeting of the Prime Minister of the Russian Federation Dmitry Medvedev with the Cambodian Prime Minister Hun Sen on the margins of the 9th East Asian Summit in November 2014 in Myanmar. The Chairman of the Government of the Russian Federation visited the Kingdom, for the first time in the history of bilateral relations, in November 2015. The signed joint documents following the talks between Dmitry Medvedev and Cambodian Prime Minister Hun Sen, were aimed, among others, at expanding cooperation in the bilateral trade and investment, law enforcement, information and humanitarian fields including the intergovernmental agreement on air traffic, the MOU and partnership between the Ministry of Economic Development of Russia and the Investment Promotion Council of Cambodia, the MOU between the State Atomic Energy Corporation 'Rosatom' of Russia and the Ministry of Environment of Cambodia on cooperation in the field of nuclear energy for peaceful purposes, etc. The first post-1991 visit of the Prime Minister of Cambodia to Russia took place in May 2016. During this visit, a weighty package of joint documents, following negotiations between Dmitry Medvedev of Russia and Hun Sen of Cambodia, was signed, including, among others, joint statement between the Ministry of Economic Development of Russia and Ministry of Commerce of Cambodia on the list of projects of Russia-Cambodia trade, economic and investment cooperation up to 2020. Cambodian Prime Minister Hun Sen also took part in the 20th anniversary of 'Russia – ASEAN' dialogue partnership in Sochi during May 18-20, 2016, and had a conversation with Russian President Vladimir Putin. The heads of the two governments met again in November 2017, October 2018, and November 2018 during 12th East Asian Summit in Manila (Philippines), ASEM summit in Brussels (Belgium), and Russia – ASEAN summit in Singapore respectively. The parliamentary dimension of bilateral cooperation is also developing dynamically. Contacts between the two countries, are also maintained through the judiciary. Defense cooperation has been strengthened during the last decade.

In terms of trade and economic cooperation, trade between Russia and Cambodia amounted to USD202.4 million in 2018, an increase of 21.5 percent compared with 2017; while bilateral trade between Cambodia and Russia was USD94.7 million in 2012. More remarkably, bilateral trade linkages between the two nations had expanded from USD10.8 million in 2006 to USD202.4 million in 2018. Cambodia's exports to Russia totaled USD191.1 million in 2018, an increase of 18.3 percent over 2017; while it was USD88.8 million in 2012. Cambodia's imports from Russia was USD11.6 million in 2018, an increase of 117.5 percent over 2017; while it was USD5.9 million in 2012. The positive balance of Cambodia in trade with Russia was USD179.5 million in 2018. Cambodia's export items to Russia, in 2018, were mainly textiles and textiles products (94.7 percent), leather raw materials, furs and products from them (2.1 percent), foodstuffs and agricultural raw materials (1.6 percent). Cambodia's imports from Russia, in 2018, were mainly machinery, equipment and vehicles (60.1 percent), mineral products (19.1 percent), chemical products (13.6 percent), wood and pulp paper products (3.3 percent). In early 2020, Cambodia and Russia have pledged to further increase bilateral trade and investment as the Kingdom aims to diversify its market through the signing of a free trade agreement (FTA) with the Eurasian Economic Union (EAEU), of which Russia is a member, together with Armenia, Belarus, Kazakhstan, and Kyrgyzstan. It has a total market of 183 million people and a GDP of USD5 trillion. Amongst the ASEAN nations, Singapore and Vietnam also have an FTA with the EAEU, while Indonesia, Malaysia and Thailand are also known to be interested.

In terms of tourism, Cambodia welcomed some 55,653 Russian tourists in 2019 and hopes to welcome an increasing number in the future. Cambodia has also students studying in Russian universities, and a history of student exchanges that date back to the Soviet era. These educational linkages will help to strengthen the bilateral relationship and will impact Kingdom's long-term policy decisions.

10. Cambodia – India Relations

Cambodia and India formally established diplomatic relations in 1952, with the first visit to the newly independent nation by an Indian Prime Minister in 1954. Cambodia's late King Norodom Sihanouk reciprocated an official visit to India in late 1954, just a few months ahead of Bandung Conference. Both countries were the architects of the non-aligned movement originated from Bandung Conference. King Sihanouk's neutral foreign policy was largely inspired by India's Jawaharlal Nehru, whose government, in terms of its foreign policy, followed the principles of non-interference, neutrality, territorial integrity, and respect for sovereignty. Cambodia and India have been enjoying friendly relations for a long time. However, despite close relations, bilateral relationship between the two nations were disrupted after Pol Pot regime took control of the country in 1975. But after the fall of Khmer Rouge regime, in 1981, Indian Prime Minister Indira Gandhi, who came to power after winning the election in 1980, decided to normalize bilateral relations with the Phnom Penh government. Accordingly, India became the first country to recognize the government of the People's Republic of Kampuchea led by Heng Samrin and resumed the diplomatic relations in 1981. Both Europe and the United States refused to recognize the Samrin government at that time and even imposed diplomatic isolation and economic embargoes against the Vietnam-backed regime in Phnom Penh. On the other hand, India's Indira Gandhi government continued to emphasize that Cambodians needed more economic and diplomatic support during that challenging time. India's such consistent support made it one of the few friends Cambodia could rely upon during that Cold War era. Again, in the late 1980s, under Rajiv Gandhi's premiership, India made noteworthy contributions to Cambodia's peace process. India took constructive political and diplomatic roles to carry out the withdrawal of Vietnamese forces from Cambodia and a peaceful settlement of Cambodia's conflicts. More particularly, India played an active role to facilitate dialogues between Cambodian political factions. India sent its Minister of state for external affairs to New York in October 1987 to meet Sihanouk, Cambodia's former head of state. That meeting was a groundbreaking measure, paving the way for the Paris meeting in December 1987 between Sihanouk and then Foreign Minister Hun Sen for the first time. Again, before the second meeting between Sihanouk and Hun Sen in Paris in January 1988, Hun Sen took decision to visit India to hold talks with Rajiv Gandhi. The meeting between Hun Sen and Sihanouk in January 1988, with India's mediation, helped kick-start regional efforts to broker peace in Cambodia. India's recognition of the Phnom Penh government and consistent sincere effort to support peace-making in Cambodia still plays a vital role in today's relationship between the two nations. Cambodian Government headed by Hun Sen hails India's consistent practice of the principles of neutrality and non-interference. Cambodian Prime Minister Hun Sen also conveyed his full support for India in 2000, to become a permanent member of the United Nations Security Council (UNSC).

Cambodia-India cultural and historical relations are more than a millennium old when Indian religion, culture, and trade emanated out of India and spread in various parts of Southeast Asia. Some Scholars are of the opinion that the religious and cultural connect between the two nations date back to 1st century. Built between 12th to 14th centuries, the magnificent structure of Angkor Wat temple is a glorious testimony of pervading influence of temple architecture of India. Indian influences are also visible on the other earlier temples of Cambodia such as Preah Vihear of Lord Shiva built from late 9th century onwards, Angkor Thom, Ta Phrom, Bayon, and other historical sites. Cambodian Society which is now predominantly Buddhist, also retains a strong influence of Indian Hindu and Buddhist rituals. In order to strengthen old age close cultural links, Cultural Exchange Program (CEP) between Cambodia and India was signed in 2000 which has been renewed from time to time. During the State Visit of Prime Minister Hun Sen to India in January 2018, the CEP has been renewed for a further period of four years till 2022. In terms of cultural assistance, Government of India had sent experts from Archaeological Survey of India for restoration and conservation of Angkor Wat temple from 1986-1993. The excellent work carried out by Indian experts is still appreciated by Cambodia. India also, in 2018, committed to help part restoration of ancient temple of Preah Vihear.

Over the past decade, as China becomes Cambodia's largest trading partner and plays an increasingly important role in the country's development, Cambodia apparently has been moving closer toward Beijing. However, with the emerging role of

India in the region, Cambodian government understands that it needs to balance relations with both Asian powers to secure maximum benefits, ranging from economics to security to politics. The bi-lateral relations have been reinforced by several high-level visits since post-colonial era until recently. In January 2018, Prime Minister Hun Sen paid a state visit to India and also participated in the ASEAN-India Commemorative Summit and as Guest of Honor at the Republic Day Parade 2018 along with other ASEAN Leaders. In the context of India's current 'Act East Policy' and the ASEAN, Cambodia is an important interlocutor and a trusted partner. Contemporary times have witnessed expansion of bilateral cooperation in diverse fields such as institutional capacity building, human resource development and extension of financial assistance in infrastructure projects, social security projects and capacity building in defense.

Cambodia-India defense ties also have been growing in recent years, with frequent goodwill visits by Indian naval forces. India expressed its determination time to time in fighting against terrorism, transnational crime, and extremism, ensuring stability, security, and peace in the region. It is also expected that India as a member of the recently revived 'Quad', the four way security dialogue which consists Japan, Australia, the United States, and India, will put its efforts to defend 'freedom of navigation and overflight' and 'rules-based international order' especially in the South China Sea.

Both Cambodia and India are members of the Mekong-Ganga Cooperation (MGC) mechanism. Therefore, besides bilateral partnership route, both the countries can enhance cooperation and relations through MGC initiative, which consists of six members – India, Cambodia, Myanmar, Thailand, Laos, and Vietnam. MGC initiative was launched in 2000, aiming to shore up cooperation in the areas of tourism, culture, education, and transport. Under MGC initiative, beginning from 2015-2016, India has been assisting Cambodia with small Socio-Economic projects known as Quick Impact Projects in the fields of agriculture, health, women empowerment, capacity building, sanitation, environment and information technology every year. As reported, these projects have received overwhelming response from the masses and created a distinct and visible impact among the beneficiaries.

In terms of trade relations, as per data from the Indian embassy in Cambodia, Cambodia-India trade has been growing steadily in the last few years. In 2019, bilateral trade volume reached USD249.92million, up 10.24 percent over 2018's USD226.69 million. Bilateral trade stood at USD188.02 million in 2015, a 10.66 percent increase over 2014 (USD169.90 million). Cambodia's exports to India reached USD82.09 million in 2019, from USD42.36million of 2015. On the contrary, Cambodia's imports from India were USD167.83 million in 2019, while it was USD145.66million in 2015. Indian investment was worth USD19.8 million as of 2019. The country is among the top ten foreign investors in Cambodia. India's main investments are in machinery, agriculture, energy, construction and mining. During a recent working lunch meeting in early July 2020 between Cambodia's Minister of Commerce Pan Sorasak and Indian ambassador to Cambodia Manika Jain, both agreed to strengthen bilateral trade relations by establishing the Cambodia-India Joint Trade and Investment Working Group to facilitate trade and investment between the two countries. Cambodian Minister, during the meeting, also expressed willingness to explore the possibility of establishing a bilateral free trade agreement (FTA) with India to open a new market with the second largest regional economy. This came as FTA with China was scheduled to be signed in August 2020 while similar negotiations between South Korea and Cambodia have also been started.

11. Cambodia – France Relations

Cambodia and France have a special relationship because of their shared history. During the 19th century, the Kingdom of Cambodia had been reduced to a vassal state of the Kingdom of Siam. On 11th August 1863, Cambodian King Norodom signed a treaty acknowledging a French protectorate over his kingdom. The main reason for King Norodom to approach France was to protect Cambodia against their two neighboring countries: Thailand and Vietnam. Under the treaty, while Cambodian monarchy was allowed to remain, powers were largely vested to a Phnom Penh based resident general. Cambodia's military protection, foreign relations, and trade relations were in the hands of France. French viewed Cambodia as a buffer zone between southern Vietnam and the British-aligned Siam (as Thailand was called earlier). They hoped that by signing the treaty, they would be protecting their own interests in southern Vietnam. In turn, as mentioned earlier, Cambodia relied on French protection to stop Vietnamese invasions on the eastern border. In 1887, Cambodia was integrated into the French Indochina union along with the French colonies and protectorates in Vietnam (Cochinchina, Annam and Tonkin). In 1897, the ruling Resident General, with the approval from Paris and citing that King Norodom was no longer fit to rule, assumed the king's powers to collect taxes, issue decrees, and even appoint royal officials and choose crown princes. The King became the figurehead and patron of the Buddhist religion in Cambodia. In 1904, King Norodom died. The French passed the succession to Norodom's brother Sisowath, instead of passing the throne on to Norodom's sons. On 3rd May, 1941, Norodom Sihanouk became the king. In 1946. Cambodia was granted self-rule within the French Union. In 1949, Cambodia's French protectorate status was abolished. Cambodia finally gained its independence from French rule on 9th November 1953.

During French colonialism in Cambodia, French made lasting contributions to Cambodia's infrastructure, urbanism, and archaeology. Also, the provinces of Battambang and Siem Reap which were annexed by Siam in the 1790s, were returned to Cambodia after France had exerted pressure on the Thai. Cambodia was not absorbed by its neighbors, as seemed almost inevitable before the French stepped in. The site of Angkor returned to Khmer jurisdiction and French archaeologists could complete its seriously needed restoration work. At the same time, the colonial period had also several negative aspects. The major defect of the French protectorate was that it failed to educate Cambodian people. They prepared the country very poorly for independence. Until World War 11, there was no university in the Kingdom, and meagre number of high schools. Cambodia's French colonial system's another flaw was the judiciary. The French administration during its colonial era in Cambodia, put no sophisticated legal system in place. Almost no local lawyers and judges received adequate legal training.

France cultivated deep cultural and political relations with Cambodia since king Norodom and Napoleon 111 approved the protectorate in 1863. However, French did not exert much influence on Cambodia as they did in Vietnam. Khmer still remained widely taught and spoken in Cambodia during colonial era. When Cambodia became independent in 1953, the French language continued to be widely taught and used in the government. In terms of economy during the French rule, the colonial government's budget originally relied largely on tax collections in Cambodia as its main source of revenue. Infrastructure and urbanization grew at a much slower rate in the early years of French rule in Cambodia. However, as French rule straightened after the Franco-Siamese War, development slowly began in Cambodia, where rice and pepper crops allowed for the economy to grow. Colonial entrepreneurs who had been granted land concessions in some provinces, introduced modern agricultural methods to foster exports. Economic diversification continued throughout the 1920s. Infrastructure and public works were also developed, and roads and railroads were constructed in Cambodian territory during the French rule. Industries were later developed but primarily designed to process raw materials for local use or for export. Foreigners dominated the work force of the economy, while higher positions were given to the French. After 1953, in the area of trade and commerce, national flavor automatically started to prevail.

France played a major role in facilitating the Paris Peace Accord in 1991. French companies are now more firmly established in Cambodia than those of any other Western country. France's economic presence in Cambodia is based both on investments from major companies like Vinci, Total, Accor, BRED, etc., and many SMEs of French business people. Trade between France and Cambodia continued to grow to reach Euro 1billion in 2017, up 8.6 percent over 2016. In 2018, bilateral trade between Cambodia and France rose by 9.2 percent year-on-year as reported by Cambodia's Ministry of Commerce. In 2018, Cambodia's exports to France worth more than USD1.1 billion, with the textile sector making up the largest share. France's exports to Cambodia, which mainly comprised agri-food products and pharmaceuticals, were valued at USD111million in 2018, the report shows. France is the third largest importer of Cambodian goods in the EU and therefore it is a very important market to Cambodia. Cambodia's main exports to France, besides textiles and garments, are footwear and rice. Cambodia mostly imports, besides medicines, wine and spirits and machinery from France (June11,2019, Khmer times).

As of 2019, French cooperation is remarkably visible in the scientific and academic spheres of Cambodia, in order to improve mainly the quality of teaching, the value of qualifications, and the professionalization of courses of study. The Agency for French Education Abroad (AEFE) through its Cambodia chapter, is providing French-language teaching through bilingual classes, French-speaking courses of study in higher education, teacher training, and diversified educational options, and it had, in 2017-2018, over 1,100 students, 60 percent of whom were Cambodians. France is also providing close cooperation to Cambodia in the area of heritage by co-chairing the International Coordinating Committee for the Safeguarding and Development of the Historic Site of Angkor and helping to restore several temples. The French Development Agency (AFD), since its inception in 1993 in Cambodia, has been helping to develop infrastructure and industry in the country. The AFD has invested Euro 300 million in Cambodia during 2012-2018, as reported by French Foreign Ministry.

In the area of tourism, Cambodia and France witnessed a regular growth in the number of tourists travelling between the countries in the recent years. In addition, a delegation from French travel agency Atout France, a government institution which works in partnership with public and private organizations in France to promote the country as a tourism destination, paid its first-ever visit, to Cambodia in June 2019 (June 13, Phnom Penh Post). Atout France's visit, as Cambodia Association of Travel Agents strongly believe, was very important for tourism development in Cambodia as it provided an opportunity for the Kingdom to be widely promoted as a holiday destination in France.

12. CAMBODIA – AUSTRALIA RELATIONS

Cambodia and Australia established diplomatic relations in 1952. Australia's strong support for the Cambodian Peace Process in the late 1980s and early 1990s, including Australia's leading role in the United Nations Transitional Authority in Cambodia (UNTAC, 1992-1993), is still well appreciated by the Cambodian people. Australia also supported the Extraordinary Chambers in the Courts of Cambodia (ECCC) to investigate and prosecute senior leaders of the Khmer Rouge regime and those most responsible for atrocities committed between 1975 and 1979. From 2004 to 2020, Australia contributed AUD44.05 million to the ECCC. As of 2019, Australia and Cambodia work together on a range of common strategic interests in regional and global contexts. Both the countries are co-members of the East Asia Summit (EAS), the ASEAN Regional Forum, and Asia-Europe Meeting (ASEM).

In terms of defense and security, Australia's modest defense cooperation program aims to assist Cambodia to develop a modern, outward-looking defense force that contributes to regional security and stability. Key focus areas for the bilateral defense engagement between Cambodia and Australia, include training and education, maritime security, and organizational reform to support the professionalization of the Cambodian Royal forces.

Australia's Anti-Money Laundering Assistance Team from the country's Department of Home Affairs and the Attorney General's Department have been assisting Cambodian officials, since 2018, with the skills to develop new laws and policies to address transnational crime. This largely helped Cambodia to develop new laws to more effectively share evidence internationally to prosecute transnational crime and to combat the financing of weapons of mass destruction. Also, Australia and Cambodia together have been working closely to combat people smuggling and trafficking, irregular migration, child sex tourism, narcotics trafficking, fraud and terrorism. In this regard, Cambodian law enforcement agencies are being assisted by an Australian Federal Police liaison office in Phnom Penh to deal with transnational crime.

People to people links between Australia and Cambodia have been forged through education, culture, and tourism. As per 2016 Census report, there are over 66,000 people of Cambodian origin living in Australia. Similarly, approximately 6000-7000 Australians reside in Cambodia, most being dual Cambodian-Australian citizens or expatriates engaged in development assistance work or business. Since 1994, more than 850 Cambodians have studied in Australia through the Australia Awards Scholarships Program. In 2019, more than 3000 Cambodians enrolled in Australian education institutes, making Australia the most popular English-speaking study destination for Cambodian students. More than 17,000 Cambodian students studied in Australia since 2002 – this includes university students, school students, VET, ELICOS (English Language Intensive Courses for Overseas Students). Since 2014, more than 1,900 Australian Students have studied and undertaken internships in Cambodia under the New Colombo Plan (NCP). The Cambodian Government and the private sector in Cambodia have been supportive of the NCP, including by offering internship opportunities.

In the area of tourism, in 2018-2019, there were 13,800 short-term visitors from Cambodia to Australia, an increase of 21.4

percent over previous year. On the other hand, approximately 127,430 Australians visited Cambodia in 2018 according to Cambodia's Ministry of Tourism.

In terms of bilateral trade and investment relationship between Cambodia and Australia, Cambodia's products are granted tariff-free access to Australia. Also, Cambodia and Australia have a bilateral market access agreement, concluded as part of Cambodia's accession to the WTO in October 2004. Bilateral trade between Cambodia and Australia reached USD196 million in 2019, up 32.6 percent from 2018, said the Australian Embassy in Phnom Penh. This includes an increase of 34.9 percent in Cambodian exports, while Cambodian imports increased by 24.8 percent in 2019. The Cambodian Chamber of Commerce (CCC) and the Australian Embassy in Phnom Penh pledged to promote trade and investment between the two countries, as it was announced in June 2020. Australia and Cambodia are also parties to the ASEAN – AUSTRALIA – NEW ZEALAND Free Trade Agreement which entered into force on 1st January 2010. Australia and Cambodia are also negotiating parties to the Regional Comprehensive Economic Partnership agreement. In 2019-2020, the Australian Government provided an estimated AUD66 million in total Official Development Assistance to Cambodia. This included an estimated AUD43.4 million in bilateral funding to Cambodia. Australian Embassy reported that Australia's aid to Cambodia during 2019-2020 compliments diplomatic and security efforts to address shared challenges including transnational crime, people smuggling and pandemics.

13. CAMBODIA – UNITED STATES RELATIONS

The United States and Cambodia, over the last several decades of the 20th century, established, broke off, and reestablished their bilateral relations as a result of armed conflict and government changes in Cambodia. Full diplomatic relations were established after the freely elected Royal Government of Cambodia was formed in September 1993. Before that, on November 11,1991, the U.S. Mission opened in Phnom Penh.

The U.S. lifted its embargo against Cambodia on January 3, 1992, thus normalizing economic relations with the country. The United States also ended its blanket opposition to lending to Cambodia by international financial institutions. In May 1994, the U.S. Mission was upgraded to a U.S. Embassy. In 1996, President Clinton signed a bill formally extending Most favored Nation (MFN) status to Cambodia. The U.S. Government subsequently designated Cambodia as a beneficiary under the Generalized System of Preferences (GSP) in 1997.

United States – Cambodia relations expanded remarkably after 2007, when Cambodia's political and human rights conditions improved and the U.S. government also lifted some restrictions on its assistance programs. Principal areas of U.S. engagement have included, among others, U.S. foreign assistance programs, demining activities, limited military assistance and cooperation, U.S. missing-in-action (MIA) recovery efforts, and U.S. naval port visits. During the November 2012 East Asia Summit in Phnom Penh, President Obama became the first incumbent U.S. President to visit the country. The United States have been working with Cambodia to further develop its democratic institutions and promote respect for human rights. The two countries also have been striving to increase bilateral trade and address challenges from promoting regional security to expanding global health and development. The United States continues to support efforts in Cambodia to improve nutrition for children, eliminate human trafficking and corruption, address environmental degradation, better manage natural resources, foster economic development, achieve the fullest possible accounting for Americans missing from the Indochina conflict in the 1960s and 1970s, and to bring to justice those most responsible for serious violations of international humanitarian law committed under the 1975-1979 Khmer Rouge regime.

In January 2019, U.S. Department of Defense Deputy Assistant Secretary for South and Southeast Asia Joseph H. Felter met with Cambodian military officials in Phnom Penh and discussed regional security issues and bilateral cooperation, including ways to improve defense ties and restart joint military activities, while in 2017, the Cambodian government unilaterally suspended Angkor Sentinel, an annual bilateral military exercise launched in 2010 that focuses on international peacekeeping, humanitarian assistance, and military-to-military cooperation; and also postponed indefinitely a U.S. humanitarian mission in the Kingdom, the U.S. Navy Mobile Construction Battalion (also known as Seabees), without explanation. Since 2008, the Seabees had worked with RCAF and performed more than USD5 million in community service projects throughout the country. In August 2019, at a US-ASEAN meeting, another positive note emerged when US Secretary of State Mike Pompeo praised Cambodia for 'protecting its sovereignty', putting a trust on the Cambodian Prime Minister's denial of a deal for Chinese Military presence in Cambodia. Phnom Penh viewed this remark as a step toward right direction by the United States.

After the factional fighting in 1997, the United States suspended bilateral assistance to the Cambodian Government. Since 1997 until recently, U.S. assistance to the Cambodian people has been provided mainly through non-government organizations in Cambodia. The United States provided roughly USD235 million in assistance related to good governance, democracy, and civil society between 1993 and 2018. Post-war Cambodia has been heavily dependent upon foreign assistance from major foreign aid donors, especially the United States, Japan, South Korea, Australia, and France. However, the Kingdom's reliance upon foreign assistance, while still significant, has declined gradually during the past decade-and-a-half. According to World Bank figures, Official Development Assistance fell from 120 percent of central government expenditures in 2002 to less than a third in 2018. The United States provided an estimated USD79.3 million in foreign assistance to Cambodia in FY2018, a decrease of 10 percent compared to FY2017. However, the Trump Administration's FY2019 foreign operations budget request reduced annual assistance to Cambodia by nearly 75 percent compared to FY2017.

In 1999, Cambodia and the United States signed a Bilateral Textile Agreement (BTA), a unique agreement that links labor standards to trade. The BTA has been an unqualified success. It has boosted Cambodia's image as a labor-friendly country and contributed significantly to its economic development by generating employment, as of 2019, for over 700,000 people and generating USD7 billion annually. The BTA is responsible for a robust and booming garment industry in Cambodia. Bilateral trade between Cambodia and the United States was valued at USD5.8 billion in 2019, a 37 percent increase compared with a year before i.e. 2018, the latest data from the US government shows. In 2018, trade between Cambodia and the U.S. reached USD4.26 billion, up 23 percent year-on-year. In 2017, US. – Cambodia bilateral trade was worth nearly USD3.46 billion, including USD3.06 billion in Cambodian goods exported to the United States. In 2019, Cambodia's exports to the World's largest market grew sharply by 40 percent, to USD5.356 million, while Cambodia's exports to the U.S. were valued at USD3.818 billion in 2018. Cambodia's exports to the US have increased remarkably since July 2016, when Cambodia was granted duty-free benefits for the exports of travel goods such as luggage, backpacks, handbags, and wallets under the Generalized System of Preferences (GSP) scheme. The United States remains the largest single overseas market for Cambodia's merchandise exports. Cambodia's imports from the United States rose by 15 percent, to USD513 million in 2019.

Tourism is another major sector of the Cambodian economy, accounted for 12.1 percent of the GDP in 2019. Cambodia welcomed 6.61 million international visitors in 2019, 6.6 percent more than in 2018, generating revenues USD4.92 billion in 2019. Since 1997, the United States has consistently been one of the top six providers of tourists to Cambodia, while in 2004, the U.S. ranked third after South Korea and Japan.

Cambodia and the United States belong to a number of the same international organizations, including the United Nations, International Monetary Fund, World Bank, and World Trade Organization.

14. CAMBODIA – CHINA RELATIONS

China has long traditional relations with Cambodia. The Sino-Khmer relationship has been sharing a historic and commercial relationship since the early twelfth century. A Chinese diplomat, Zhou Daguan, under the Emperor Chengzong of Yuan, arrived at Angkor in 1296 and remained at the court of King Indravarman 111 until 1297 (Hingham, 2001). He was the first Chinese representative to visit Khmer Empire. At modern time, after Cambodia gained full independence from France in 1953, the first diplomatic relations between Cambodia and China were established on July 19, 1958 and never officially broke after that. China, since then, have gradually developed its relations with Cambodia through various stages. In 1993, Cambodia's first democratically elected government came into power after Paris Peace Agreement in 1991. From 1993 to 1997, Cambodia's new administration had a close relationship with its major aid donors and FDI source countries, as the country was in urgent need for foreign aid, budget support, and FDI for reconstruction. Cambodia's major aid donors include countries led by Japan, the United States, and key European Union countries such as France and Germany. Similarly, major FDI source countries were Taiwan, Malaysia, Hong Kong, Vietnam, and Thailand in order. During this period, China maintained a stable bilateral relations with Cambodia, with China's intimate relationship with late King Sihanouk and royalist party FUNCINPEC.

Cambodia's 1997 conflict between its two major parties and major political leaders – FUNCINPEC's Prince Norodom Ranariddh and Hun Sen of the Cambodian People's Party (CPP), dramatically changed the Sino-Cambodia relations. Cambodia's major aid source partners decided to suspend the aid flow to Cambodia to contain CPP immediately after the military conflict broke out in 1997, and that was the time when China emerged with its full financial and diplomatic support for Cambodia. In return, Hun Sen shut down Taiwan's representative office and offered his firm support of the One-China policy. China and Cambodia, from then on, have gradually grown their close relation in every dimension.

During 1997-2013, before BRI (formerly known as OBOR) was launched, China's Cambodian policy, and its FDI and trade amount to Cambodia used to change according to mutual needs. China's aids to Cambodia became a central political tool in enhancing bilateral connection. The pattern of China's aid to Cambodia from 1997 to 2013 was relatively supply-demand base, in sense of the various types of aid projects. Industrial concentration and market orientation of Chinese capital flow to Cambodia emerged after 2008 and strengthened after 2012, when concept of BRI was initiated in 2013. In other words, before BRI initiative, during one and half decades of tentative gestation, cultivation, and development, China and Cambodia gradually developed solid mutual trust and interdependence, comprehensive cooperation, and a multi-level dialogue framework towards viable partnership. However, still China – Cambodia relation during these one and half decades should be considered as an extension of Cambodia's political history succeeding from late King Sihanouk's principles of neutrality, non-alignment, power balancing, internal stability, and national consolidation.

BRI is the first grand state strategy of China's government to utilize its foreign policy as an embodiment to externalize its domestic economic pressure (Shihlun Allen Chen, 2018). Based on China's need of a grand geopolitical strategy, internal economic overcapacity pressure, and hence industrial transformation needs, BRI is supposedly a response of regional economic and trade development strategy through large, systematic, and multilateral cooperation. BRI with more clear industrial focus on infrastructure, energy, communication technology, and finance, has clearly changed the original aid pattern and decision making of China's foreign policy. Accordingly, there are changes in the operation, process, and planning of China - Cambodia relations from 2013.

The major projects, under BRI implementation in Cambodia, that both China and Cambodia agreed upon are transportation and hydroelectric power infrastructures that have been under construction since 1997; and the other projects are based on Cambodia's National Strategic Development Plan: 2014-2018 and National Industrial Development Policy: 2015-2025. The Mekong River Development Plan is also core project in which both China and Cambodia are attempting to cooperate under a current complex multinational framework. Beijing has so far funded construction of seven hydropower dams that are collectively capable of generating half of Cambodia's entire electricity needs. China has also built about 3,000 kilometers (1,864 miles) of highways and numerous bridges since 1997. All these investments have turned China into Cambodia's largest foreign direct investor and closest ally. As a whole, after 2013, BRI appears to the Cambodian government as a great chance to gain economic benefit in infrastructure construction and industrial development. However, although Chinese investments have significantly contributed to Cambodia's economic growth, the benefits of Chinese money have not been widely shared with the local population. It appeared to have benefited only some privileged sections of Cambodian society, who own lands or operate businesses that cater to Chinese nationals. As reported, instead of hiring local workers, many Chinese businesses tend to bring workers from China, fueling resentment among Cambodians. A report published by Cambodia's Interior Ministry stated that over 250,000 Chinese nationals currently reside in the country. This is over 60 percent of all foreign residents in Cambodia. Cambodia's national Police website, in August 2019, quoted a secretary of state as saying that of the Chinese nationals living in the country, over 78,000 reside in Preah Sihanouk province and only 20,000 have work permits. The ministry also reported that from 2014 until the end of July 2019, more than 2,700 Chinese nationals were deported. Also it is widely alleged that Chinese workers are, in most cases, offered a higher wage than Cambodians. It is true that in the recent times, there is growing concern over Chinese domination of the local economy. However, amid those concerns and doubt how much the general public of Cambodians can finally benefit from China's investment and aids, Hun Sen administration has expressed its sincere and firm commitments time to time to ensure the benefits of the Cambodian masses while working as a beneficiary state within the parameter of China's grand strategy.

China has also been playing a key role in improving Cambodia's military inventory since 2010, when Beijing donated 250 jeeps and trucks to Cambodia's army after the US scrapped a similar plan. China has also been helping Cambodia by enhancing the capacity and expertise of the Royal Cambodian Armed Forces by offering training courses and providing military equipment and materials. In June 2018, China granted military aid of more than USD100 million during China's Defense Minister's visit to Phnom Penh to attend a China-Cambodia military exhibition. Cambodia has suspended joint military exercises with the United States indefinitely, but has held exercises with China twice since 2016.

Trade between Cambodia and China has increased since Cambodia's admission as a full member of the ASEAN in 1999. Two-way trade between the two countries stood at USD9.42 billion in 2019, while trade between Cambodia and China was USD4.8 billion in 2016. In 2019, China exported goods with a value of around USD7.53 billion to Cambodia, while the Kingdom exported USD1.3 billion worth of goods to the Chinese market in 2018, an increase of 37 percent year-on-year. Cambodia's current exports to China are milled rice, sliced and dried cassava, bananas, and corn. From China, Cambodia imports raw materials for garments, construction materials, and electronic devices. Cambodia has asked China to open the door wider for Cambodian products and not only of the agricultural type. Cambodia wants China to accept more garments as well as textiles and science-based goods among others (Khmer Times, 6th March 2020). The two countries began to discuss the feasibility of a bilateral FTA in December 2019 and launched the first round of negotiations in January 2020. Chinese Commerce Minister and his Cambodian counterpart jointly announced the completion of China-Cambodia Free Trade agreement (FTA) talks in July, 2020 (Global Times, 20th July 2020).

In terms of tourism, according to the Cambodian Ministry of Tourism, about 2 million Chinese tourists visited Cambodia in 2018, up 70 percent from a year earlier. The year 2019 marked the year of closer China-Cambodia cooperation in culture and tourism, as experts said. Cambodia's Tourism minister said that Chinese tourists topped the list of foreign visitors coming to Cambodia in the first 10 months of 2019, with 2.02 million, a 24.4 percent increase year-on-year, accounted for 38 percent of all of Cambodia's international tourists.

Conclusion

Current international geo-political and economic environment offered Cambodia both challenges and opportunities for development and proactive engagement with the regional and international communities. As of early 2020, diplomatic efforts to rebuild its prestige in the region is one of the priorities of Cambodia's foreign policy. Cambodia needs an active foreign policy so that it can mobilize resources and international assistance for its development, especially in reducing the distribution-gap of developmental benefits and poverty eradication. After decades of civil war and chaos, now is the time for Cambodia to improve its status in regional and international forums. Cambodia also requires a grand vision to reap opportunities and address challenges in the long run. This vision must entail its already accepted path of democracy, rule of law, good governance, a free market economy, and peace and stability.

CHAPTER-ELEVEN
COVID-19 : HEALTH, SOCIO-ECONOMIC, AND GEO-POLITICAL CONSEQUENCES IN THE WORLD

The continuing COVID-19 pandemic has become an international public health emergency. It has changed the world economically, socially and geo-politically as never before. While public health experts have long warned of an emerging global major pandemic and asked for greater preparedness, policymakers around the globe failed to give importance to that warning and considered it less-priority issue to invest money, time, and political capital to tackle the abstract possibility of a future crisis. As a result, the whole world was unprepared when novel coronavirus posed a global public health threat with a massive magnitude. As the pandemic has spread across the globe, the policy responses of different countries have been continuing to be tempered by political realities. A global pandemic like COVID-19 of such a magnitude necessarily requires a global response. A coordinated international response is undoubtedly the best way to confront an international public health emergency. It is quite understandable that Governments around the world, since February 2019, have been facing tough time while taking decisions about the appropriate measures to address the pandemic: what restrictions to impose and when to loosen them, where monetary assistance to be provided and also how it is to be raised, and importantly what national concerns can be limited to favour international cooperation. Public health recommendations, economic considerations, and political constraints are the basic factors to be taken into account while taking the above decisions. Therefore, it is also understandable that the national policy responses to COVID-19 pandemic of different governments around the globe vary according to their respective health, socio-economic, and political reasons. However, as Jeffry Frieden, a professor of government at Harvard university explained, a basic economic principle is that any policy that is good for society as a whole can be made to be good for everyone in society, even if the policy creates winners and losers. It requires only that the winners be taxed just a bit to compensate the losers – and everyone is better off.

A basic political economic principle is that the winners don't like being taxed to compensate losers. What is best for the country may not be best for my region, or group, or industry, or class – and so I will fight it. Political economy is the integration of political and economic factors in our analysis of modern society. In as much as just about everyone would agree that politics and economics are intricately and irretrievably interwoven – politics affects the economy and the economy affects politics – this approach seems natural. Political economy has proved itself powerful in understanding governments and societies. Most of the policymakers who are tackling COVID-19 pandemic around the world, are appeared to be more influenced by political economic principles than basic economic principles. The COVID-19 pandemic has unquestionably presented an era-defining challenge to the global economy and public health. Additionally, while the economic consequences and health challenges are devastating, the geopolitical impact has continued to unfold – and might be a trigger for change in global political order.

ORIGIN OF COVID-19 AND HOW IT MORPHED INTO A GLOBAL PANDEMIC

COVID-19 pandemic, so far, evolved at a rapid pace. The first case of COVID-19 presented in Wuhan, China on 17th

November 2019. Eight more cases of viral pneumonia of unknown origin were diagnosed there in early December 2019. Genomic sequencing determined the illnesses were caused by infection from SARS-CoV-2, a coronavirus that originated in wildlife (i.e. animal-to-human transmission followed by person-to-person). The China Centre for Disease Control notified the World Health Organization (WHO) on 31st December 2019 about pneumonia cases of unknown etiology, released the SARS-CoV-2 sequence to the international community on 10th January 2020, and confirmed person-to-person transmission to WHO on 20th January 2020. At that point, coherent albeit preliminary scientific and medical understanding existed that a novel and highly contagious beta-coronavirus with greater virulence than influenza was being transmitted from person-to-person by aerosol inhalation. That understanding should have informed nations' risk mitigation authorities. The December 2019 outbreak was initially localized to Wuhan in China's Hubei province. Over the next three months, the total number of infections increased rapidly emulating exponential growth: 67 days to reach 100,000 confirmed cases of infection worldwide; only four more days were needed to go from 200,000 to 300,000 cases. On 27th January 2020, Europe's first cluster of infections with person-to-person transmission was reported in Germany. On 30th January 2020, WHO Director General declared a Public Health Emergency of International Concern. The United States also reported its first locally transmitted case in Chicago. On 31st January 2020, the United States declared COVID-19 a public health emergency and imposed a mandatory 14-day quarantine to any U.S. citizen that had visited Hubei province in China. For non-U.S. nationals who travelled to China within two weeks before their flight to U.S. denied entry. Also, the first two COVID-19 cases were confirmed in the United Kingdom. On 2nd February 2020, the first COVID-19 death was reported outside of China, a 44-year old Wuhan resident who died in the Philippines. On 11th February 2020, Corona virus was officially named COVID-19. On 12th February 2020, 175 people were detected to have infected onboard a cruise ship docked in Yokohama, Japan. Finally almost 700 people on board of the same ship were infected over the following weeks. On 19th February 2020, the outbreak of COVID-19 cluster in Daegu, South Korea began. On 20th February 2020, COVID-19 epidemic started taking toll in Italy. On 6th March 2020, the United States reported an increasing number of COVID-19 cases, including Washington, California, Florida, Arizona, Indiana, and New York. Actually, it was the beginning of U.S's COVID-19 epidemic. On 14th March 2020, China introduced 14-day quarantine for any overseas arrival. On 17th March 2020, the first human trials of a coronavirus vaccine began in Seattle, United States. On 24th March 2020, the United Kingdom went into lockdown. By 26th March 2020, the total confirmed positive COVID-19 cases reached 531,860, and 24,057 deaths reported in 160+ countries and territories. On 2nd April 2020, total COVID-19 cases all-over the world surpassed 1 million. On 6th April 2020, China reported its first day with no COVID-19 deaths since the outbreak began. On 27th June 2020, world-wide total COVID-19 cases surpassed 10 million. On 3rd July 2020, total number of cases surpassed 11 million. On 10th August 2020, world-wide COVID-19 cases surpassed 20 million. On 12th August 2020, Europe's COVID-19 cases surged because of the surge of cases in Germany, France, and Spain. On 17th September 2020, global coronavirus cases touched 30 million. It took only 18 days for global cases to surge from 25 million to more than 30 million, while it took 20 days for the world to go from 20 million to 25 million, and 19 days to go from 15 million to 20 million cases. However, the global rate of new daily cases was slowing as of 3rd week of September 2020. While the trajectory of COVID-19 still fell far short of the 1918 Spanish flu, which infected an estimated 500 million people, killing at least 10 percent of them, experts expressed their worries that the available data might be underplaying the true impact of the pandemic. Actual prevalence and mortality, inevitably, are higher than the reported data during a pandemic especially when it is a new disease like COVID-19. The difference comes from testing backlogs and shortages, underreporting of mild cases, non-reporting of asymptomatic infections, misattribution of cause of death, and the likelihood that some countries are concealing the magnitude of their outbreaks. Inevitably, the global economy has been devastated by the pandemic, with many nations, as of 22nd September 2020, still maintaining strict restrictions on their population to contain fresh outbreaks.

Table: 11.1

As of 21st September 2020:

Officially Confirmed Global COVID-19 Total Cases (of 216 Countries, areas or territories): 30, 905,162.

Officially Confirmed Global COVID-19 Total Deaths (of 216 countries): 958,703.

Officially Confirmed Global COVID-19 Total Recovered Cases (of 216 Countries, areas or territories): 20,597,914.

Top Five Infected Countries

Country	Total cases	Deaths
United States	6,703,698	198,509
India	5,487,580	84,372
Brazil	4,528,240	137,363
Russia	1,103,399	19,418
Peru	762,865	31,369

Sources: Johns Hopkins University, WHO and health authorities.

SOCIO-ECONOMIC AND HEALTH CONSEQUENCES

As of 22nd September 2020, the day of writing this chapter, it has become clear that the world has changed almost beyond recognition during the last eight and half months. No country in this world has escaped the health, economic, and social impacts of the COVID-19 crisis. As the health and human toll grows, devastating economic damage is already evident and represents the largest economic shock the world has experienced in decades. Global economic activities have already been declined drastically during the last eight and half months, and are projected to continue to decline on a scale not seen since the Great Depression. It is truly a crisis like no other in our memory. The pandemic is expected to plunge most countries into recession in 2020, with per capita income contracting in the largest fraction of countries globally since 1870. For emerging markets and developing countries, many of which face daunting vulnerabilities, it is critical to strengthen public health systems, address the challenges posed by informality, and implement reforms that will support strong and sustainable growth once the health crisis abates. COVID-19 crisis highlighted the need for urgent action to cushion the pandemic's health and economic consequences, protect vulnerable populations, and set the stage for a lasting recovery. The downturns causing by the pandemic, are estimated to reverse years of progress toward development goals and tip tens of millions of people back into extreme poverty. Emerging markets and developing economies will mostly be buffeted by economic headwinds from multiple quarters: pressure on weak healthcare systems, loss of trade and tourism, dwindling remittances, subdued capital flows, and tight financial conditions amid mounting debt. Exporters of energy or industrial commodities are particularly hard hit. COVID-19 and efforts to contain it have triggered an unprecedented collapse in oil demand and a crash in oil prices. Demand for metals and transport-related commodities such as rubber and platinum used for vehicle parts have also tumbled. While agriculture markets are well supplied globally, trade restrictions and supply chain disruptions could yet raise food security issues in some places. Should COVID-19 outbreaks persist, should restrictions on movement be extended or reintroduced, or should disruptions to economic activity be prolonged, the recession could be deeper. Looking at the speed with which the crisis has overtaken the global economy may provide a clue to how deep the recession will be.

Alliance Bernstein in its Global macro outlook as of August 2020 forecasted that the global economic growth for 2020 would be -4.5 percent, with an upward revision of euro area growth of -7.5 percent, and a downward revision to the United States with -5.4 percent growth. They also expected the global economy to expand by nearly 5 percent in 2021. They predicted that output levels for the advanced economies to still be 2 percent below those at year-end 2019 and roughly 6 percent below an extrapolation of the pre-crisis trend. However, the global economy's growth prospects will depend critically on the virus's future path. Additionally, the ongoing policy support is also essential. There is little that monetary policy can do to directly influence the future path of output, but it can play an important supporting role by suppressing bond yields, keeping debt-servicing costs low and providing fiscal space for governments to support their economies.

The euro area contracted by a record 12.1 percent in the second quarter of 2020, dwarfing its 3.6 percent decline in the first quarter of 2020. Among the larger countries, the decline in output ranged from 10.1 percent in Germany to 18.5 percent in Spain. With Spain heavily dependent on summer tourism and signs emerging in September 2020 that virus is picking up steam there more quickly as well as in France, euro area's economic performance in the third quarter of 2020 will surely continue to be further adversely affected. It would be relevant to note that Europe's leaders already agreed on Euro 750 billion of joint funding to help the worst-hit economies recover. Overall, the second-quarter decline in output in euro area was slightly better than initially suggested. In France, GDP fell 12.4 percent in the second quarter of 2020, smaller than the preliminary estimate of 17 percent published by the National Statistics Institute. However, from middle of September, 2020, France started to face fresh new clusters of COVID-19 outbreaks. Hope, this can be handled by targeted measures and that the risk of new national lockdowns can be avoided.

The U.S. economy suffered its biggest blow since the Great Depression, in the second quarter of 2020, as the COVID-19 pandemic shattered consumer and business spending, and a nascent recovery is under threat from a resurgence in new cases of coronavirus. The bulk of the deepest contraction in at least 73 years reported by the Commerce Department occurred in April 2020 when activity almost grounded to an abrupt halt after restaurants, bars, and factories among others were shuttered in mid-March to slow the spread of coronavirus. More than five years of growth have been wiped out. Gross domestic product (GDP) collapsed at a 32.9 percent annualized rate in the second quarter of 2020, the deepest decline in output since the government started keeping records in 1947. The drop in GDP was more than triple the previous all-time decline of 10 percent in the second quarter of 1958. The U.S. economy contracted at a 5 percent pace in the first quarter 2020. It fell into recession in February 2020. Output shrank 10.6 percent in the first half of 2020. Though activity picked up starting in May 2020, momentum slowed subsequently amid the explosion of COVID-19 infections, especially in the densely populated South and West regions where authorities in hard-hit areas were closing businesses again and paused re-openings. That tempered hopes of a sharp rebound in growth in the third quarter of 2020. The U.S. Central Bank kept interest rates near zero and pledged to continue pumping money into the economy. Economists insist without the historic fiscal package of nearly USD3 trillion during the peak period of pandemic, the economic contraction of United States would have been deeper. The package offered companies help paying wages and gave millions of unemployed Americans a weekly USD600 supplement. A staggering 30.2 million Americans were receiving unemployment checks in the week ending July 11, 2020. However, consumer spending, which accounts for more than two-thirds of the U.S. economy, plunged at a 34.6 percent pace in the second quarter of 2020. Business investments also tumbled at a 27 percent rate during the same period. Boeing reported a bigger than expected quarterly loss in July 2020 and slashed production on its widebody programs. The pandemic also crushed oil prices, leading to deep cuts in shale oil production and layoffs. Spending on non-residential structures such as mining exploration, shafts and wells plunged at a record 34.9 percent rate. Investment in homebuilding tumbled at a 38.7 percent rate. Government spending rose during the period, though state and local government outlays fell. Trade added to GDP, but inventories were a drag.

China's official real GDP growth rate, as forecasted, will like be 1.1 percent in 2020, down from 6.1 percent in 2019. However, 2021 growth is expected to rebound to about 8.8 percent. Since the corona virus pandemic battered China's economy, tens of millions of urban and factory jobs have evaporated. But many of the newly unemployed have instead returned to their rural villages. China's vast countryside now serves as an unemployment sponge, soaking up floating migrant workers in temporary agricultural work on small family plots. In late April 2020, only about half of the last year's number of rural workers were still working, as mentioned by Scot Rozelle, a Stanford economist. The situation got worse as only about 10 percent of China's jobless normally receive state unemployment benefits because of stringent requirements. Unemployment insurance is only available to those who have paid into public funds for more than 12 months along with contributions from their employers. A vast majority of migrant laborers, whose jobs are seasonal, do not qualify. Instead, the only recourse for hundreds of millions of migrant workers lies in a return to the land. For the first time in China's modern history, Beijing did not set an annual economic growth target rate in 2020, citing uncertainty because of the global corona virus pandemic. The global economic slowdown could imperil China's goal to eradicate rural poverty by the end of 2020, a centrepiece initiative of Chinese leader Xi Jinping when he took power in 2012. In terms of risk factors, policy easing in China may be less effective than expected if new economic data offer big surprises to the downside. This would put a sustained economic stabilization at risk for 2020 and the next.

In Japan, substantial improvements were noticed after state of emergency was lifted on May 25, 2020. Restrictions were relaxed, and mobility measures were undertaken. The Japan government announced, to cushion the COVID-19 impact, the second fiscal package in May 2020 – amounting to Y117 trillion or 21 percent of GDP – on top of a nearly Y100 trillion package revealed in April 2020. However, the surge in COVID-19 cases through July 2020 generated significant second-wave concerns and there is a clear risk that the country's growth profile of 2020 will remain patchy.

In Australia and New Zealand, until late June 2020, the COVID-19 pandemic looked well under control. As a result, lockdowns and other restrictions were lifted, and activity was recovering smartly. However, subsequently, a ' Stage 4' lockdown was required to reimpose in the city of Melbourne because of the exponential surge in virus cases particularly in the state of Victoria. While substantial stimulus package, including a range of support measures like wage subsidies, are intended to cushion the economies through the shutdown, there remain questions over how long these measures will remain in place. In New Zealand, there is a continuous debate over whether the Reserve Bank of New Zealand (RBNZ) needs to do more, including a move to a negative interest rate policy.

Canada's economy went into recession in the second quarter of 2020, alongside the global economy. However, the policymakers have responded aggressively and effectively. The Bank of Canada is also expected to remain accommodative for the foreseeable future.

In the United Kingdom, the monthly GDP series published by the Office for National Statistics shows that UK output rose by a disappointing 1.8 percent in May, following a cumulative decline of 25.9 percent for March and April 2020. Barring significant upward revisions to these numbers, UK second-quarter GDP is more likely to approach (or be worse than) the 18.5 percent decline in Spain than the 12.1 percent drop in the euro area. The key risk factors likely to affect the economic outlook are how quickly the economy emerges from lockdown and Brexit negotiations. The UK outlook continues to be clouded by inconsistent communication. In September 2020, the Bank of England warned that the rising rate of coronavirus infections and a lack of clarity over the UK's future trade relationship with the EU could threaten the economic recovery. The UK is still in a deep recession in September 2020, while COVID-19 infections are at their highest level since mid-May. The UK's Chief Scientific Adviser warned that UK could hit 50,000 cases a day in mid- October without further action. He also stressed while the figures given were not a prediction, 'speed' and 'action' are required to halt the regular rise in cases. Citing the uncertainty, the Bank of England held interest rates at 0.1 percent, a historic low. The bank added that it would continue its monetary support for the economy, but stopped short of increasing its bond-buying program or reducing interest rate further.

In Asia ex Japan and China, COVID-19 remains the key factor influencing the economic outlook. Taiwan and South Korea stand out on the responses to the virus itself. In Thailand, Vietnam, and Malaysia, the case counts also remain low. Trends in India, Indonesia, and the Philippines are still concerning, and these countries have rolled back their time lines to relax restrictions. The economic policy response to date with monetary easing and substantial fiscal support being delivered across the board. The anticipated headwind of weaker domestic demand from the US and Europe remains, particularly as those regions attempt to navigate the prospect of a second virus wave. It's a reminder that even if COVID-19 related uncertainty begins to clear, the headwinds from other factors such as deglobalization and US-China tensions, will remain stiff.

India, in late March 2020, declared a nationwide 21-day lockdown to stop the spread of the coronavirus among the population of 1.3 billion people. India tried to tame COVID-19 by short-term sacrificing it's economy. But such trade-off never materialized. In fact, India – far more than its peers – has been facing the worst of both worlds. Some economic hardship was certainly expected, given the nation's lockdown, but the way in which India imposed its coronavirus restrictions reduced any public health benefit and complicated any rebound. As on 19th September 2020, India's official coronavirus tally stood at 5,214,677 – second behind the U.S. – with 84,372 reported deaths. On the other hand, as of middle of September 2020, India's economy was experiencing it's deepest recession since it started publishing GDP numbers in 1996. India also recorded fastest growing number of coronavirus cases of any country on earth. India's GDP shrank nearly 24 percent in the second quarter of 2020 compared with the same period last year. The contraction is the Country's biggest in decades and the worst second quarter decline among the world's top five economies. Besides India's agricultural sector which grew 3.4 percent in the second quarter, compared with the same period last year, the results of other sectors were grim. In the second quarter 2020, India's construction industry shrank 50 percent, manufacturing shrank 39 percent, and trade, hotels, and other services shrank 47 percent. India's dual crisis – a flailing economy and an unchecked public health catastrophe – left the government with few options. India released a USD266 billion stimulus package, worth nearly 10 percent of the Country's annual GDP in May 2020, while Government revenue generation remained all time low during the period owing to the financial impacts of the lockdown. The government's tax revenue fell 32.6 percent in the April – June quarter, 2020, underscoring the damage done to the economy by the COVID-19 pandemic and the lock down that followed. The revenue shortfall widened the country's fiscal deficit at 83.2 percent of the full-year budget estimate. The central goods and services tax (GST) took the maximum 53 percent knock, suggesting extreme consumer distress or caution. In terms of prospects of recovery, some better numbers are expected in the third quarter since the period will be reflecting the economic reopening. The International Monetary Fund, in June 2020, projected the Indian economy to contract 4.5 percent in 2020, while its economy grew by 3.1 percent in the first quarter.

In Latin America, COVID-19 cases in Brazil are still on the rise and the consumer sector remains severely impacted. However, there are some early signs of an improving economy. The July manufacturing PMI was 58.2, up from 51.6 in June and a low of 36 in April 2020. GDP increased 1.3 percent month over month in May, but is still down significantly from pre-pandemic levels. Higher activities in non-retail sectors are expected to grow in the coming months, as factories and primary sector operations resume. However, the recovery of the domestic economy will take more time, especially in the retail and consumer service segments. The Central Bank of Brazil cut the Selic rate by 25 basis points in August 2020, likely ending the easing cycle. Mexico's second-quarter GDP release confirmed the sharp year-on-year drop in the industrial (-26 percent) and services sectors (-15.6 percent) due to the COVID-19 crisis. However, the quarterly result implies a strong activity rebound in June (+8.5 percent month over month). Domestic demand remains weak. External accounts show a picture with exports recovering and imports subdued in June 2020. The Central Bank of Mexico is still expected to continue gradually cutting the intervention rate. Chile's Congress passed a constitutional amendment that allows emergency withdrawals of up to 10 percent from individual retirement accounts. The Government strongly opposed the change believing it would decrease the expected income replacement ratio for retirees. The new law enjoyed large support from Chileans and congressional members. In early August, Argentina finished debt negotiations with external creditors, The deal restructured around USD60 billion in external debt and provided around USD36 billion of debt relief through substantive interest payment reductions and extension in maturities. The Argentina government announced that the country would need to negotiate with the IMF to postpone upcoming payments to that multilateral organization. The Government's constraints on financing and an increase in the primary deficit have forced it to rely on credit from the Central Bank, increasing the likelihood of a spike in inflation that could hinder economic stability once activity resumes after the COVID-19 lockdown.

Real growth prospects of Eastern Europe, Middle East, and Africa (EEMEA) have deteriorated sharply for 2020, owing to weaker external demand (largely because of euro area recession) and domestic lockdown measures to contain the COVID-19 spread. Lower energy prices also weigh on real GDP growth for the region's oil exporters. Central banks, given a challenging outlook, have eased respective monetary policies and implemented bond purchase programs to support domestic financial liquidity. While further modest interest rate cuts are possible in Russia, other countries such as South Africa and Turkey have likely come to the end of their easing cycles. In terms of risk factors, while the extent of the economic downturn in 2020 is becoming clearer, the shape of the recovery beyond this year remains highly uncertain.

In the Frontier markets, Angola's short-term liquidity concerns have largely been addressed by a three year debt moratorium from China and the G20 Debt Service Suspension Initiative (DSSI). The IMF was expected to approve a rapid financing facility at the end of July 2020, but it was postponed at short notice. Elevated medium-term financing needs, and the dominance of external debt, point to Angola's challenging time ahead. In Ukraine, July and August 2020 proved volatile on the domestic political front following the resignation of the Governor of the National Bank of Ukraine (NBU). Against ongoing significant refinancing needs in 2021, a resumption of IMF funding program is still expected in late 2020 or early 2021. Ecuador, while facing significant fiscal challenges, reached an agreement to restructure its external debt with bondholders and its largest bilateral creditor, China. Ecuador amended the terms of its bonds with nearly 98 percent approval from bondholders and reduced financing costs by nearly USD16billion over 10 years, including eliminating interest payments for the rest of 2020. Ecuador also expects to receive an additional USD2.4 billion in new financing from China as part of the restructuring, which will help the country to close its nearly USD4 billion funding gap before the end of 2020. The next step is to finalize a new agreement with the IMF, which will help to keep Ecuador's fiscal consolidation reforms on track.

The overall global economic and health scenario, as of middle of September 2020, is after collapsing in the first half of the year, economic output recovered swiftly following the easing of measures to contain the COVID-19 pandemic and the initial re-opening of businesses. As OECD suggested, all G20 countries with the exception of China, will suffer recession in 2020. Although a fragile recovery is expected in 2021, in many countries output at the end of 2021 will still be below levels compared to 2019, and of course well below than what was projected prior to the pandemic. Restoring confidence will be crucial to how successfully economies can recover. Policymakers mostly reacted rapidly and massively to buffer the initial blow to incomes and jobs. As of September 2020, while the global economic outlook seems less pessimistic, risks and uncertainty still remain high. Prospects for global economic growth will depend on various factors, including the likelihood of new virus outbreak, the impact on consumer and business confidence, and the extent to which governments aid for jobs and businesses can boost demand. The unprecedented policy support by governments needs to continue, but should be more targeted and be flexible enough to adapt to changing conditions.

GEO-POLITICAL CONSEQUENCES

The COVID-19 pandemic undoubtedly unleashed dramatic effects on everyday life in each and every country of the world. However, the geopolitical implications of COVID-19 could prove even more profound. COVID-19 has already exacerbated and is increasingly creating pressure points in the global order, that could fundamentally reshape global geopolitics.

Besides the direct effect of the pandemic being the loss of human life, there are wide concerns regarding the political and economic side-effects of COVID-19. In this context, two vital questions come to the fore: What will the post-COVID-19 world look like? What opportunities and threats will be presented by the new international order? Based on the estimates provided by the World Bank, 60 million people could fall into extreme poverty during post-COVID-19 period, and developing and emerging economies could be severely afflicted by the health and economic impacts of the pandemic. Unemployment is on rise even in developed economies. Countries with weak welfare systems are failing to meet the expectations of their people during these extremely difficult times. Economic recession in almost all the countries of the world has already triggered political consequences in many of them, as it will act as a multiplier of already existing social, economic and political problems. Many argue that post-COVID-19 world economy will require a recovery program similar to that of the post-WW11 era, while countries with the means to lead such a program will increase their ambit of influence.

The current multilateral order has shown its weaknesses globally. It has failed to provide the necessary decisions to counter the crisis and effectively tackle its social, political and economic effects. Similarly, multilateral institutions also have fallen short in meeting the expectations of the international community. As a consequence, this fact has already been used by many nationalist movements across the globe, especially in Europe, to question the efficacy of multilateralism and to spread nationalist, unilateralist, and even in some cases isolationist agendas. However, while many argue for an end to multilateralism, the COVID-19 pandemic has actually proved the opposite. It has revealed the need for global responses to a global crisis and also for multilateral approaches. In fact, the problems unfolded by the COVID-19 pandemic are not entirely about multilateralism itself, but rather the inefficiency of existing multilateral mechanisms. The pandemic is also expected to emphasize the concept of strong, self-sufficient states. As a provider of security, welfare, and healthcare services, the state alone comes to the forefront during global pandemics and national epidemics alike. The pandemic has demonstrated that existing tools for gauging state power fall short in determining actual state power. While assessing state power, one must now take into account healthcare systems, supply chains, and emergency response capabilities, in addition to military and economic power, and population size, on which the realist approach frequently concentrates. COVID-19 pandemic and the ensuing recession have placed the countries under a prospective new geo-political regime and also have offered stress tests for the doctrines of decreasing global cooperation, increasing regionalism, and a resurgence of nationalism and great-power politics. It is to be noted that several interconnected challenges were already salient before the pandemic. One is localisation-mounting pressure to reduce reliance on greenhouse-gas-emitting transportation is rendering just in time, globe-straddling supply chains more fragile. Second is regionalisation, notably but not exclusively promoted by Trump's America-centric trade policy, and facilitated by the mainstreaming of onshore means of production and the reduced reliance on oil and gas produced in geopolitically fraught regions such as Russia and the Persian Gulf. Third is decoupling, with the aim of unwinding key value chains in China and reducing dependency on Chinese exports.

Since Xi Jinping became President of China in 2013, the U.S.-China relationship has grown more confrontational. Xi adopted a more assertive foreign policy and reinforced domestic authoritarianism. The 2017 National Security Strategy of the United States of America declared the return of great-power rivalry with Russia and China to be the foremost threat to U.S. security and economic well-being. The COVID-19 pandemic thus comes at a time when the reigning global power (the United States) has been getting increasingly ready to confront the rising power (China) politically, economically, diplomatically, and even militarily. Xi's geopolitical and geo-economic assertiveness, combined with China's diplomatic bullying and predatory approach to intellectual property rights and one-sided digital imperialism, have helped cement a bipartisan consensus behind getting tough with China in an otherwise polarised United states and led to growing pushback in the EU.

The impact of COVID-19 on America's geopolitical heft and positioning depends crucially on the duration of the pandemic and involves inordinate uncertainty. If COVID-19 is reduced to predictable and manageable proportions, the U.S. economy could emerge from a one-off 'corona recession' relatively intact, which would attenuate the virus's geopolitical impact on the United States. However, unlike previous recessions, the virus-induced one will push all of America's main trading partners, including China into negative territory, thus depriving the U.S. of outside engines of growth. Even though the U.S. economy is less dependent on exports in terms of their share of GDP than other countries – 12 percent against a global average of 30 percent – it would still suffer from such a globally depressed environment . So even this scenario would be comparatively more difficult for the U.S. than previous economic crisis. On the other hand, China was the first to suffer the onslaught of COVID-19 and the first to move carefully out of confinement, the bulk of the country's firms having returned to business. But there still remain credible doubts about the official figures on the virus's level of infection in China. Also, China's 'mask diplomacy' during the initial infection period in Europe, has been often maladroit and sometimes malicious. For China, the larger problem is economic. China's authorities have long considered 6 percent growth necessary to avoid unemployment. In the Chinese system, delivering close to full employment is seen as a key element of regime legitimacy. China has become less reliant on foreign trade for its economic prosperity, but its exports in goods and services still represent some 21 percent of its GDP. It is also reliant on the same value chains as its foreign partners. The global recession will inevitably affect China's growth and employment prospects. The Chinese response will unlikely be isolationist. If the people are upset, an authoritarian regime will often resort to diverting their attention to foreign targets. Assertive patriotism has been part of Xi's thinking at least since the 19th CCP congress in 2017. Turning it into angry nationalism is clearly an option. A telling historical analogy here may be the aggressive surge of Japanese nationalism during the Great Depression in the 1930s. As mentioned, tensions have escalated between the U.S. and China on multiple fronts in 2020, from the coronavirus pandemic to Hong Kong, but it is in the field of trade and technology where the Trump administration has worked most diligently to put pressure on Beijing. Semiconductors are the cornerstone technology of the information age and key to the US-China tech war, as well as both nations' relationship with Taiwan. The U.S. has embarked on a two-pronged technology strategy of cutting China's access to high-tech supply chains through sanctions on companies like Huawei, while bringing Taiwan closer into its orbit. What's at stake is mastery of the tiny electronic devices that power the modern economy by acting as data-processing brains for products, from smartphones to cars and spacecraft. The semiconductor industry is also critical to a suite of advanced technologies - including the next generation of wireless networks, artificial intelligence and connected devices – that could give either country an economic edge in the future. The current U.S. administration is looking for a simple way to gain control over China's industrial growth. Since probably every semiconductor in the world is made using at least one tool from a U.S.-based company, the U.S. Department of Commerce expects to be able to use semiconductor trade restrictions to give its control over China's participation in the electronics market, said Jim Handy, semiconductor analyst from Objective Analysis in California. Even after several decades and billions of dollars investment, China trails the U.S., South Korea, and Taiwan in the complex and capital intensive production of semiconductors. China imported USD312 billion and USD305 billion worth of chips in 2018 and 2019 respectively, exceeding the amount it spent on oil, data from the General Administration of Customs showed. In the political front, while Beijing was optimistic over an early conclusion of its ongoing talks with ASEAN for a code of conduct in the disputed South China Sea, the Southeast Asian researchers suggested instead that the talks' suspension due to the coronavirus pandemic meant Beijing now lacked the use of the ongoing negotiations as a 'pretext' for saying all was well in the sea dispute. With recent stand-offs in the waters, as well as Southeast Asian claimants (Malaysia, Vietnam, Brunei, Indonesia, and the Philippines) ramping up 'lawfare' tactics of citing international maritime law to press their respective cases – much to Beijing's annoyance – an amicable resolution looks farther away than before, the analysts said. In another front, Australia 'has painted itself into a geopolitical corner' with China as Australia agreed to lead the investigation into the origins of the coronavirus following a call between its Prime Minister Scott Morrison and U.S. President Donald Trump. China has since imposed anti-dumping tariffs on Australian barley and launched two investigations into wine imports. Australia's over reliance on the goodwill generated by its free trade agreement with China to shield it from the ramifications of its political alliance with the United States could result in problems with Beijing for years to come, trade and foreign affairs experts said.

The EU's future, to a significant degree, is riding on its ability to handle the COVID-19 crisis. Since the beginning of this century, the EU's growth rate has been one percentage point lower than that of the U.S., and its nations are divided between a frugal north and an indebted south. Europe's ageing societies are finding it difficult to cope with the integration of unskilled immigrants and refugees in the west and north, and with the mass exodus of its youth from the east and south. The EU has proven insufficiently attractive to convince the United Kingdom to remain a member and is challenged by strong Europhobic parties in many member states. To make matters worse, health policy before COVID-19 struck was and still is a national competency, which helps to explain the extraordinary diversity of COVID-19 related clinical outcomes among the nations of the euro area. Given the EU's high exposure to international trade, it stands to suffer correspondingly from a global corona recession. In this backdrop, the question is what will happen next in EU? The most likely or rather no less likely scenario in EU, as mentioned by Francois Heisbourg, IISS senior adviser for Europe, will be : most of the EU's labour force is on partial employment, and its return to work is quicker than that in the U.S. The eurozone's members agree on a recovery package on top of the European Central Bank's financial support and national efforts, with business picking up in an intact single market and eurozone. EU member states rediscover the political virtues of external borders, reaching a de facto consensus on immigration policy and also forging a muscular approach to trade backed up by feasible industrial policy and data management. China itself will no longer have unfettered IT access to Europe while forbidding foreign access behind its Great Firewall. The above outcome is more likely. Because the world witnessed that the EU proved time to time to have strong survival instincts. Neither the euro crisis nor the migration tensions of the last decade laid it irretrievably low. China's active pursuit of economic and strategic advantage has not met with great success. Chinese foreign direct investment in Europe is sinking and the more blustering of China's ambassadors have become targets of ridicule. Regionalisation and decoupling at China's expense have become new normal. Therefore, the EU could be one of the bigger geopolitical surprises of the COVID-19 crisis.

FUTURE EXPECTATIONS

Despite lots of uncertainties, there are some obvious next steps for the United States and its allies and partners. The people of the world who sincerely love and nurture democratic values are eagerly looking forward to the U.S. and its allies and partners to take the leading roles to face this pandemic crisis of the century. The U.S. with its allies and partners need to develop a comprehensive joint strategy to address COVID-19 and shape the post -pandemic global order. The United states together with its allies and partners should lead a counter-coronavirus coalition to implement strong joint measures to curb the virus's spread, and also unleash its economic might to ensure those afflicted with the illness receive care. The U.S. should work more closely with its allies and partners, supporting them with medical resources and acting as a much more reliable partner than China. The United States should act as the global leader in this crisis period. The United States' vast resources, partnerships, and capacity for innovation puts it in a capable position to take up the mantle of leadership, produce medical supplies and vaccines, and quash the pandemic. While the United States should be tough on the WHO for its deference to China, it should also seek to strengthen global public health institutions, erect new ones where necessary, and reassert its influence in them. The Chinese government, despite its alleged culpability in allowing the virus to spiral into a pandemic, is also pushing for a new multilateral public health initiative in the form of the Health Silk Road. The United States should not cede global leadership in refashioning and constructing multilateral institutions in order to ensure to have the capacity to response to the pandemic, address outbreaks, facilitate cooperation, and avoid influence of authoritarian regimes. Finally, transparency is a major attribute in stemming fast -breaking global health crisis, and democratic countries led by the United States, therefore, have an advantage over authoritarians who suppress and destroy important health data.

COVID-19 will most likely cause a global recession and possibly a depression. In that scenario, protectionism will become tempting. However, we learned from the history that protectionism failed to stem the Great Depression in the 1930s and only worsened an inward, nationalistic turn among global powers that fed into World War 11. Instead, the united States and its partners and allies should immediately work together to facilitate quicker economic recovery and to rebuild the global economy with resolute actions. The United States' USD3 trillion stimulus is surely a positive step in that direction, as are the recent steps taken by the EU. Additionally, whereas China has limited experience with booms and busts due to an extended period of economic growth, the United States and its partners are more used to market cycles, and this should give them added resilience to the current crisis.

The United States and its partners, while working together, can amass an impressive degree of economic, diplomatic, and military clout, and scientific knowledge – all of which are integral to a strong bonding for comprehensive response to the pandemic. Where relationships have been frayed in previous months, the U.S. should work to repair them and be positioning to take the lead of a coalition of states dedicated to countering all the consequences of corona virus. The concept of national security, as western publics rightly demanded, be broadened to include security against pandemics. How this new concept is integrated into national security – should be a policy priority for planners in the near future.

Finally, the COVID-19 pandemic, in just a few months, has upended global health security, pushed the world economy into a tailspin, and intensified great-power rivalry. Even if the COVID-19 downturn is not as long and brutal as the Great Depression, the wholesale disruption it has already provoked in the lives of all will deeply change the internal and external dynamics of our politics and societies.

CHAPTER-TWELVE
CONCLUDING OBSERVATIONS

Cambodia, as of end-2019, was synonymous with progress. A prolonged period of mostly political and social stability since the Paris Peace Accord of 1991 provided the basis for the country's rapid economic development. Since the early 2000s to 2019, Cambodia's average economic growth rate had been among the highest in the world; the success of its garment industry, its attractiveness to tourists and the growth in construction have driven a transformation of the economy. Poverty had fallen dramatically during the period as a result, accompanied by a decline in inequality. In 2015, Cambodia graduated to become a lower middle-income economy.

As on 31st May 2020, Cambodia's total export values amounted to USD5.9 billion, a year-on-year increase of 11.7 percent in the first five months of 2020. The value of Cambodia's total imports amounted to USD8.1 billion, a decrease by 1 percent in the same period, compared with 2019, according to data from Economic Diplomacy—Socio-Economic trends from the Ministry of Foreign Affairs and International Cooperation (MFAIC). The decline in the growth of import values was because of the sluggish economic activity in March (0.4 percent) and negative growth in April (13.9 percent) and May 2020 (26.5 percent). Meanwhile, the import of major goods decreased, especially construction materials, textile products (mainly cloth) and machinery, the report said. The growth of exports stem from an increase of electronics by 45 percent, bikes by 18 percent, rice by 29 percent and other products by 30 percent while exports of manufacturing dropped around 6 percent and rubber by 27 percent during the period. Cambodia exported USD1.96 billion worth of goods to the U.S. in the first five months of 2020, registering a sharp growth of 33.4 percent compared to the same period in 2019, according to data from the United States International Trade Commission (USITC). A breakdown of the export statistics shows that Cambodia's apparel exports to the U.S. increased, in first four months of 2020, by 17.4 percent year-on-year to USD0.95 billion, while exports of travel goods, during the same period, surged by 42.7 percent year-on-year to USD0.36 billion. Exports of footwear, Cambodia's third largest export category to the U.S. during the period, grew by 32.2 percent year-on-year to USD0.19 billion. It is noteworthy that Cambodia became the US's second largest supplier of travel goods in the January-April 2020 period, accounting for 13.1 percent of travel goods imported by the U.S., while the country represented only 7.6 percent of U.S. travel goods imports during the same period in 2019. Cambodia's positive export performance in the period was due to the fact that the US did not see a serious COVID-19 outbreak until March 2020. Cambodian factories had continued to fulfil orders well into the period until mass order cancellations began around mid-March, 2020. The COVID-19 outbreak led to higher demand for food and storage in all the countries, causing increased demand for rice exports from Cambodia. Cambodia's total rice exports to international markets reached more than 300,000 tonnes by 30th April 2020, up 40.46 percent on the same period of 2019, with China accounting for 41 percent of exports, the UK and the EU 32 percent, ASEAN countries 13 percent, and the others 14 percent. The Cambodian government initially on 5th April 2020 put in place export restrictions on fish, white rice and paddy rice to ensure local food security for its own people, but subsequently on 20th May 2020, the government lifted the ban on exports of white rice, paddy rice and fish (Khmer Times).

Cambodia's growth momentum quickly disappeared in early 2020 due to the global COVID-19 outbreak. Although growth was strong, reaching 7.1 percent in 2019, the COVID-19 outbreak caused sharp decelerations in most of Cambodia's main engines of growth in the first quarter of 2020, including weakened tourism (and hospitality), construction activity, and mostly from mid-March 2020, the export sector. In Cambodia, the first case of corona virus was confirmed on January 27, 2020 and as of September 26, 2020, there were total 276 confirmed COVID-19 cases, out of which 274 patients already recovered and only 2 active cases were still there. A geographic breakdown revealed that the top three locations where COVID-19 was found were Sihanouk Ville, Phnom Penh, and Kampong Cham, which had 32.5 percent, 22.8 percent, and 13.8 percent of the cases respectively. Most of the infected cases were imported cases. Until end-September 2020, the country also reported zero deaths from COVID-19. The Cambodian government fought three battles simultaneously in order to contain the outbreak: (i) Imposed a travel ban on visitors from severely infected countries as a measure against imported cases. Although the country did not apply a ban on arrivals from China, in mid-March the Cambodian government announced a ban on arrivals from Italy, France, Germany, Spain, the U.S. and Iran. Subsequently, it also closed its borders with Vietnam and Thailand. Effective from 30th March, Cambodia also suspended the visa exemption policy for a month and made it mandatory for foreign travellers to provide a COVID-19—free medical certificate obtained within the last 72 hours before arrival. (ii) Raising awareness on self-protection, social distancing, early school break, a ban on gatherings, and cancellation of mass celebrations of the Khmer New Year ceremony in mid-April together with temporary interprovincial travel restrictions, among others. In April 2020, a 'State of Emergency' law was also urgently adopted to be ready to be declared if there are public health emergencies; and (iii) Striving to offer effective treatment, which, in turn, resulted in the recovery of all infected patients. Towards preparing for a bigger battle, 3,000 rooms have been made available throughout the country with 422 additional staff mobilized (World Bank). While Cambodia has, so far, avoided a health crisis, it has not been immune from the economic crisis sweeping the global economy. The global economic crisis unleashed by COVID-19 poses the greatest threat to Cambodia's development in its 30 years of modern history. The three most affected sectors – tourism, manufacturing exports, and construction – contributed more than 70 percent of growth and 39.4 percent of total paid employment in 2019. The Asian Development outlook (ADO) 2020, September update forecasted a 4.0 percent contraction for Cambodia's gross domestic product in 2020, compared to its June forecast of a 5.5 percent contraction. As predicted by World Bank, poverty could increase between 3 and 11 percentage points from a 50 percent income loss that lasts for six months for households engaged in tourism, wholesale and retail trade, garment, construction, and manufacturing. Cambodia's fiscal deficit is expected to reach its highest level in 22 years, and the country's public debt could rise to 35 percent of GDP by 2022.

The spill-overs of COVID-19 are already being felt in Cambodia largely through three key channels: tourism, exports, and construction & foreign direct investment.

TOURISM

Impact of the COVID-19 outbreak on Cambodia's tourism sector is unprecedented. The demand for tourism and hospitality services has almost collapsed especially in the second quarter of 2020. The global response to contain the COVID-19 outbreak has resulted in prolonged international travel restrictions and internal lockdowns. During January and February 2020, tourist arrivals, as reported, contracted by 25.1 percent year-on-year, the first contraction since the 2008-2009 global financial crisis. Cambodia's most popular tourist attraction, Siem Reap, experienced a 45.6 percent decline in tourist arrivals during the first quarter and a 99.6 percent reduction year-on-year in April 2020. Cambodia has been heavily reliant on tourists from the East Asia and Pacific region, especially Chinese tourists. Arrivals from the East Asia and Pacific region as a whole accounted for about 80 percent of total arrival in Cambodia in 2019. The structural slowdown in Cambodia's tourism sector has occurred over the past few years as indicated because of low repeat visit rate of less than 20 percent. However, Cambodia's tourism sector initially received a substantial boost when the authorities' 'China ready' initiative introduced in 2016 paid off. This has resulted in a significant rise in the share of Chinese visitors, which peaked at 35.7 percent in 2019, more than offsetting the overall decline of arrivals from the rest of the world. However, in 2020, international arrivals rapidly declined after the COVID-19 outbreak in China. As the virus spread from China to the rest of the world, tourism activity in Cambodia has come to a standstill. Tourism and hospitality services is the second largest growth driver in Cambodia, contributed about 18.7 percent of the country's real GDP growth in 2019. More importantly, the tourism sector is an important foreign exchange earner, accounted for more than three-quarters of Cambodia's services exports, and about one-fifth of its total goods and services exports. In September 2020, the Asian development Bank estimated that the service sector will drop 15.1 percent in 2020, on account of a massive drop in tourist arrivals, leading to the shutdown of some 3,000 tourism businesses and the layoff of some 45,000 workers in the industry.

In response, the Cambodian government have introduced multiple measures to support the tourism industry with tax relief and social security contribution exemptions in order to ease the liquidity crunch, while the Central Bank advised commercial banks as well as microfinance institutions to reschedule loan repayments by hard-hit borrowers including restaurants, hotels, guesthouses, beverage shops, and others. Additionally, efforts have also been made to restore the attractiveness of the temple complexes, with conservation and rehabilitation works, and restoration of physical infrastructure to make it better organized. The tourism authorities are also taking the time to identify new potential tourism products for the entire Siem Reap province, particularly in Kulen Mountain, the Tonle Sap area, and the areas located within the temples of Angkor.

THE EXPORT SECTOR

Factories in Cambodia have been hit hard by the COVID-19 global economic slowdown because of falling orders. An unprecedented export demand shock has resulted in the cancellation of a large part of garment, footwear, and travel goods orders from the two main destinations, the United States and EU. This occurred after Cambodia's manufacturing export industries experienced supply chain disruptions causing closures of some garment factories in early March 2020. As stated earlier, in 2019, the garment and footwear industry of Cambodia contributed to almost one-fifth of the country's GDP growth. In addition, the European Union's partial suspension of trade privileges for Cambodia kicked in on 12th August 2020, leaving the country to absorb a potential loss in exports in light of a COVID-19 induced economic slowdown. With the sanctions, some 20 percent of Cambodia's total exports to the European markets are affected, including those of garment and footwear products and travel goods. EU's withdrawal of tariff preferences and their replacement with the EU's standard tariffs (most-favoured nation or MFN), which will affect selected garment and footwear products, and all travel goods and sugar, amounting to around Euro 1 billion or one-fifth of Cambodia's yearly exports to the EU. The suspension, the EU said, was necessitated because of Cambodia's systematic human rights violations. In February 2020, the European commission completed a year-long investigation and evaluation period and decided to suspend the 'Everything But Arms' (EBA) trade privileges on 40 types of products, accounted for USD1.4 billion exports to the economic bloc in 2019. EU was one of the largest export destination of Cambodia. In 2019, bilateral trades rose to USD6.59 billion in which Cambodia had vast surplus.

The latest updates from the industry show that most factories have only limited orders after the first half of 2020. This is because many orders have been either frozen or cancelled. Consequently, as of 15th September 2020, a third of GTF (garment, textile, and footwear) factories of Cambodia had been either halted their production or temporarily closed with a total of more than 95,000 workers out of work, according to Labour Ministry. Official data show that as of February 2020, the garment, footwear, and travel goods industry consisted of 1,087 factories and employed 941,000 workers. The formal garment sector is the main source of government revenue, especially direct revenue. The sector is the largest formal and paid employment industry in the economy, although it is ranked third in terms of its contribution to real economic growth, providing about 17 percent of real GDP growth in 2019. As factory orders have slowed down, global brands have also expressed concern over Cambodia's embracing of coal power plants, which they say contradicts their commitment to moving towards renewable energies. Global brands, at the same time, also sounded that this could affect their sourcing negatively from Cambodia.

The Cambodian government has allocated around USD1.164 billion as a leeway to bolster the economy struggling with the impacts by the EBA's partial loss and the COVID-19 pandemic, said Finance Ministry's spokes-person Meas Soksensan.

CONSTRUCTION AND FDI INFLOWS

Prior to the COVID-19 outbreak, Cambodia's construction (and real estate) sector had been one of the main drivers of the economic growth in the country, registering average growth of 18.1 percent during 2014 – 2019. Construction and real estate sector contributed more than a third of Cambodia's GDP growth in 2019. This was a result of rising foreign investment in the country, with the country's ASEAN membership, location between Thailand and Vietnam, and close proximity with China making it an attractive destination. However, in view of the expected economic slowdown in the country, GlobalData predicted that growth in the construction industry to slow down to 4.9 percent in 2020 as compared to a previous forecast of 9.7 percent, with a high likelihood of further downward revisions as the COVID-19 outbreak extends globally and affects global growth. During the first two months of 2020, both construction activity and approved FDI inflows significantly weakened. Imports of steel, which is largely used for construction, dipped by 47.4 percent year-on-year in the first two months of 2020. Likewise, approved FDI projects for the construction sector contracted by 40.2 percent year-on-year during the same period. This would greatly diminish economic growth of Cambodia. Apart from the continuing slowdown, since the beginning of 2020, in demand for new housing due to rising unemployment and funding crisis, the problems in the construction industry have been compounded by the government's announcement of halting the launch of new construction projects in the country in 2020. In March 2020, Prime Minister Hun Sen announced that the government would delay all new construction projects (excluding those funded by foreign developers) that were expected to be started in 2020. This would likely affect the infrastructure and energy & utilities construction market in the country.

Cambodia's construction boom has been, so far, driven by foreign investments. Chinese companies, in particular, have been investing heavily in the country's infrastructure and commercial and residential real estate markets. This includes investments under the ambitious Belt and Road Initiative (BRI), with Cambodia being a member of the programme since its launch in 2013. However, with the Chinese economy expected to slow down dramatically in 2020, investments from China are expected to be more limited at least in the short term. Moreover, supply chain disruptions which has led to shortage of construction materials, has affected BRI projects in the country. Foreign investments from other countries also are expected to be muted in the short term.

Cambodia's commercial construction segment is expected to be the most adversely affected, especially the leisure & hospitality and outdoor leisure segments. With global tourism expected to decline by 60-80 percent in 2020, the industry is destined to face cash flow problems which would affect expansion plans, thereby putting on hold ongoing projects in the short term i.e. at least in 2020 for the time being. The industrial construction market is also witnessing headwinds, with the garment manufacturers in the country adversely affected due to unprecedented export demand shock inflicted by COVID-19 pandemic around the globe.

As part of the COVID-19 response, the authorities have granted an exemption of the ownership transfer tax for property valued at USD70,000 or less. However, the COVID-19 outbreak has generated an unprecedented demand shocks, while the property market already appears well saturated after almost a decade-long construction and real estate boom. In 2020, Cambodia is expected to experience its lowest growth rate since 1991. The COVID-19 shock, propagated through falling global demand, supply chain disruptions, and nation-wide lockdowns, is hitting most of Cambodia's main drivers of growth hard. Cambodia's construction industry is expected to regain growth momentum gradually from 2021, assuming COVID-19 containment measures are going to achieve success globally. Moreover, as an export driven economy, Cambodia's recovery depends on what happens world-wide. Indeed, Cambodia's economy won't begin to return to normal until the economies of China, Europe and the U.S. return to normalcy.

While COVID-19 outbreak has caused a sharp deceleration in most of Cambodia's main engines of growth so far and is also expected to continue to weakened those sectors in the coming months, if not year, unless and until the pandemic situation comes to normalcy world-wide. The outbreak has also immensely disrupted many other segments of Cambodia's economy. As World Bank reported, by end- May 2020, at least 1.76 million jobs were at risk due to the COVID-19 outbreak. The collapse of the growth drivers not only hurt economic growth but has also caused unemployment to potentially sore to nearly 20 percent. The weak performance of the agriculture sector will make it harder for the sector to absorb laid-off workers from the tourism and export sectors. Rice production in 2020 has been so far slow due largely to less favourable weather conditions. Like rainy season rice production, 2020's dry season rice cultivation has been relatively slow. As a result, total rice production during the 2019-2020 harvesting season reached 10.885 million metric tons, marginally lower than the 10.892million metric tons produced during the 2018-2019 harvesting season. In addition, yield also marginally declined by 0.5 percent, reaching 3.09 metric tons per hectare. While recent efforts to modernize the agriculture sector have intensified as Cambodia endeavours to increase productivity within its major crops, COVID-19 pandemic has grossly disrupted such focused endeavour because of pandemic related diverted priorities. Returning migrant workers have put further pressure on Cambodia's shrinking job market. In the absence of significant mitigation measures, the COVID-19 pandemic could lead to a sharp increase of poverty. Poverty simulations show that poverty would increase to nearly 11 percentage points from a 50 percent income loss that lasts for six months for households engaged in tourism, wholesale and retail trade, garment, construction, or manufacturing. Returning migrants from Thailand and their households that relied on their remittances, are also likely to face significant income losses and elevated risk of falling into poverty.

The local Khmer Times newspaper quoted industry experts saying in mid-May 2020, that many tourism-related businesses are increasingly going under. Bankruptcies could rise even further considering the delicate state of the microfinance industry. In mid-May 2020, an estimated 2.6 million Cambodians had outstanding microfinance loans worth more than USD10 billion collectively, according to figures from the Cambodia Microfinance Association quoted in media reports. Cambodia reportedly has the highest microloan debt rate per borrower in the world at around USD3,804, representing more than twice Cambodia's GDP per capita. Anecdotal reports suggest many Cambodians are selling off assets like land, vehicles and gold to ensure they have enough money to meet basic expenses in the months ahead. Many are doing so just to keep up with debt repayments; several others are already falling behind. The National Bank of Cambodia has asked MFIs and banks to offer loan deferments on a case by case basis. But a statement by 135 civil society groups in late April 2020 called on the government 'to ensure that MFIs immediately suspend all loan repayments as well as interest accrual on loans for at least three months and return the millions of land titles currently held as collateral by MFIs to their owners'. But many microfinance lenders, as well as formal banks, argue that they cannot accept delayed payments from all clients and warn that a blanket amnesty would endanger the financial sector longer term if it prompts a rise of non-payment or over-indebtedness. In addition, COVID-19 induced the spill-over effects from a slowdown in the real sector to the banking and financial sector could also be sizeable. The tapering of capital inflows is triggering the easing of real estate market prices, likely ending the construction boom. With the current large outstanding credit of the construction, real estate, and mortgage sector, non-performing loans are expected to rise. The share of outstanding bank credit (excluding microfinance and shadow banking credits) financing to the combined construction, real estate, and mortgage businesses peaked at 31.1 percent or USD7.7 billion (28.6 percent of GDP) by end-2019. Importantly, a real estate market correction has already started, following a prolonged construction and property boom. Under the circumstances, COVID-19 pandemic situation will undoubtedly put extra sizeable pressure on Cambodia's banking and financial sector. Implementing monetary policy easing, Cambodia's Central Bank reduced the reserve requirements ratio to 7 percent for both local and foreign currencies for six months starting in April 2020 from 8 percent for riel and 12.5 percent for foreign currencies.

Cambodia's public debt-to-GDP ratio remained stable at below 30 percent of GDP until 2019. It is projected to increase from 2020, as the country's overall fiscal deficit is widening. Cambodia's debt-to-GDP ratio is expected to reach 35 percent by the end of 2022. In 2019, Cambodia remained at low risk of external debt distress as per Debt Sustainability Analysis

Concluding Observations

(DSA) using the joint IMF / World Bank Debt Sustainability Framework for Low Income Countries. However, the scenario has been changed since the DSA conducted in 2019. Due to COVID-19 pandemic, in 2020, with the fiscal deficit estimated at 9 percent and 99.6 percent of the debt external (and in an external currency), overseas financing requirement will be large and, therefore, exchange rate also will come under further pressure. By the end of 2019, Cambodia had a total outstanding public debt of USD7.6 billion of which 0.04 percent or USD2.74 million is public domestic debt. Overall borrowing terms apparently remained concessional, with a interest rate (weighted average) and maturity of 0.8 percent and 28.51years respectively. Outstanding debt, in terms of currency, in U.S. Dollars is the largest, accounting for 43.9 percent of total outstanding debt; SDR (Special Drawing Rights) and Chinese Yuan are next, covering 25.9 percent and 14.6 percent respectively.

In terms of implications for domestic revenue and foreign exchange reserves, as World Bank pointed out that the COVID-19 outbreak is hitting Cambodia's revenue base. Terribly affected export and construction sectors of Cambodia, as discussed above, are the main sources of direct and indirect revenues. The least affected agriculture sector is tax exempt. Therefore, it is highly likely that revenue collection in 2020 will be significantly below the budget target. The overall fiscal deficit (including grants) is therefore projected by World Bank, to widen to 9.0 percent of GDP in 2020, down from a surplus of 0.5 percent in 2019. The shortfall in domestic revenue collection will surely require the authorities to dip into government savings, and the domestic financing need is projected to amount to 5.3 percent of GDP. Government savings, in 2019, stood at 22 trillion riels (or 20.2 percent of GDP) after several years of accumulation. Given the authorities' sufficient liquidity, recourse to Central Bank financing to fill the widening overall fiscal deficit is not usually expected. However, more worrying is the country's declining 'fiscal space', the money the government has left to spend after making it's allocated and mandated payments such as public-sector wages, social security contributions and loan repayments. Under the worst case scenario, the World Bank forecasted – which is now far from the worst-case scenario in view of the COVID-19 global pandemic – the Cambodian government's 'fiscal space' will fall from 55 percent of GDP in 2016 to just 28 percent of GDP in 2023. In other words, less than a third of the state budget will be available soon for investment and new social programs, arguably at a time when the country need them most.

Given that the country's key foreign exchange earners, namely tourism and exports, are being severely impacted by the coronavirus outbreak and while FDI inflows are also slowing, Cambodia's foreign exchange reserves position is also projected to deteriorate. The country's foreign exchange reserves, in 2020, are expected to decline to USD16.8 billion (6.8 months of prospective imports), down from USD18.7 billion (7.6 months of prospective imports).

Cambodia's nearly thirty-years long growth momentum quickly disappeared in early 2020 due to the global COVID-19 outbreak. The Cambodian government already introduced emergency measures to contain the outbreak and provided fiscal assistance to affected households, workers, and enterprises. However, the risks stemming from an overleveraged financial sector are rising. Several financial sector vulnerabilities including high credit concentration, related party lending risks, lack of consolidated cross-border supervision and gaps in implementation of risk-based supervision, could exacerbate the COVID-19 shock. The concentration of FDI inflows in a few sectors namely banking, construction and real estate, combined with bank lending mainly in construction and real estates poses an additional source of risk.

Under the above circumstances, firstly, as the pandemic is still far from over, Cambodia needs to be ready to respond to a possible future outbreak. Another most urgent step is to continuously monitor and provide support to households to alleviate poverty. This includes leveraging existing programs and relief as well as targeting mechanisms to support the poor and vulnerable through social assistance to maintain their living conditions. After fulfilling immediate relief requirements, it is crucial to strengthen the existing mechanism to identify the poor through its IDPoor program in order to scale up Cambodia's existing social assistance and social insurance schemes. To facilitate a robust recovery, the government will also require to continue to ensure macro-economic and financial sector stability as well as accelerate trade and investment reforms and encourage faster adoption of technologies. The COVID-19 pandemic will still likely have major implications on how regional and global trade and investment will be conducted going forward, with expected major shifts in trade and migrant policies, and flow of goods and services. In that case, effective government intervention will be essential to facilitate economic recovery. The success of the government measures hinges on targeting appropriate small, medium, and large firms and enterprises that are viable and efficient but lack timely and cheaper financing sources to become feasible to run and to create jobs. As and when the outbreak comes under control, refocusing and reenergizing efforts and sources that might have been interrupted or diverted to cope with the COVID-19 outbreak to moving forward with key structural and sectoral reforms is crucial. Economic resiliency is also to be ensured. In order to achieve economic resiliency, it is necessary to further promote ease of doing business, the investment climate, and a reduction of energy and logistics costs to reintegrate with regional and global value chains after a period of devastating interruption caused by the outbreak.

APPENDIX

ANNEX 1 : CAMBODIA'S KEY INDICATORS

Output and Economic Growth	2016	2017	2018	2019
GDP (annual variation in %)	7.0	7.0	7.5	7.1
Exports GNFS*	61.3	60.7	63.3	63.6
Imports GNFS	65.7	64.1	66.6	65.3
Domestic demand (annual variation in %)	9.9	8.5	10.0	9.9
GDP per capita (USD, Nominal)	1,264.90	1,375.80	1,476.80	1,620.64

Money and Prices

	2016	2017	2018	2019
Inflation, consumer Prices (annual %)	3.5	3.1	3.2	3.3
M2 (% of GDP)	70.9	79.4	88.8	96.0
Domestic Credit to the Private sector (% of GDP)	69.5	74.5	82.8	91.1
Nominal Exchange Rate (local currency per USD)	4,058.0	4,062.0	4,067.0.	4,075.0
Short term interest rate (% per annum)	11.9	11.7	11.3	11.0

Fiscal

Revenue (%of GDP)	20.7	21.4	22.3	21.2
Expenditure (%of GDP)	22.1	23.1	24.2	23.9
Overall Fiscal Balance (%of GDP)	-1.4	-1.6	-1.9	-2.6
General Govt. Debt (%of GDP)	29.1	30.3	30.6	30.0

External Accounts

Exports growth, FOB (USD, annual %)	8.6	5.3	5.3	9.0
Imports growth, CIF (USD, annual %)	8.6	4.0.	4.1.	7.6
Merchandise exports (% of GDP)	45.5	45.2	46.8	46.8
Merchandise imports (% of GDP)	56.9	55.6	57.6	56.6
Services, net (% of GDP)	7.0	7.0	7.4	8.1
Current account balance (current USDmillions)	-2,040.2	-2,155.5	-2,502.9	-2,540.7
Current account balance (% of GDP)	-10.2	-9.7	-10.5	-9.5
Foreign Direct Investment (Net inflows, USDmillions)	2,164.40	2,381.0	3,238.6	2,835.80
Foreign Direct Investment Net inflows, (% of GDP)	10.8	10.8	13.4	10.4
Gross International Reserves (millions USD)	6,730.80	8,757.90	10,143.70	10,650.90

Sources: Cambodian Authorities, IMF, and World Bank
GNFS* = Goods and Non-factor Services.

Appendix

ANNEX 2 : GDP Indicator of Combodia

Cambodia GDP	2019	2018	1960-2019 Highest	1960-2019 Lowest	Unit
GDP (annual growth %)	7.10	7.50	13.30	0.10	percent
GDP	27.09	24.57	27.09	0.51	USD billion
GDP per capita	1,269.00	1,202.60	1,269.00	321.30	USD
GDP per capita PPP	4,388.80	4,159.30	4,388.80	1,111.20	USD
GDP Constant Prices	52,976.00	49,262.00	52,976.00	14,175.00	KHR billion
GDP from Agriculture	9,504.50	9,401.20	9,504.50	4,756.90	KHR billion
GDP from Construction	5,293.00	4,480.00	5,293.00	420.00	KHR billion
GDP from Manufacturing	12,275.60	11,252.60	12,275.60	1,445.50	"
GDP from Mining	836.30	720.50	836.30	20.10	"
GDP from Services	20,772.50	19,457.20	20,772.50	4,192.90	"
GDP from Transport	3,507.40	3,248.70	3,507.40	681.70	"
GDP from Utilities	353.90	328.40	353.90	50.80	"

GDP* (Gross Domestic Product) measures of national income and output for a given country's economy. The gross domestic product is equal to the total expenditures for all final goods and services produced within the country in a stipulated period of time.

ANNEX 3
Destination of Cambodia garment, footwear and travel good exports

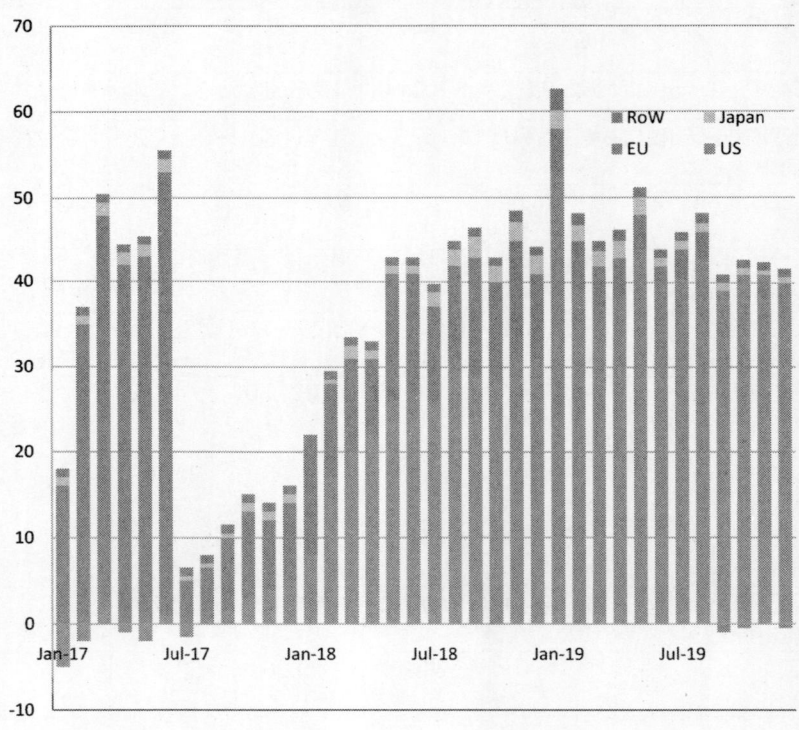

Appendix

ANNEX 4
Economic Performance
GDP constant prices*

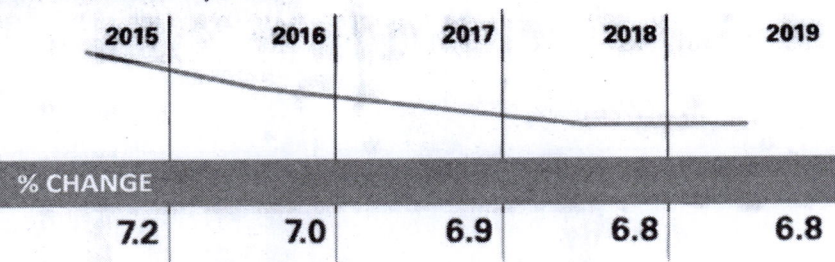

*2010 market price; percentage change estimates start after 2016
Source: International Monetary Fund, World Economic Outlook Database, October 2017

GDP per capita, current prices (CAGR 8.37%)

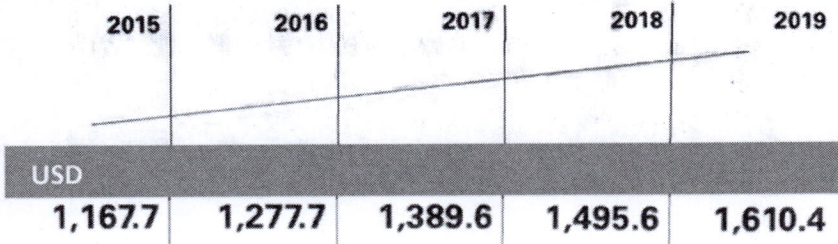

Figures after 2012 are estimates
Source: International Monetary Fund, World Economic Outlook Database, October 2017

Foreign direct investment inflows

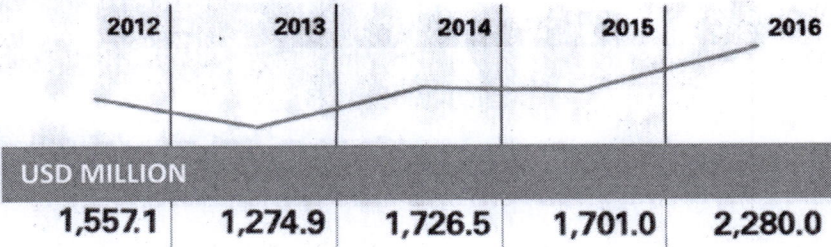

Source: ASEAN Secretariat

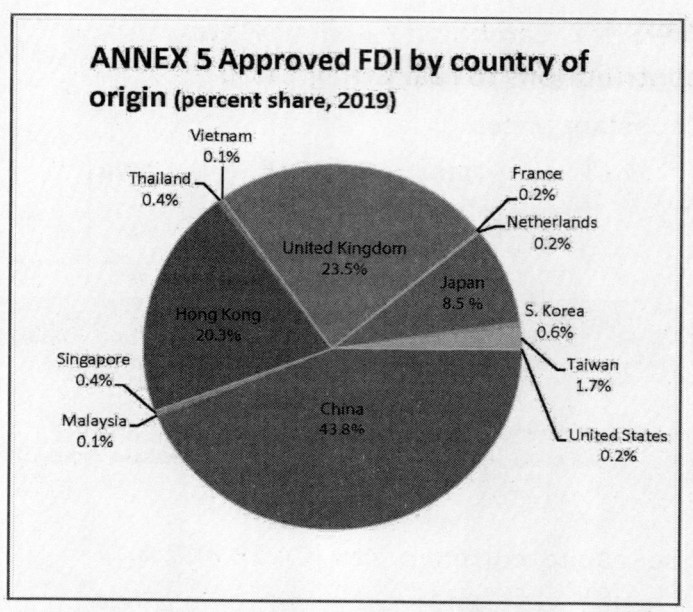

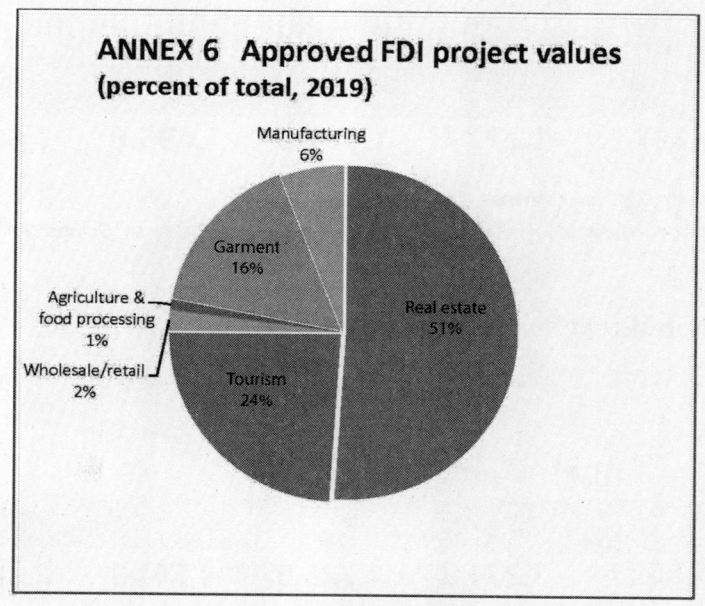

ANNEX 7 Cambodia / Real GDP growth and contributions to real GDP growth

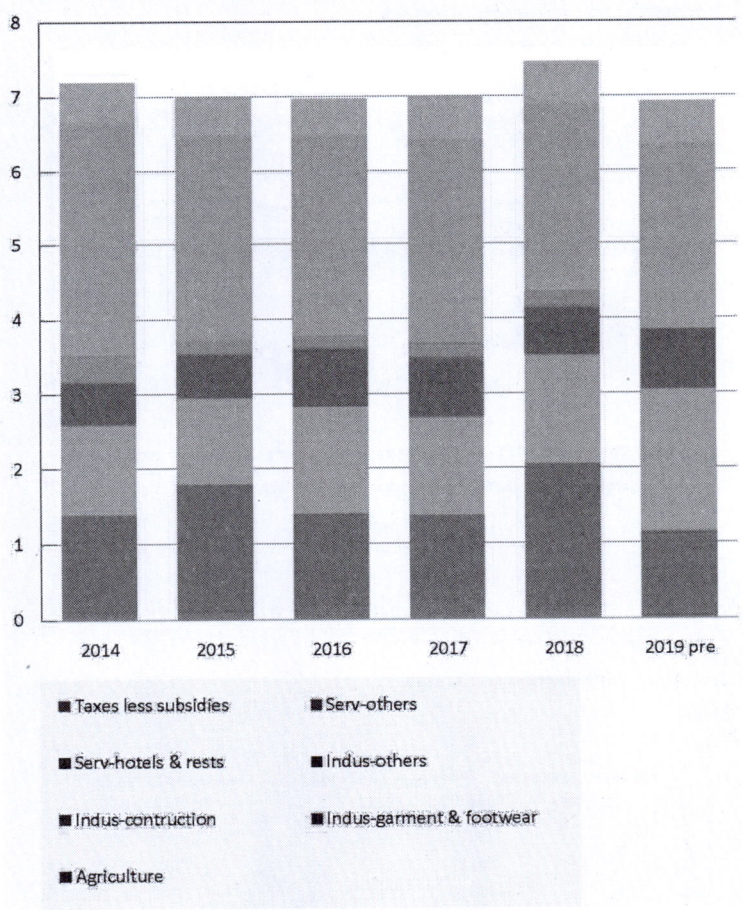

ANNEX 8 Cambodia : Robust Growth and Low Inflation

Economic growth remains strong supported by construction, garment, and trade and finance.

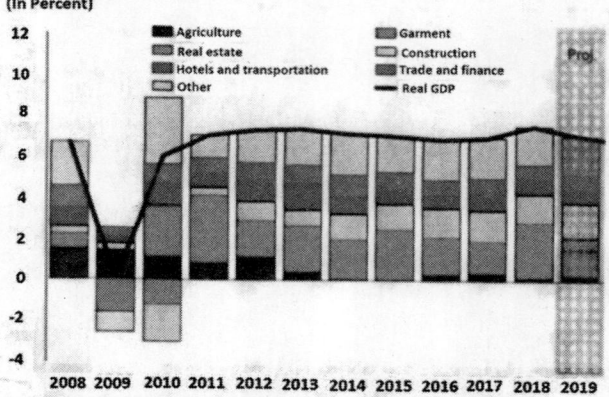

Inflation remains at low levels due to subdued food prices.

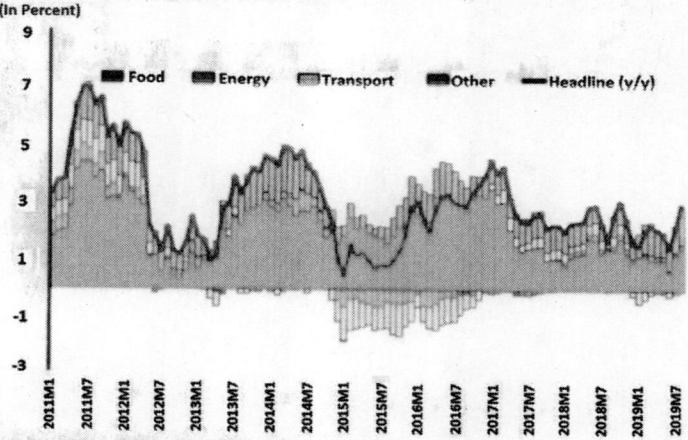

Appendix

ANNEX 9 Cambodia : Robust Revenue Performance Amid Spending Pressures
Fiscal performance remains strong...

Fiscal Balance
(In Percent of GDP)

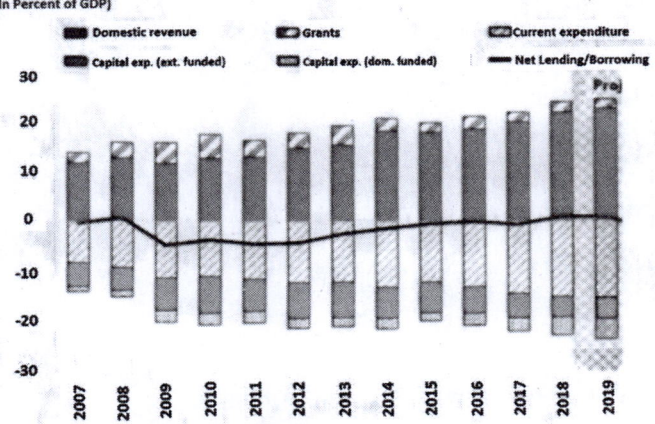

Sources: Cambodian authorities, and IMF staff calculations

...and revenues continue to increase, supported by strong administrative efforts.
Fiscal Revenues
(In Percent of GDP)

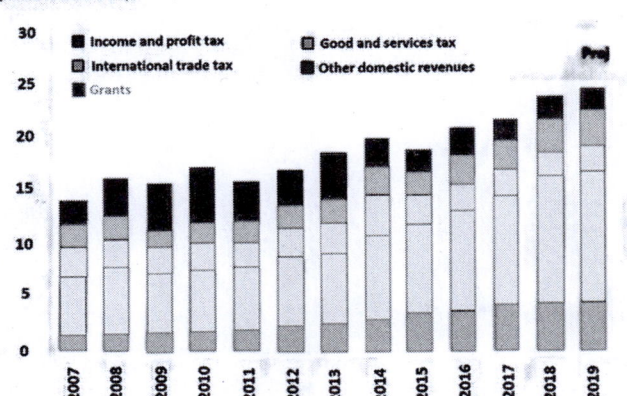

Sources: Cambodian authorities, and IMF staff calculations

ANNEX 10 Cambodia : Worsening External Position

The correct account deficit widend owing to high imports...

Current Account
(In Precent GDP)

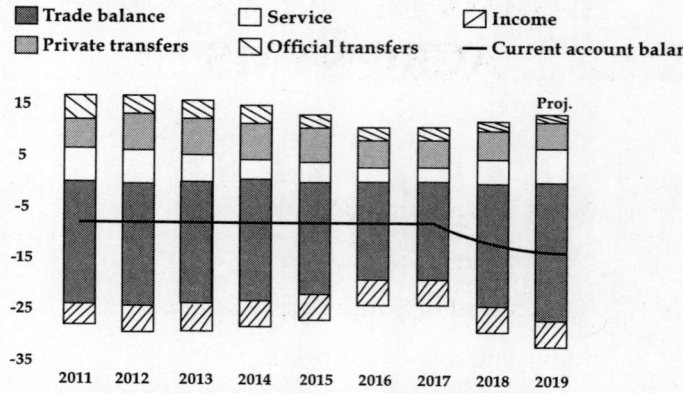

Source: Cambodian authorites; IMF staff calculations

... and was financed by FDI inflows and incresing ST inflows.

Current Account Financing
(In Precent GDP)

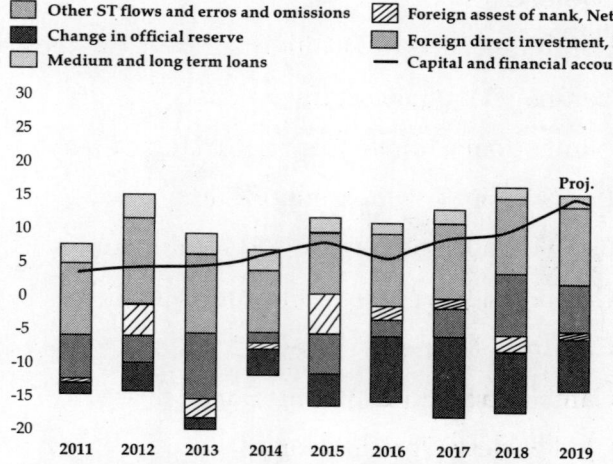

Source: Cambodian authorities; IMF staff calculations.

ABBREVIATIONS AND ACRONYMS

ADB	Asian Development Bank
AFTA	ASEAN Free Trade Area
ASEAN	Association of Southeast Asian Nations
BFC	Better Factories Cambodia
BISC	Business Information Services Counters
BPO	Business Process Outsourcing
BSP	Budget Strategic Plan
CARD	Council of Agricultural and Rural Development, Cambodia
CBHI	Community-based Health Insurance, Cambodia
CCCA	Cambodia Climate Change Alliance
CCCSP	Cambodian Climate Change Strategic Plan
CDC	Council for Development of Cambodia
CDHS	Cambodia Demographic and Health Survey
CDRI	Cambodia Development Resource Institute
CPF	Country Planning Framework
CSES	Cambodia Socio-Economic Survey
CSO	Civil Society Organization

DCPS	Development Cooperation and Partnership strategy
DFA	Development finance Assessment
DHS	Demographic and Health Survey
DP	Development Partner
DTIS	Diagnostic Trade Integration Study
EBA	Everything but Arms, European Union
ECE	Early Childhood Education
EFAP	Emergency Food Assistance Project
EGL	Early Grade Learning
EIA	Environmental Impact Assessment
EIC	Economic Institute of Cambodia
EII	Employment Injury Insurance
EPA	Export potential Assessment
ERW	Explosive Remnants of War
EU	European Union
FDI	Foreign Direct Investment
FRS	Food Reserve System, Cambodia
GCF	Green Climate Fund
GDP	Gross Domestic Product
GER	Gross Enrolment Rate
GGGI	Global Green Growth Institute
GMAC	Garment Manufacturing Association in Cambodia
GNI	Gross National Income
GUDP	Green Urban Development Program
GVC	Global Value Chain

Abbreviations and Acronyms

HDI	Human Development Index, UNDP
HDIA	Human Development Impact Assessment
HEF	Health Equity Fund (s), Cambodia
HIP	Health Insurance Projects
HSP	Health Strategic Plan
ICT	Information and Communication Technology
IDP	Industrial Development Policy
ID	Poor Identification of Poor Households Programme, Cambodia
IF	Integration Framework
IFTF	Integrated Framework Trust Fund
ILO	International Labour Organization
IMF	International Monetary Fund
INDC	Intended Nationally Determined Contribution
IP	Intellectual Property
IT	Information Technology
ITC	International Trade Centre
IWRM	Integrated Water Resources Management
JICA	Japanese International Cooperation Agency
JMI	Joint Monitoring Indicator
KAS	Konrad-Adenauer-Stiftung
KHR	Cambodian riel
LCA	Latent Class Analysis
LDC.	Least Developed Country
MAFF	Ministry of Agriculture, Fishery and Forestry
MCS	Ministry of Civil Service

MDG	Millennium Development Goal
MIC	Medium Income Country
MIH	Ministry of Industry and Handicraft
MME	Ministry of Mine and Energy
MoC	Ministry of Commerce, Cambodia
MoE	Ministry of Environment, Cambodia
MoEF	Ministry of Economy and Finance, Cambodia
MoEYS	Ministry of Education, Youth and Sport, Cambodia
MoH	Ministry of Health, Cambodia
MoLVT	Ministry of Labour and Vocational Training, Cambodia
MoP	Ministry of Planning, Cambodia
MRD	Ministry of Rural Development, Cambodia
MoSVY	Ministry of Social Affairs, Veterans and Youth Rehabilitation, Cambodia
MoWA	Ministry of Women's Affairs, Cambodia
MPI	Multidimensional Poverty Index
MSMEs	Micro, Small, and Medium Enterprises
NCC	National Coordinating Committee
NCD	Non-Communicable Disease
NCDM	National Committee for Disaster Management, Cambodia
NCSD	National Council for Sustainable Development
NCT	National Core Team
NEP	National Employment Policy
NESAP	National Environmental Strategy and Action Plan
NGO	Non-Governmental Organization

Abbreviations and Acronyms

NIP	National Implementation Plan
NIS	National Institute of Statistics, Cambodia
NPGG	National Policy for Green Growth
NSDP	National Strategic Development Plan
NSFSN	National Strategy for Food Security and Nutrition, Cambodia
NSPGG	National Strategic Plan for Green Growth
NSPS	National Social Protection Strategy for the Poor and Vulnerable, Cambodia
NSSF	National Social Security Fund, Cambodia
NYDP	National Youth Development Policy, Cambodia
OD	Operating District
ODA	Official Development Assistance
ODI	Overseas Development Institute
OECD	Organisation for Economic Co-operation and Development
OPHI	Oxford Poverty and Human Development Institute
OVOP	One Village One Product
PPP	Purchasing Power Parity
PRAKAS	A proclamation signed by a minister or inter-ministerial entity
PRSP	Poverty Reduction Strategy Papers
PWP	Public Works Programme
RGC	Royal Government of Cambodia
RIA	Rapid Integration Assessment
RS-IV	Rectangular Strategy Phase IV
SDF	Skill Development Fund

SDG	Sustainable Development Goal
SEA	Southeast Asia
SEDP	Socio-Economic Development Plan
SEZ	Special Economic Zone
SHI	Social Health Insurance
SME	Small and Medium-sized Enterprise
SNL	Sub-National Level
SPI	Social Protection Index, Asian Development Bank
SPPF	Social Protection Policy Framework, Cambodia
STEM	Science, Technology, Engineering, and Mathematics
TRADE	Trade Related Assistance for Development and Equity
TRIPS	Trade Related Aspects of Intellectual Property Rights
TRTA	Trade Related Technical Assistance
TSI	Trade Support Institutions
TVET	Technical Vocational Education and Training
TWGs	Technical Working Groups
UHC	Universal Health Coverage
UN	United Nations
UNCT	United Nations Country Team
UNCTAD	United Nations Conference on Trade and Development
UNDG	United Nations Development Group
UNDP	United Nations Development Programme
UNCAC	United Nations Convention against Corruption
UNEP	United Nations Environment Programme

Abbreviations and Acronyms

UNESCO	United Nations Educational, Scientific and Cultural Organization
UNFCCC	United Nations Framework Convention on Climate Change
UNICEF	United Nations Children's Fund
UNIDO	United Nations Industrial Development Organization
USAID	United States Agency for International Development
USD	United States Dollar
VAT	Value-added Tax
VRG	Village Representative Group, ID Poor Programme, Cambodia
WDI	World Development Indicators
WFP	World Food Programme
WHO	World Health Organization
WTTC	World Travel & Tourism Council
WTO	World Trade Organization

BIBLIOGRAPHY

Anderson, K. and S. J. Smith. 2001. Editorial: Emotional geographies. Transactions of the Institute of British Geographers.

ADB (2018). Asian Development Outlook 2018 Update: Maintaining Stability Amid Heightened Uncertainty. Asian Development Bank, Manila.

ADB (2018). Cambodia's New Technical and Vocational Education And Training Policy. Asian Development Bank. Manila.

ADB (2014). Cambodia: Country Partnership Strategy 2014-2018. Asian Development Bank, Manila.

ADB (2014). Cambodia – Country Poverty Analysis 2014. Manila.

ADB (2014). Improving Rice Production and Commercialization in Cambodia: Findings from the Farm Investment Climate Assessment. Metro Manila: Asian Development Bank.

ADB (2018). Technology Innovation for Agricultural Statistics. Asian Development Bank, Manila.

ADB (2019). Key Indicators for Asia and the Pacific. Manila.

ADB (2019). 'Cambodia, 2019-2023 – Inclusive Pathways to a Competitive Economy. Asian Development Bank, Manila.

Andersen, Henry. (2019). 'Multidimensional Poverty Analysis – Cambodia'. Final Report.

ASEAN Secretariat, "Agreements on Agriculture and Forestry," http://www.aseansec.org.

Acharya, A. (2017). "The Myth of ASEAN centrality?" Contemporary Southeast Asia: A Journal of International and Strategic Affairs.

ASEAN Secretariat (2019). "Fact Sheet on ASEAN Economic Community". Jakarta.

ASEAN Secretariat (2019). "Final Chairman's Statement of the 34th ASEAN Summit," Bangkok, July 23, 2019.

ASEAN Secretariat (2019). Joint Communique of The 52nd ASEAN Foreign Ministers' Meeting, Bangkok.

ASEAN Secretariat (2018). ASEAN – China Strategic Partnership Vision 2030. Jakarta: Asean Secretariat.

Associated Press (2006). 'Cambodia Gives Garment Companies Tax Holiday'. 16th June 2006.

Ayres, D.M. (2000). Tradition, modernity, and the development of Education in Cambodia. Comparative education Review.

Bansok, R., Phirun, N., and Chhun, C. (2011). Agricultural Development and climate Change: The Case of Cambodia. Working Paper Series No.65. CDRI, December.

BBC News – BBC.com

Beeson, M. (2013). "Living with Giants: ASEAN and the Evolution of Asian Regionalism." Trans-regional and trans-national Studies of Southeast Asia.

Bingxin, Yu. and Xinshen, Diao. (2011). Cambodia's Agricultural Strategy: Future Development Options for the Rice sector. A Policy Discussion Paper, Special Report 9. Phnom Penh: Cambodian Development Resource Institute.

Brickell, K. 2014. 'The whole world is watching': Intimate geopolitics of forced eviction and women's activism in Cambodia.

CARDI (2017). Summary report on Main Achievements of Research and Agricultural Technology Development in 2016 and Strategic Directions for 2017. Cambodian Agricultural Research and Development Institute.

CCC (Cooperation Committee for Cambodia) (2018). Civic Space for Civil Society Organizations in Cambodia. Phnom Penh.

CDRI (Cambodia Development Resource Institute) (2007). 'Youth Migration and Urbanization in Cambodia.' Working Paper 36. Phnom Penh: CDRI.

CDRI (2017). Existing Non-Tariff Measures In Cambodia. Cambodia Development Review. Phnom Penh: Cambodian Development Resource Institute.

CDRI (Cambodian Development Resource Institute) (2017). Political Economy of Civil Society in Cambodia. Phnom Penh: CDRI.

Chandler, D. 1993. The Tragedy of Cambodian History: Politics, War, and Revolution since 1945.

Chap, Sotharith and Vannarith Chheang. 2010. 'ERIA Study to Further Improve the ASEAN Economic Community (AEC) Score Card.

Cambodia Country Study. 2010. "Trade Liberalization under ACFTA and its possible Impacts on Cambodian Industries." ADB Research Paper.

Chhair, S., and L. Ung (2013). 'Economic History of Industrialization in Cambodia'. WIDER Working Paper No. 2013/134. Helsinki: UNU-WIDER.

Chhair, Sokty and Ung, Luyna (2018). 'Cambodia's Path to Industrial Development – Policies, Lessons, and Opportunities. Oxford Scholarship Online.

Chhun, Chhim., Bora, Buth., and Sothy Ear. (2015). Effect of Labor Movement on Agricultural Mechanization in Cambodia. CDRI Working Paper Series No.107. Phnom Penh: Cambodian Development Resource Institute.

Council for the Development of Cambodia (CDC) (2012). Cambodia Investment Guidebook. Phnom Penh: Japan International Cooperation Agencies.

Cramb, R., Sareth, C., and Vuthy, T. (2020). The Commercialization Of Rice Farming in Cambodia.

Dary, phon., Sokcheng, Sim., and Pirom, K. (2017). Synergies and Trade-offs with Intensification of Rice and Livestock Production in Cambodia. CDRI Special Report No.16. Phnom Penh: Cambodian Development resource Institute, June.

Dasgupta, S. and D. Williams (2010). "Women Facing the Economic Crisis – The Garment Sector in Cambodia", in Poverty and Sustainable Development in Asia, edited by A. Bauer & M. Thant, Asian Development Bank; Manila.

Dawson, W. (2010). 'Private Tutoring and Mass Schooling in East Asia: Reflections of Inequality in Japan, South Korea, and Cambodia.' Asia Pacific Economic Review.

Deininger, K. and L. Squire (1996). "Measuring Inequality: A New Data Base". World Bank Economic Review.

Department for Economic and Social Affairs (2015). "Valuing the Environment From Sustained to Sustainable Growth." United Nations: New York.

Desai, S. (2017). "ASEAN and India Converge on Connectivity." The Diplomat, December 19. https://thediplomat.com/2017/12/asean-and-india-converge-on-connectivity/.

Donovan, D.A. (1993). Cambodia: Building a Legal System from Scratch. International Lawyer (ABA) 27.

Duggan, S.J. (1996). Education, teacher training and prospects for Economic recovery in Cambodia. Comparative Education Review.

Dy, K. 2013. Challenges of teaching genocide in Cambodian secondary Schools. Policy and Practice: Pedagogy about the Holocaust and Genocide Papers.

Ear, S. (2009). 'Sowing and Sewing Growth: The political Economy of Rice and Garments in Cambodia'. Stanford Centre for International Development.

East-West Management Institute (EWMI) (2003). Land Law of Cambodia: A Study and Research Manual.

EIC (Economic Institute of Cambodia) (2007). 'Addressing the Impact of the Agreement on Textile and Clothing Expiration on Cambodia'. EIC, June.

EIC (Economic Institute of Cambodia) (2009). 'Export Diversification and Value Addition for Human Development'. Phnom Penh: EIC.

FAO (2018). Crop Prospects and Food Situation. Quarterly Global Report No. 2. Food and Agriculture Organization, June.

FAO (2018). Trade Policy Briefs: WTO Negotiations. No. 31. Food and Agriculture Organization. February.

FAO (2018). Trade Policy Technical Notes: Trade and Food Security. No. 21. Food and Agriculture organization, January.

Fernandes Antunes, A., B. Jacobs, R. de Groot, K. Thin, P. Hanvoravongchai & S. Flessa, (2018). "Equality in financial Access to healthcare in Cambodia from 2004 to 2014". Health Policy and Planning.

Garment Manufacturers Association in Cambodia (GMAC) (2015). Bulletin 2015. Phnom Penh: Garment Manufacturers Association in Cambodia.

Garment Manufacturers Association in Cambodia (GMAC) (2019). Bulletin 2019. Phnom Penh: GMAC.

Global Witness. 2016. Hostile Takeover: The Corporate Empire of Cambodia's Ruling Family. London, UK: Global Witness.

Goh, E. (2016). "Southeast Asian Strategies toward the Great Powers: Still Hedging after All These Years?" The Asian Forum.

Hang, C. (2010). 'Cambodia's Macroeconomic Development'. Phnom Penh: Presentation at the Annual Meeting of Cambodian Economic Association, February, Phnom Penh.

Harvard Business School (HBS) (2004). 'Worker Rights and Global Trade: The U.S. – Cambodia Bilateral Textile Trade Agreement'. Case Study, Harvard Business School.

Hem, S. (2015). Political Economy of Institutional Reform to restore Trust in Public Institutions in Cambodia: Design of a Specialized Court to end Land Disputes. Nagoya University Graduate School of Law.

Hiebart, M., and Nguyen (2014). 'Cambodian Regime Realigns its Foreign Relations'. Yale Global Online. 4th February.

Hughes, C. and Conway, T. (2003). Towards Pro-Poor Political Change In Cambodia: Policy Process. London: ODI.

Hsieh, P.L. (2017). "The RCEP, New Asian regionalism and the Global South." MegaReg Series 4, New York: New York University of Law.

Irvin, G. (1993). 'Rebuilding Cambodia's Economy: UNTAC and Beyond'. The Hague: Institute of Social Studies.

ILO (2017). 'Recent Trade Policy developments and possible Implications for Cambodia's garment and footwear sector', Cambodian Garment and Footwear Sector Bulletin, Iss. 5, International Labor Organization, Geneva, ilo.org/asia/publications/WCMS_541288/lang-en/index.htm.

ILO (2018). Association of South-East Asian Nations: Employment and Environmental Sustainability Fact Sheets 2018. Asia and the Pacific: International Labor Organization.

ILO (International Labor Organization) (2018). Extending Social Protection to Informal Workers in Cambodia.

IMF (2019). CAMBODIA: 2019 Article IV Consultation – Press Release Staff Report; and Statement by the Executive Director for Cambodia. IMF Country Report No. 19/387, December.

Inspection Panel (2010). Cambodia: Land Management and Administration Project. Investigation Report. World Bank.

Jain-Chandra, S., T. Kinda, K. Kochhar, S. Piao, and J. Schauer, (2016). "Sharing the growth dividend: Analysis of inequality in Asia". IMF Working Paper 16/48, International Monetary Fund: Washington D.C.

Kaneko, Y. (2010). An Alternative Way of Harmonizing Ownership with Customary Rights: Japanese Approach to Cambodian Land Reform. Journal of International Cooperation Studies 18.

Khmer Times. Several issues of 2018, 2019, and 2020. Phnom Penh.

Kiernan, B. 2004. How Pol Pot came to power: Colonialism, Nationalism, and Communism in Cambodia, 1930 – 1975. 2nd ed. London: Yale University Press.

Konrad-Adenaur-Stiftung (KAS) (2018). Economic Transformation in Cambodia and Abroad.

Kraft, H.J. (2017). "Great Power Dynamics and the Waning of ASEAN Centrality in Regional Security." Asian Politics &Policy 9, no.4.

Krueger, D., and F. Perri. (2006). " Does income inequality lead to Consumption inequality? Evidence and theory." The Review of Economic Studies.

Kunmin, Kim. And Paula, P. Plaza. (2018). Building Food Security in Asia through International Agreements on Rice Reserves. Policy Brief 2018 No. 01. Tokyo: Asian Development Bank Institute, August.

Le Thu, H. (2018). "China's Dual Strategy of Coercion and Inducement Towards ASEAN." The Pacific Review 35, no.4.

Leifer, M. (2013). Dictionary of the Modern Politics of Southeast Asia. Routledge.

Luch, L. (2010). 'The Impact of Remittances from the Garment Factory Workers on Income – A Case Study in Rural Cambodia'. Journal of Rural Economics, 82 (special issue).

Makara, Ouk., Vang, Seng., Sophany, Sakhan., and Chanthy, P. (2017) Achievements in Research and Technology Development 1999-2017. CARDI. Phnom Penh: Cambodian Agricultural Research and Development Institute, August.

MAFF (2013). Bulletin of Agricultural Statistics and Studies. Phnom Penh: Department of Planning and Statistics, Ministry of Agriculture, Forestry and Fisheries.

MAFF (2015). Agricultural Sector Strategic Development Plan 2014-2018. Ministry of Agriculture, Forestry and Fisheries, May.

Ministry of Agriculture, Forestry and Fisheries, Cambodia. http://www.maff.gov.kh/en---------. 2005. "Agricultural Sector Strategic Development Plan (2006-2010).

MEF (Ministry of Economy and Finance) (2018). Economic Developments, Outlook and Challenges. Phnom Penh.

MEF (Ministry of Economy and Finance) (2018-2019). Cambodia Public Debt Statistical bulletin.

MoEYS (Ministry of Education, Youth and Sports) (2005). Education Strategic Plan 2006 – 2010. Phnom Penh.

MoEYS (Ministry of Education, Youth and Sports) (2014a). Education Strategic Plan 2014-2018. Cambodia. Phnom Penh.

MoEYS (Ministry of Education, Youth and Sports) (2018). Public Education Statistics and Indicators, 2016-2017.Phnom Penh.

MoFAIC (Ministry of Foreign Affairs and International Cooperation) (2018). Cambodia Stability and Development First. To Tell The Truth. Version 2. Phnom Penh.

Ministry of Industry (1998). 'Industrial Development Action Plan'. Phnom Penh: Ministry of Industry.

Ministry of Land Management, Urban Planning, and Construction (2017). Report on Total Result of Implementing 2016 Action Plan and Ongoing 2017 Action Plan. Phnom Penh.

Ministry of Tourism (2012). Tourism Statistics: Annual Report in 2012. Phnom Penh: Ministry of Tourism.

Ministry of Tourism (MoT) (2012). Tourism Strategic Development Plan 2012-2020. Phnom Penh: Ministry of Tourism.

Minitry of Tourism (MoT) (2015). Cambodia Tourism Marketing Strategy 2015-2020. Phnom Penh: Ministry of Tourism.

Ministry of Tourism (2019). Tourism Statistics: Annual Report in 2019. Phnom Penh: Ministry of Tourism.

MoWA (Ministry of Women's Affairs) (2015). National Study on Women's Health and Life Experiences, Cambodia. Phnom Penh.

Mueller, L. M. (2019). 'ASEAN centrality under threat – the cases of RCEP and connectivity'. Journal of Contemporary East Asia Studies.

National Bank of Cambodia (NBC) (2012). Annual Report 2011. National Bank of Cambodia, Phnom Penh.

National Bank of Cambodia (NBC) (2016-2019). NBC Annual Report 2016-2019. Phnom Penh: National Bank of Cambodia.

National Bank of Cambodia (2019). Monetary Statistics Bulletin.

National Bank of Cambodia (NBC) (2018-2019). Balance of Payments Statistics.

National Institute of Statistics and Ministry of Planning (2010). Labor and Social Trends in Cambodia 2010. National Institute of Statistics and Ministry of Planning supported by International Labor Organization, Phnom Penh, Cambodia.

NEA (National Employment Agency) (2018). Skills Shortages and Skill Gaps in the Cambodian Labor Market: Evidence from Employer Survey, 2017. Phnom Penh.

Neef, A., Touch, S., and Chiengthong, J. (2013). The Politics and Ethics Of Land Concessions in Rural Cambodia. Journal of Agricultural Ethics 26.

Oba, M. (2016). "TPP, RCEP, and FTAAP: Multilayered Regional Economic Integration and International Relations." Asia Pacific Review 23, no.1.

OECD (2017), Social Protection System Review of Cambodia: OECD Development Pathways. Paris: OECD Publishing.

OPHI (Oxford Poverty and Human Development Initiative) (2018). Global MPI Country Briefing 2018: Cambodia (East Asia and the Pacific).

Osborne, M. 1997. The French Presence in Cochinchina and Cambodia.

Penh National Institute of Statistics. (2016). Cambodia Socio-Economic Survey 2015.

Peou, S. 2007. International Democracy Assistance for Peacebuilding: Cambodia and Beyond. New York: Palgrave Macmillan. The Phnom Penh Post. Several issues of 2018, 2019, and 2020.

Pomfret, R. (2013). "ASEAN's New Frontiers: Integrating the Newest Members into the ASEAN Economic Community." Asian Economic Policy Review 8, no.1.

Ratcliffe, M. (2009). 'Study on Governance Challenges for Education in Fragile Situations: Cambodia Country Report.' Report to the EC.

RGC (2010). Policy Document on Promotion of Paddy Rice Production and Export of Milled Rice. Phnom Penh: Royal Government of Cambodia.

RGC (2013). 'Rectangular Strategy Phase 111'. Phnom Penh: The Ministry of Planning.

RGC (2018). Rectangular strategy – Phase 4 of Samdech Techo Hun Sen. The Royal Government of Cambodia, August.

RGC (Royal Government of Cambodia) (2017). Social Protection Policy Framework (SPPF) (2016-2025). Phnom Penh.

Royal Government of Cambodia. Rice Export Policy

Royal Government of Cambodia (2009). 'National Strategic Development Plan Update, 2009-2013'. Phnom Penh: The Ministry of Planning.

Royal Government of Cambodia (RGC) (2015). Cambodia Industrial Development Policy 2015-2025. Phnom Penh: Council of the Development of Cambodia.

Sida (2018b). Sectoral Analysis Study of Sub-national Governance in Cambodia. Phnom Penh.

Sik, B. (2000). Land Ownership, Sales and Concentration in Cambodia. Cambodia Development Research Institute.

Slocomb, M. 2010. An Economic History of Cambodia in the Twentieth Century. Singapore: NUS Press.

Sodeth, Ly. and Miguel Eduardo, S.M. (2018). Cambodia Economic Update: Recent Economic Developments and Outlook. World Bank Group, April.

Sotharith, Chap and Sotheara, Chhorn (2019). 'Cambodia's Development Strategy: Connecting Neighbors'.

Springer, S. 2009. The neo-liberalization of security and violence in Cambodia's transition, in S. Peou (ed.), Human Security in East Asia: Challenges for Collaborative Action. New York: Routledge. 2010. Cambodia's Neoliberal Order: Violence, Authoritarianism, and the Contestation of Public Space, London: Routledge. 2015. Violent Neoliberalism: Development, Discourse and Dispossession in Cambodia. London: Palgrave Macmillan.

Stranger, R., J. Slater and C. Molteni. (2000). The European Union and ASEAN: Trade and Investment issues. Basingstoke: Macmillan, 2000.

Tan, C. (2007). 'Education Reforms in Cambodia: Issues and Concerns.' Educational Research for Policy and Practice.

Thiel, F. (2010). Donor-driven land reform in Cambodia – Property Rights, planning, and land value taxation. Erdkunde 64.

Tuan, Ngo. (2012). 'Cambodia: Garment exports soar 9.9 percent in 9-months'.

UNDP Cambodia. (2007). Land and Human Development in Cambodia Discussion Paper No. 5.

UNESCO (2010). EFA (Education for All) Global Monitoring Report, 2010: Reaching the Marginalized. Oxford: Oxford University Press.

Wang, Y. (2013). "The RCEP Initiative and ASEAN Centrality." China International Studies, No.42.

World Bank (2005). Cambodia: Quality Basic Education for All. Washington D.C.

World Bank (2009b). Sustaining rapid Growth in a challenging Environment. Phnom Penh: World Bank.

World Bank (2010). Providing Skills for Equity and Growth: Preparing Cambodia's Youth for the Labor Market. World Bank Human Development Department, East Asia Pacific Region.

World Bank (2015). Cambodian Agriculture in Transition: Opportunities and Risks. Economic and Sector Work. Report No. 96308-KH. Washington, D.C.: World Bank.

World bank (2017). Atlas of Sustainable Development Goals 2018 From World Development Indicators. Washington: The World Bank Group.

World Bank (2017). Cambodia Economic Update: Staying Competitive Through Improving Productivity. Washington, D.C.

World Bank (2017). Cambodia Overview. Available at http://www.worldbank.org/en/country/Cambodia/overview (viewed 5th June 2017)

World Bank (2017). "Cambodia – Sustaining strong growth for the benefit of all." https://www.worldbank.org/en/country/Cambodia/publication/Cambodia-Systematic-Country Diagnostics.

World Bank (2016). Leveraging the Rice Value Chain for Poverty Reduction in Cambodia, Lao PDR, and Myanmar. Economic and Sector Work Report No. 105285-EAP. The World Bank, May.

World Bank (2018). World Development Indicators, http://datatopics.worldbank.org/world-development-indicators/.

World Bank (2019). Microfinance and Household Welfare. Cambodia Policy Note. Washington DC.

World Bank (2019b). Recent Economic Developments and Outlook. Selected Issue: Investing in Cambodia's Future: Early Childhood Health and Nutrition. Phnom Penh.

World Bank (2019c). Cambodia's Future Jobs: Linking to the Economy of Tomorrow. Phnom Penh.

World Bank (2019d). Recent Economic Developments and Outlook. Special Focus: Upgrading Cambodia in Global Value Chains. Phnom Penh.

World Bank (2019). East Asia and Pacific Economic Update, April,'19.

World Bank (2019). Cambodia Investment Climate Assessment. Phnom Penh.

World Bank (2020). Cambodia Overview. Available at http://www.worldbank.org/en/ country/cambodia/overview.

WFP (World Food Program) (2019). Urban Vulnerability in Phnom Penh. Phnom Penh: Cambodia Country Office.

WFP (World Food Program) (2019b). Vulnerability and Migration in Cambodia. Phnom Penh: Cambodia Country Office.

Xinhua (2011). 'Cambodian garment exports rise 26 percent to 3bln USDin 2010'. ASEAN-China Centre, 27th January 2011.   http://www.asean-china-centre.org/english/2011-01/27/c_13709843.htm

Yagura, K. (2011). 'does Labor Migration Offer Opportunities for Meeting Prospective Spouses? The case of Migrant Workers In Cambodia'. Population, space, and Place.

Ye, M. (2015). "China and Competing Cooperation in Asia-Pacific: TPP, RCEP, and the New Silk Road." Asian Security 11, no.3.